Blueprint for Exceptional Writing

Jennifer Fontenot

Garden City Public Schools

Karen Carney

Eastern Michigan University

Boston   New York   San Francisco
Mexico City   Montreal   Toronto   London   Madrid   Munich   Paris
Hong Kong   Singapore   Tokyo   Cape Town   Sydney

Executive Editor: Aurora Martínez Ramos

Series Editorial Assistant: Kara Kikel

Director of Professional Development: Alison Maloney

Marketing Manager: Danae April

Production Editor: Janet Domingo

Editorial Production Service: DB Publishing Services, Inc.

Composition Buyer: Linda Cox

Manufacturing Buyer: Linda Morris

Electronic Composition: Schneck-DePippo Graphics

Interior Design: Schneck-DePippo Graphics

Cover Administrator: Kristina Mose-Libon

Between the time website information is gathered and then published, it is not unusual for some sites to have closed. Also, the transcription of URLs can result in typographical errors. The publisher would appreciate notification where these errors occur so that they may be corrected in subsequent editions.

ISBN-10: 0-205-57174-3   ISBN-13: 978-0-205-57174-1

Library of Congress Cataloging-in-Publication Data
Fontenot, Jennifer.
  Blueprint for exceptional writing / Jennifer Fontenot, Karen Carney.
    p. cm.
  Includes bibliographical references and index.
  ISBN-13: 978-0-205-57174-1 (alk. paper)
  ISBN-10: 0-205-57174-3 (alk. paper)
1. English language—Composition and exercises—Study and teaching (Elementary) 2. English language—Composition and exercises—Study and teaching (Middle school) I. Carney, Karen. II. Title.

LB1576.F625 2009
372.62'3044—dc22   2008018458

Printed in the United States of America

10 9 8 7 6 5 4 3 2 1 Bind-Rite 12 11 10 09 08

Allyn and Bacon
is an imprint of

www.allynbaconmerrill.com

This book is dedicated to the children and teachers with whom we have worked and from whom we have learned much throughout our careers.

It is also dedicated to all the students for whom *Blueprint for Exceptional Writing* may open the door to creative and meaningful expression.

Contents

Acknowledgments   x

Let's Begin   xi

Section I   The Master Blueprint Plan

Chapter 1   Phase I: Teaching Authentic Vocabulary   2

Before You Start: Student Rough Draft Writing Folders   3

Steps in Phase I: Teaching Authentic Vocabulary   3

Step 1: Written Expression Vocabulary   4

Step 2: Conventions and Grammar   15

Step 3: General Vocabulary   21

In Summary: Authentic Vocabulary Phase   23

Chapter 2   Phase II: Teaching Prewriting Strategies   33

Five Steps in Phase II: Prewriting   34

Step 1: Multisensory Experiences   35

Step 2: Wheel of Thought   38

Step 3: Genre Format and Voice   40

Step 4: Blueprint Note Taking   45

Step 5: Talking Paragraphs   47

In Summary: Prewriting Phase   49

Chapter 3   Phase III: Teaching Writing   52

Two Steps in Phase III: Writing   53

Step 1: Draft Writing   54

Step 2: Title Writing   58

In Summary: Writing Phase   60

Chapter 4   Phase IV: Teaching Authentic Editing   61

Five Steps in Phase IV: Authentic Editing   62

Creating the Assessment Rubric   63

Step 1: Self-editing   67

Step 2: Peer Editing   68

Step 3: Teacher Conference   69

Step 4: Final Copy Writing   70

Step 5: Teacher Assessment   70

In Summary: Editing Phase   71

Chapter 5   Phase V: Publishing—Sharing the Purpose   72

Three Steps in Phase V: Publishing   73

Step 1: Within the School   74

Step 2: For the Community   82

Step 3: Student Portfolios and Keepsakes   84

In Summary: Publishing Phase   86

Section II: Teaching Genres Using BEW

Chapter 6   Personal Narrative Writing   88

What Is a Personal Narrative?   88

Personal Narrative Building Blocks   89

Common Student Mistakes: What a Personal Narrative
    Is *Not*   90

Teach the Genre Using BEW Phases   94

In Summary: Personal Narrative   113

Chapter 7   Persuasive Writing   120

What Is Persuasive Writing?   120

Persuasive Writing Building Blocks   121

Common Student Mistakes: What Persuasive Writing
    Is *Not*   124

Teach the Genre Using BEW Phases   125

In Summary: Persuasive Writing   142

Chapter 8   Research Papers 156

What Is a Research Paper?   156

Research Paper Building Blocks   158

Common Student Mistakes: What a Research Paper
    Is *Not*   159

Teach the Genre Using BEW Phases   161

In Summary: Research Writing   182

Chapter 9   Poetry Writing 187

What Is Poetry?   187

Poetry Building Blocks   188

Common Student Mistakes: What Poetry Is *Not*   188

So, Why Teach Poetry?   190

Teach the Genre Using BEW Phases   190

In Summary: Poetry Writing   202

Chapter 10   Response to Reading   211

What Is Response to Reading?   211

Response to Reading Building Blocks   212

Common Student Mistakes: What Response to Reading
    Is *Not*   213

Teach Response to Reading Using BEW Phases   214

In Summary: Response to Reading   223

Section III: Interactive Creative Activities for Teaching Writing

Chapter 11   Kindergarten through Grade 2   228

Interactive Strategies for Teaching Writing and Genre
    Vocabulary—Genre Format   229

Interactive Strategies for Teaching Writing and Genre
    Vocabulary—Genre Elements   230

Skill-Building Activities for Learning Personal Narrative
    Building Blocks   232

Skill-Building Activities for Learning Persuasive Writing
    Building Blocks   237

Skill-Building Activities for Learning Research Building
    Blocks   240

Skill-Building Activities for Learning Poetry Building
    Blocks   243

Chapter 12   Grades 3 through 5   248

Interactive Strategies for Teaching Writing and Genre
    Vocabulary—Genre Format   249

Interactive Strategies for Teaching Writing and Genre
    Vocabulary—Genre Elements   250

Skill-Building Activities for Learning Personal Narrative
    Building Blocks   253

Skill-Building Activities for Learning Persuasive Writing
    Building Blocks   256

Skill-Building Activities for Learning Research Building
    Blocks   259

Skill-Building Activities for Learning Poetry Building
    Blocks   263

Chapter 13   Grades 6 through 8   268

Interactive Strategies for Teaching Writing and Genre
    Vocabulary—Genre Format   269

Interactive Strategies for Teaching Writing and Genre
    Vocabulary—Genre Elements   271

Skill-Building Activities for Learning Personal Narrative
    Building Blocks   273

Skill-Building Activities for Learning Persuasive Writing
    Building Blocks   277

Skill-Building Activities for Learning Research Building
    Blocks   280

Skill-Building Activities for Learning Poetry Building
    Blocks   283

Chapter 14   Planning for the Future   288

Maintaining the Momentum   288

At the Classroom Level   289

At the Building Level   290

At the District Level   292

Our Final Words   292

**Appendixes   BEW and Researched-Validated
Practices**

Appendix A NCLB and Teaching to Diverse Learners   297

Appendix B Classroom Instruction   300

Glossary   304

Bibliography   307

Index   309

Acknowledgments

Our heartfelt thanks to family and friends who gave freely of their time and talents to support this venture.

Many thanks to Len Gajda for your sharp eye and editing. Gina Abraham, Dr. Deb Christian, Antoinette Gurney, Auleen Jarrett, and Kim Peach, your editing and writing suggestions helped us tremendously. Our artist friend Doraina DeSanto, your sketches are awesome. Eric Bedoun, our fantastic photographer, you've captured those teachable moments! Abraham Marashi, our high school student, you did an awesome job on video editing and technical work. Wendy Hazlett, Katie Bell, and Gayle Seals, you deserve rich thanks for sharing your time and expertise to proofread and provide suggestions from a teacher's point of view. Finally, special thanks to Kevin and Daniel Carney, our support team and fan club. Our gratitude goes out to our friends and family for their encouragement during this adventure. Finally, we thank our mothers who inspired us as teachers. We hope this book is a measure of joy in teaching.

Let's Begin

Welcome to Blueprint for Exceptional Writing

This book is designed for you, the teachers in grades K through 8 who are dedicated to helping students think, plan, and then write interesting and meaningful essays. This book provides a Master Plan to help you build successful writers and to help your students produce successful writing. Blueprint for Exceptional Writing (called BEW for short) provides strategies that you add to your lessons as you teach your writing curriculum.

General Questions and Answers

Q: What is Blueprint for Exceptional Writing?

A: BEW strategies are organized around *five phases* that are designed to help students understand the complex process involved in taking an unadorned idea to a polished writing selection. Here's a short summary of the key features that BEW strategies provide:

- Phases broken down into manageable steps or lesson components, which are taught with *best-practice strategies*, using jingles (spoken or sung), hand or arm motions, and a number of specialized graphic organizers to be used as teaching aids. BEW strategies allow for *differentiation* based on student needs. They involve language enrichment techniques, multisensory experiences, visual tools, and the use of constant repetition to assist learners of all abilities.

- Lessons that demonstrate how to *teach skills in a direct way.* You will find examples of lessons that tell you specific steps you can use such as *ask, answer, teach, model,* and *review.*

- A focus on vocabulary and concepts that are taught and *reviewed* constantly for every genre selection that you cover during the school year.

BEW is a complete system of strategies that fully complements your curriculum instruction. The secret is to adopt a set of strategies that you will use *consistently* so that even your most challenged learners will come to know each step.

Q: **Is BEW a writing curriculum?**

A: No. It's a systematic set of clear, differential teaching strategies designed to teach students all the steps involved in becoming good writers for every genre. These strategies have the added benefit of being compatible with the more popular writing programs and district and state curricula.

Q: **Do I have to use everything in BEW for it to be effective?**

A: Yes. Writing instruction is most powerful if all teachers at a grade level or schoolwide use the same approach. This is true of BEW. You will find a variety of strategies to select from to match your grade level and genre units.

Q: **What does the Master Plan Blueprint for Exceptional Writing look like?**

A: The flowchart in Figure 1 shows the Master Plan for our BEW model. Note the five phases and the multiple steps within each phase that contain strategies for teaching your students to be successful writers. Refer to the Master Plan as you proceed through the sections of this book.

Book Format

Q: **How do I find information in this book?**

A: This book provides three different sections to assist you in your instruction, as well as appendices, a glossary, and a bibliography. Throughout the book we provide examples of black-line masters of our Blueprints and other graphic organizers and student worksheets. Feel free to duplicate any of these teaching and learning aids for classroom use. We know they will bring you great success in your teaching!

Section I

Section I includes five chapters, one for each of the phases in the writing process that we use in BEW. This section develops teaching strategies to help you teach each of the steps in each of these phases of the writing process. All the steps and phases in the BEW Master Plan are appropriate for writing

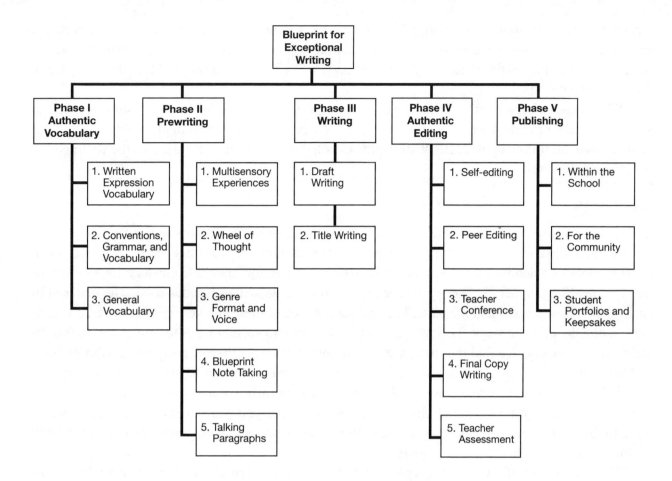

FIGURE 1

The Master Plan

instruction at any grade level. The specific content you teach, however, will align with your grade-level curriculum expectations.

Section II

We have found that teachers want to know more about how to teach writing and what good writing looks like in each genre. Therefore, Sections II and III are provided to help you in these areas.

Many teachers know they have to teach different genres, but have little experience regarding which elements should be included. The chapters in Section II are intended to give you a clear picture of the four most commonly taught genres in grades K through 8. We provide a chapter for each of the following genres: personal narrative, persuasive writing, research, and poetry. In addition, we added a chapter called "Response to Reading." Although not a genre, this chapter teaches your students analytical higher-order thinking skills in combination with a writing activity. This type of writing is valued by the International Reading Association (IRA) and is beginning to be included in many district curricula.

Within each chapter you will find a genre description and the *building blocks* students need to learn to become proficient writers within the genre. We provide real-life student writing samples for your review. We follow up with BEW strategies to help you teach all five phases of the writing process for each genre.

Section III

Section III is designed to be used as a workbook section. The three chapters in this section provide specific interactive strategies and creative activities for teaching the steps in each BEW phase. Each chapter contains teaching strategies that apply to one of the following grade clusters: lower elementary (grades K–2), upper elementary (grades 3–5), and middle school (grades 6–8). The material in each chapter is organized in three parts. The first part of each of these chapters teaches specific vocabulary words in strategic ways. This includes catchy jingles and special ways to remember each writing word or concept. We find that having a memorable strategy (a rhyme, a saying, a hand motion) and using it consistently is the key to helping *all* your learners connect to abstract vocabulary. We also include an area where you can record strategies of your own that apply to the same vocabulary or concept, just in case you already have a great strategy that you want to keep using. Feel free to write in this section and then use your written reference to help build consistent patterns for teaching writing vocabulary words and genre units.

The second part of each of the chapters includes creative activities related to each the four commonly taught genres. You will find several suggestions to help you get started teaching the components of each genre. We hope you find a few fresh ideas to add to your teaching.

The final part of each of the chapters provides frequently seen student grammatical errors with creative remedies for correcting those errors.

Planning for the Future

All the sections in this book are designed to help you instruct your students so that they can demonstrate *content power* in their compositions and produce high-proficiency writing selections. "Planning for the Future" is written to give you ideas for building a schoolwide writing program. Students need to build writing skills from grade to grade, and continuity needs to be provided in teaching instruction for this to happen. Constant assessment and training are necessary to improve teacher and student skills. Student mastery in writing requires refining and developing new school improvement goals each and every year.

Appendix

In the appendices we provide background information on the research that will help your school and district identify the connection between BEW strategies and current research-validated practices.

Glossary

We know that some of the words associated with writing instruction can be confusing. We include a glossary of words and terms related to expressive writing to assist you in this area. Are you unsure of a writing term? Just look it up in our glossary.

Bibliography

This section includes references cited in the text as well as other helpful writing sources.

Blueprint for Exceptional Writing DVD

If you're wondering what BEW looks like in action, just play the enclosed DVD, in which we highlight some of the features of the BEW process with our students for you to see. These special features include teaching vocabulary, authentic editing, and examples of students sharing their published pieces.

BEW Instructional Schedule

Q: **How should I plan my teaching schedule when I use BEW strategies?**

A: We've included some suggestions to follow for teaching BEW throughout your school year.

Yearly

Follow your district and state curriculum guidelines to plan the genre units and skills you want to cover during the school year. Typically, you want to spend two to three weeks on a unit to go through all five phases of the writing process. Repeat this cycle for each genre unit several times. Constant repetition of the same key steps in writing increases your students' understanding and performance.

Remember that you can teach writing in cross-curricular units. You may want to teach the research genre when studying a science unit, or the persuasive writing genre when conducting a social studies unit.

Genre Units

Your grade-level curriculum will dictate which genres should be taught during your school year. You may have four or five genres to cover in a year, and you will teach some of the genres several times, depending on how they relate to your overall curriculum. This results in having multiple writing cycles during which you teach a genre from the Vocabulary Phase to the Publishing Phase of that writing selection. A typical writing cycle lasts three weeks for lower elementary, and two weeks for upper elementary and middle school. We find it is best that students write five to six selections for each genre interspersed throughout the year. For example, you might teach a cycle starting with a personal narrative in September. This might be followed by a persuasive writing selection. After the persuasive selection, you might return to do another personal narrative, and then a research paper. If you use the concept of this spiral repetition, it provides an ongoing review of the requirements of each genre.

Daily Instruction

You will be teaching a genre and asking students to publish a selection every two to three weeks. For each of these units, give each of your students a Rough Draft Writing Folder (see the Student Worksheets at the end of Chapter 1).

Before you begin teaching the BEW process, hand out a Rough Draft Writing Folder to each student. These folders include the word *genre*, the central theme for that genre, and the student topic on its cover sheet. Begin your five- to ten-minute daily vocabulary review with the aid of these folders. Next you will teach, model, and review prewriting strategies that activate student background experiences and language so the students have something real and meaningful to say. This typically takes one to two days. Then you will teach, model, and review the steps in writing the rough draft and title. This takes one to three days. The genre cycle is completed by moving through the Editing Phase (one to two days) and the Publishing Phase (one to two days). Table 1 presents what these schedules might look like. Notice how the plan for each day calls for reviewing all previous learning.

Table 1 Two-Week Teaching Schedule of Personal Narrative

	Monday	Tuesday	Wednesday	Thursday	Friday
Week 1	Vocabulary	Vocabulary Review	Vocabulary Review	Vocabulary Review	Vocabulary Review
	Prewriting Activities	Prewriting Activities	Prewriting Review as Needed*		

	Monday	Tuesday	Wednesday	Thursday	Friday
Week 2	Vocabulary Review	Vocabulary Review	Vocabulary Review	Vocabulary Review	Vocabulary Review
	Writing Activities 1. Writing the Draft	Writing Activities 1. Writing the Draft 2. Title Writing	Editing 1. Self-editing 2. Peer Editing	Editing Review 1. Teacher Conferencing 2. Writing the Final Copy 3. Teacher Assessment	Publishing

*The Prewriting review includes review of the Wheel of Thought and Web of Words graphic organizers to assist students in writing.

BEW and Research-Validated Practices

No Child Left Behind and Teaching to Diverse Learners

Q: **Does the 2001 federal mandate of No Child Left Behind (NCLB) require teachers to use *research-validated* practices in their classrooms?**

A: Yes. NCLB calls for teachers to use *research-validated* strategies with all students. This NCLB mandate provides monies through Title funds that pass through the states to local districts for the education of students at risk. To receive these funds, schools must prove they are using research-validated instructional strategies to improve school achievement.

Q: **Is BEW based on research-validated practices that apply to teaching diverse learners?**

A: Yes. BEW strategies are in line with the recent mandates of NCLB, which requires all teachers to use research-validated practices. BEW strategies were developed over many years, with constant attention paid to updating the strategies to match research for best practice in instructional design to support *all* learners.

The National Center to Improve Tools for Educators (NCITE, 2001) conducted an in-depth review investigating best-practice strategies for diverse learners. NCITE's objective was to find effective strategies and use them to format a specific instructional design. This resulted in the identification of six specific strategies for teaching called the *Effective Teaching Strategies That Accommodate Diverse Learners*. In fact, the combined effect on student learning when all six strategies are used is a very powerful tool that can nearly close the gap between diverse learners and general education students (Coyne, Kame'enui, & Carnine, 2007). These principles have become widely accepted as valid practices to be used with diverse learners across the United States.

When the research-validated six principles of accommodation are compared with the differential teaching strategies used in BEW, you will easily see why our techniques are so effective. Each and every accommodation recommended for teaching by NCITE is present in the differential strategies of BEW. We provide more detailed information about these practices in Appendix A and in Table 2.

Classroom Instruction

Q: **What does research say are good instructional strategies for all students? Is BEW research-validated in this area?**

A: Yes. BEW is directly aligned with *research-validated* strategies for classroom instruction. The Association for Supervision and Curriculum Development (ASCD) is a leading national organization that provides sound research for best practices in education. ASCD has endorsed the research findings of Robert Marzano, a leading researcher, who lists nine strategies that research finds improves student learning (Marzano et al., 2004). When compared with BEW, we find that every principle shown to be effective by this cutting-edge researcher is present in our model (Table 3 on pages xx–xxi). For more detailed information on this research, see Appendix B.

Aligning BEW with Your Writing Program

Q: **Can BEW strategies be used in conjunction with other writing programs that have been adopted by your school district?**

A: Absolutely! These strategies can be used in combination with other programs to enhance your teaching curriculum. BEW strategies will fit hand-in-hand with any writing program that your school or school district is using. You may pick and choose which BEW writing strategy or activity you want to incorporate, or use all five phases with your current writing curriculum.

Table 2 BEW Strategies and the Six Principles of Accommodation for Diverse Learners

Six Principles of Accommodation	BEW Strategies
Principle One–Big Ideas The large concepts that provide the foundation and meaning for the daily and weekly lessons	**All Phases** *Master Plan* composed of five phases of the writing process: vocabulary, prewriting, writing, editing, and publishing
Principle Two–Primed Background Knowledge Connecting instruction to students' background and experiences so that it will be more easily understood	**Phase I** Ongoing review of the *"Big Ten" vocabulary words* and genre-specific vocabulary **Phases I and II** *Multisensory experiences* to support sensory connections and *language development* on topics prior to writing
Principle Three–Conspicuous Strategies Special techniques that help diverse students learn the vocabulary, concepts, steps, and patterns related to the big idea	**Phase I** *Catchy jingles and hand motions* to support the Big Ten vocabulary words **Phases I and II** *Graphic organizers* with specific shapes to provide visual support for language and genre formatting
Principle Four–Mediated Scaffolding Guidance and support provided to learners until they can be successfully independent	**All Phases** *Direct instruction and modeling* for initial teaching in each genre unit **Phases II and III** *Blueprint graphic organizer* with shapes and colors for different paragraphs, and matching writing paper used until they can be phased out
Principle Five–Judicious Review Scheduled opportunities during units and throughout the school year for students to review previous skills and concepts	**All Phases** All five phases in the writing process are reviewed cyclically for *every two- to three-week genre unit* throughout the year **Phase I** Vocabulary reviewed *daily* **Phases II and IV** Student ideas and writing reviewed via talking paragraphs, self-editing, peer editing, and teacher conferencing for *each genre unit* **Phase IV** The creation of student-generated editing rubrics for genre format and voice, vocabulary and usage, and spelling and grammar for *each genre unit*
Principle Six–Strategic Integration Opportunities for students to integrate learning with other areas, helping them advance their skills for authentic purposes	**Phase V** Students write for *real audiences and authentic purposes*. Genre units are tied to other content areas (*cross-curricular writing*)

Source: Adapted from Coyne et al. (2007).
For more detail on the alignment between BEW and these six accommodations, please see Appendix A.

Table 3 BEW Strategies and Nine Effective Instructional Strategies

Nine Effective Instructional Strategies	BEW Strategies
Strategy One–Identifying Similarities and Differences Students connect new learning to previous learning by comparing, contrasting, and classifying information	**All Phases** When teaching genre units, students write their selections based on the *building blocks* of that genre. They must compare and contrast each specific building block correctly to distinguish the appropriate genre format
Strategy Two–Summarizing and Note Taking Students need to practice these skills to learn to sort out important details from unimportant ones.	**Phases I and II** *Graphic organizers* in BEW help students summarize their ideas on a topic and record notes. The *Blueprint* requires students to put notes into sequential order
Strategy Three–Reinforcing Effort and Providing Recognition Teachers can improve student learning by reinforcing student effort on tasks and providing recognition as they progress in their learning	**All Phases** All phases include *direct instruction* with student input, resulting in praise, student applause, and recognition of effort. Phase IV (editing) provides opportunities for students and the teacher to provide positive *feedback*. Phase V (publishing) results in public accolades
Strategy Four–Homework and Practice Students should complete homework as independently as possible. Immediate feedback from the teacher is needed when homework is assessed	**Phase II** In elementary grades, homework entails bringing *pictures* and *memorabilia* that coordinate with *writing topics*. In higher grades, it includes writing final copies and collecting research
Strategy Five–Nonlinguistic Representations Students learn by using words, but also when there are images or motor responses that can be added	**Phase I** BEW strategies include jingles and hand motions to help remember key *vocabulary words* **Phase II** BEW strategies include *graphic organizers* in which shapes and colors trigger expectations; also use literary bags and boxes
Strategy Six–Cooperative Learning Student learning is enhanced by having students work in small groups	**Phase II** Students *talk out* selections prior to writing **Phase IV** Students work with each other and provide support for each other during *editing*
Strategy Seven–Setting Objectives and Providing Feedback Learning should be goal oriented, with corrective feedback that is immediate and varied. Students should buy into the goals	**All Phases** Corrective feedback occurs during explicit instruction, modeled lessons, and the *editing phase*. Each genre unit has the expectation of a *final published piece*—a *presentation* for a specific *audience*

Table 3 BEW Strategies and Nine Effective Instructional Strategies (continued)

Nine Effective Instructional Strategies	BEW Strategies
Strategy Eight–Generating and Testing Hypotheses Teaching this skill involves open-ended questions that allow students to analyze, problem solve, make decisions, and investigate concepts	**Phase II** *Open-ended questions* are used during the Prewriting Phase to stimulate thoughts on the topic (e.g., What would happen if . . . ? What would you do then?)
Strategy Nine–Cues, Questions, and Advance Organizers Using these three techniques can trigger student memories and stimulate learning	**All Phases** BEW utilizes all three techniques to stimulate student language and writing. This includes *picture cues, hand motions, multisensory experiences* and the *Blueprint graphic organizer*

Source: Adapted from Marzano et al. (2004).
For more detail on the alignment between BEW and these nine strategies, please see Appendix B.

One of the most widely used program in our schools today is *6 Traits of Writing* (Spandel, 2008). There are also various programs involving student writing workshops. These programs are a perfect fit with BEW instructional strategies. *6 Traits of Writing* bases instruction on six critical elements of writing. These elements are eventually blended together to produce a finished writing selection. The key traits are instructed one trait at a time using a systematic method. Students apply each trait to their own writing and are assessed according to the appropriate six-trait rubric. Students blend these traits into all writing selections as they become more proficient writers. According to Spandel (2008), these six traits are so widely used that many school districts are incorporating them into district teaching standards. This method of teaching helps students break down the complex process of writing into manageable steps. It gives teachers and students a common vehicle for evaluating writing, and a common vocabulary with which to discuss it. This writing program has the key advantage of being compatible with the language arts curriculum used for reading instruction.

BEW and 6 Traits have many complementary features. In fact, you will find that adding BEW strategies to your instruction helps all your students, but particularly targets your diverse learners and helps them become more successful as they progress through the writing process. Table 4 presents how BEW and 6 Traits can enhance writing instruction in your classroom when used together.

Table 4 BEW and 6 Traits Writing

6 Traits Writing	BEW Strategies
Overall This is a *process writing program* designed to support curriculum and instruction especially through revision and editing.	**Overall** This is a five-phase set of process writing strategies that supports curriculum and instruction with heavy emphasis on prewriting activities and genre format. BEW strategies are designed to stand alone or to complement and enhance any process writing program. For example, teach the 6 Traits using BEW instructional strategies.
Organizational Structure Instruction centers on teaching and assessing *one trait* at a time as students progress through multiple writing assignments. It provides a common writing *vocabulary* with focus lessons and examples of student work at different proficiency levels for each of the traits.	**Organizational Structure** Instruction centers on strategies for teaching all phases of the writing process—including genre format and voice—for each writing assignment in any genre. The 6 Traits can be introduced *one trait* at a time with BEW's interactive teaching strategies. After each trait is mastered, the next trait can be introduced in the next BEW writing assignment. This strategy fits with BEW teaching *authentic vocabulary*.
Prewriting Activities Emphasis is on *modeling* and *showing examples* in class as students *plan* their writing. It is important to recognize that ideas for a writing selection often change during the revision stage.	**Prewriting Activities** This phase provides *daily* vocabulary and language-building activities related to *topics* and *genres*. It uses graphic organizers and multisensory activities to stimulate student language and experiences. Use BEW strategies to help all writers find their own topics. The prewriting strategies can enhance student learning and understanding when used with 6 Traits by assisting students to connect a writing *topic* to their own *experiences*.
Assessment *Rubrics* with samples of student work at each *proficiency level* are provided for each trait. Teachers are supported in understanding what proficient writing looks like for each trait and at different grade levels. This allows them to understand and assist students more thoroughly in gaining those skills.	**Assessment** *Rubrics* in BEW teaching involve editing student-writing selections three different times for genre format and voice, vocabulary and usage, and grammar and spelling. Students create each rubric as a class, reviewing skills they have learned. The 6 Traits can be added to this rubric. *Both types of rubric* can be used with students as they develop the six traits and as they learn to proofread their work.

A second very popular process-writing approach widely used in schools today is a concept called *writing workshops*. This student-centered teaching approach advocates the creation of a writing environment that encourages students to see themselves as writers. Writing workshops use small-group dynamics to help students collaborate with one another to generate writing ideas and then to develop these ideas into their personal writing concepts. Students share ideas in small groups, self-discover topics for writing, and then write routinely and frequently about these topics. Instruction is most often conducted in minilessons driven by student need. Teacher modeling and modeling by using many professionally written examples are key elements in teaching process writing with these strategies. Currently there are a wide variety of titles available using the writing workshop idea for instruction, including *Directing the Writer's Workshop* (Gillet & Beverly), *Writing Workshop: The Essential Guide* (Fletcher & Portalupi), *A Writer's Workshop: Crafting Paragraphs, Building Essays* (Brannon), and *Writing Like Writers: Guiding Elementary Children through a Writer's Workshop* (Johnson).

BEW strategies can enhance instruction in any classroom that uses the *writing workshop* process. Teachers who use the workshop approach can incorporate many BEW teaching strategies into their minilessons. For instance, BEW teaching strategies assist diverse learners in finding topics to write about using the Wheel of Thought. BEW strategies also help develop voice and provide guidance in understanding the overall structure of writing selections. Even with the safe atmosphere of a writer's workshop format, your students benefit from BEW's strategies for teaching language experiences and multisensory activities to stimulate their ideas for writing. Table 5 (page xxiv) shows how writing workshop ideas can be aligned with BEW concepts to provide a more effective writing program.

Table 5 BEW and Writing Workshop Ideas

Writing Workshop Ideas	BEW Strategies
Overall A *process writing* approach that promotes the development of a strong *writing community* within the classroom. The steps in this *writing cycle* emphasize prewriting, revising, editing, and publishing. The concept teaches the *doing of writing* rather than talking about it, resulting in the *flow* of student writing.	**Overall** A *process writing* set of strategies organized in five phases. The strategies can be used in their entirety or they may be used selectively to fit with your teaching style and your students' needs. BEW strategies can be used effectively with writing workshops by enhancing the *writing climate* of classrooms and making sure students *understand the steps* in the writing process.
Organizational Structure Student writing time is *scheduled* in a *consistent and predictable* way. Writing is practiced *daily*. Direct instruction occurs in *minilessons* driven by student need.	**Organizational Structure** Daily writing instruction is organized into five phases with logical, *consistent* steps in each phase taught explicitly to accelerate student learning. BEW strategies can be incorporated easily into *minilessons*. Enhance *minilessons* by using the strategies to instruct character dialogue and voice, or grammar rules, such as using quotation marks.
Prewriting Activities Students are shown *examples* from professionally published works, such as storybooks, picture books, or specific genre-related selections. *Teachers model, and students often self-select topics*.	**Prewriting Activities** The first two phases of BEW provide strategies for *daily vocabulary development* and for developing *language and ideas* to help with writing genres. In BEW, teachers are advised to *model each step* involved in the writing process. Graphic organizers, such as the Wheel of Thought, help students easily develop *the individual writing topics* needed in *writing workshops*.
Assessment The procedure for assessing skills is embedded as part of the writing cycle. It frequently involves *students being their own first editor*, and *teacher conferencing* focused on one or two skills specific to each student's needs.	**Assessment** Student-generated classroom *rubrics* are used for assessing each student selection during three steps: self-editing, peer editing, and teacher conferencing. Using *student-generated rubrics* enhances the assessment process in writing workshops. Also, *peer editing* is a natural small-group activity.
Sharing Student Work Writers workshops strongly advocate *sharing* student selections. Writing for an audience and a specific purpose is seen as key.	**Student Publishing** BEW advocates using *purposeful student publishing ideas* for every writing selection. Students are *motivated* to do their best when they know their writing will be shared. BEW publishing strategies advocate a *real-life* method of publishing, just like that of writing workshops. We provide a lengthy list of ways to make *publishing purposeful*. These publishing activities can add motivation to writing workshop classroom activities.

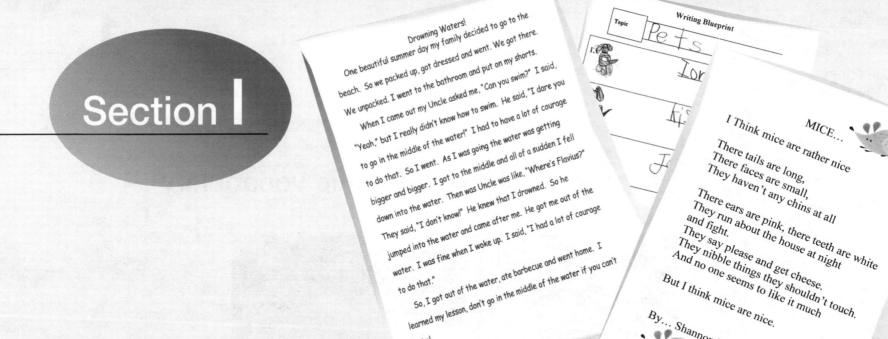

The Master Blueprint Plan

Chapter 1   Phase I: Teaching Authentic Vocabulary

Chapter 2   Phase II: Teaching Prewriting Strategies

Chapter 3   Phase III: Teaching Writing

Chapter 4   Phase IV: Teaching Authentic Editing

Chapter 5   Phase V: Publishing—Sharing the Purpose

Section **I**

*Children speak before they
write. Enrich their writing
vocabulary orally before
you ask them to use the
concepts in their writing.
Do this in an authentic
way so that it is clear
and memorable for them.
Review these words often.*

Phase I: Teaching Authentic Vocabulary

Using the BEW process, we teach written expressive vocabulary by using an authentic learning approach. We offer tried-and-true strategies (gestures, pantomime, and creative teaching techniques) to help add a visual, auditory, or kinesthetic action to assist students in learning a skill or concept. You can use our strategies just as they are or modify them to reflect your teaching style. By using

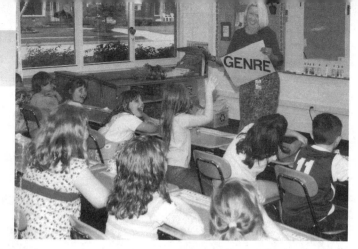

Mrs. Demski's second-grade class has a great time learning new writing vocabulary words!

BEW's interactive strategies systematically and repeatedly, the added visual and verbal cues will help all learners to have a quick multisensory connection to the concept. During the past twenty years, we've also found that using BEW's differential teaching strategies with students identified as at risk, and with special needs, and English language learners (ELLs) have dramatically increased their expressive writing skills.

Before You Start: Student Rough Draft Writing Folders

Before you begin Phase I of BEW, every one of your students will need a Rough Draft Writing Folder. This simple-to-make folder has two purposes. First, it is designed to hold all the graphic organizers, webs, and writing prompts for one student assignment. This eliminates students losing papers. Second, it acts as a stepping-stone to teaching expressive writing vocabulary, because the cover of the Rough Draft Writing Folder contains some of the key vocabulary words that will be taught. The black-line master student worksheets for grade-level-appropriate Rough Draft Writing Folders are included at the end of this chapter.

The Rough Draft Writing Folder is set up with a cover sheet, on which the students write their name, project start and finish dates, theme, and student topic. When you open the folder, you will find a Blueprint Graphic Organizer (the purpose of this organizer is discussed later in this chapter) on the left side and corresponding writing paper on the right side. Students should have one of these folders for every genre writing selection that you teach throughout the year.

Steps in Phase I: Teaching Authentic Vocabulary

There is no need to tell you that teaching writing can be difficult when students in a single classroom have widely diverse abilities and backgrounds. The first phase in our Master Plan (see Figure 1.1) involves teaching writing vocabulary to your students in a way that even the students with special needs, ELLs, or students with other risk factors will actually know what you are talking about. When you teach vocabulary authentically, students retain more than they do by looking up the definition of

ELL–BEWCONNECTION

ELL students lack age-appropriate vocabulary. Teach writing vocabulary first the BEW way.

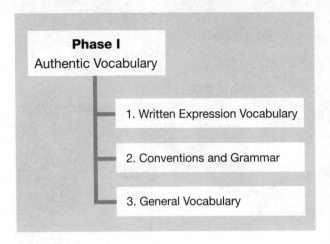

Phase I
Authentic Vocabulary

1. Written Expression Vocabulary

2. Conventions and Grammar

3. General Vocabulary

FIGURE 1.1

The Master Plan Branch

writing vocabulary words in a dictionary and recording them in their notebooks. So, put away the notebooks and you'll be surprised to see how much your students retain by using our methods.

Students often find the words used with writing to be abstract. Using the BEW process, we provide strategies for a concrete way of teaching vocabulary and having fun while you're doing it. Students learn by mimicking these strategies and master the concepts by repeated practice.

The three areas of vocabulary addressed during Phase I of BEW teaching strategies are as follows:

Step 1: Written Expression Vocabulary. Vocabulary words used during the writing process (such as genre, theme, topic) as well as genre-specific vocabulary words (such as plot, research question, argument)

Step 2: Conventions and Grammar. Vocabulary words used in conventions and grammar (such as indenting, transitions, adverbs) as well as genre-specific vocabulary words (such as author's point of view, verb tense, chronological order)

Step 3: General Vocabulary. Vocabulary words that enhance written communication (such as imagery, powerful verbs, metaphors) on any given topic

Step 1: Written Expression Vocabulary

The Big Ten Words that are appropriate for grades K through 8 are

1. Genre: the kind of writing
2. Central Theme: large topic
3. Topic: that's what it's all about
4. Illustration: a picture drawn by the author or an artist
5. Blueprint: graphic organizer
6. Rough Draft: learning copy
7. Editing: fixing our mistakes
8. Final Copy: finished writing selection
9. Publishing: sharing with others
10. Student Portfolio: collection of our work

FIGURE 1.2

Autumn, one of our young authors, certainly knows her writing vocabulary words! She shows her artistic talent by drawing her teacher reviewing the Big Ten Written Expression words.

When we observe master teachers instructing reading, social studies, or history, the first step they teach involves the critical vocabulary associated with the subject. For years, students have increased their knowledge base and reading skills by learning new vocabulary words associated with a subject. Why should writing be any different? Before students can complete a writing assignment effectively, they must understand all the writing vocabulary associated with their writing project and appropriate to their specific grade level.

When teaching written expression vocabulary, there are ten key vocabulary words we recommend for grades K through 8. These words and concepts must be taught in an interactive way.

Big Ten Vocabulary Word 1: Genre

Genre comes first, whether you're teaching beginning writers, such as kindergarten students, or more experienced writers like eighth-grade students. Genre can be taught as early as kindergarten and should be expanded upon throughout a student's entire school career. Keep in mind that all literature is categorized according to its genre. For instance, your literacy curriculum more than likely gives your students examples of short stories, poems, letters, research reports, and biographies—to name a few.

> **KEY:** Understanding genre in reading and writing is the critical first step in teaching writing vocabulary.

In addition, increasing student understanding of literacy genres will improve their expressive writing scores on state high-stake tests. The sections of state proficiency writing tests are organized according to very specific genres. When students understand the specific genres being evaluated by your state's standards, they will successfully compose a genre-appropriate selection. For example, if your state writing test instructs students to develop a persuasive argument on a given writing prompt, and students being tested are unaware of the building blocks needed for composing a persuasive argument, they will be unsuccessful in meeting state requirements. Consequently, students must be made aware of genre-specific writing format and style through teaching strategies. To teach this in an interactive way, follow Professor Write on page 6.

> **SUGGESTION:**
> Use the associated, catchy hand jive, pantomime, or rhyme we've created for each writing genre (listed by grade-level clusters in Section III).

Professor Write's Interactive Teaching Strategy

Genre

Ask: "What is genre?"

Give Them a Precise Answer: "Genre is the kind of writing."

Explain: Give examples of categorizing different types of letters. For example, ask your students: "How many of you have written a friendly letter or email? You write a friendly letter or email to a friend—somebody that you know well." Students might respond affirmatively. Then ask: "How many of you have written a business letter or email? You write a business letter or email to somebody other than a friend, maybe a teacher or the principal." Next, ask them: "How are these two types of email or letters different?" They may tell you that a friendly letter or email uses different vocabulary and sentence types than a business letter. Explain to your students that, just as there are different types of letters, there are also many different genres in writing. Different writing genres sound different, use different words, and have a different purpose just like different types of letters or email.

Repeat the Question and Answer: "What is genre? Genre is the kind of writing." Have your students repeat the definition to you, to their neighbor, and then to another neighbor in exactly the same way. Repetition and oral responses give additional support to your students with special needs, ELLs, and students with other risk factors. They will remember and recall these important vocabulary words just as quickly as your other students, and everybody will have fun with words at the same time!

WRITING TIPS

Writing Tips: Teaching *Genre*

- Bring a variety of songs from different music genres to your class. Play them and ask your students to categorize each song according to its genre.

- Bring a variety of reading selections from different genres to your class. Read them aloud to students and ask your students to categorize each selection according to its genre. Ask them to state reasons for their answers.

- Discuss current movies and have the class group the movies into the correct genre and give reasons for their answers.

- Discuss current television programs and have the class group the television programs into the correct genre and give reasons for their answers.

Big Ten Vocabulary Word 2: Central Theme

Following the concept of genre, the next authentic vocabulary concept that should be taught is central theme. Do your students shrug their shoulders and say, "I don't know what to write about"? Getting started on a topic is the most difficult part of any expressive writing assignment.

Central theme is a broad concept that encompasses a whole spectrum of more narrowly focused topics that students actually use as subject matter to compose their writing. For example, a reading series may have a central theme of courage. Each student may think about a time in their own lives when they demonstrated courage. This event becomes the student topic—our next vocabulary word. Knowing the difference between theme and topic will help students narrow their writing focus and follow the writing prompt more accurately.

Professor Write's Interactive Teaching Strategy

Central Theme

Ask: "What is the central theme?"

Give a Precise Answer: "It is the big idea that each of our stories must be about."

Explain: Many times your elementary reading program will provide a central theme that relates to a series of stories you are reading, so connect this theme to your writing. This helps students see that reading and writing are related. Use a central theme from your reading program. Tell students that it is important to be able to write on a topic related to a big idea. This helps students understand that big idea in different ways. Every student should pick a topic that relates to the same central theme.

Repeat the Question and Answer: "What is the central theme? It is the big idea that each of our stories must be about." Have your students repeat the definition to you, to their neighbor, and then to another neighbor in exactly the same way. Repetition and oral responses give additional support to your students with special needs, ELLs, or students with other risk factors.

Big Ten Vocabulary Word 3: Topic

It is important to teach your students what a topic is in writing. The word *topic*, however, can't be taught in a vacuum; it must be taught in relation to a central theme. Frequently, educators confuse the central theme with the topic. The difference between these two concepts must be clear to students in order for them to write. Therefore, after teaching about a central theme, teach students that they will pick a topic that tells something about that theme—something they know about and can describe. We use a graphic organizer—the Wheel of Thought (see Student Worksheet 2.1 at the end of Chapter 2)—to help students brainstorm topics related to a theme. Then teach a little jingle (to the tune of "The Hokey Pokey") that will help your students remember the meaning of the word *topic:* "That's what it's all about: [each student adds a word or two about their own topic to complete the jingle]."

Professor Write's Interactive Teaching Strategy

Topic

Ask: "What is a writing topic?"

Give a Precise Answer: Have the students sing, "That's what it's all about [add a word for the student's topic]," to the tune of "The Hokey Pokey."

Explain: Read a short paragraph to the students. Ask them to identify the topic: "What is this paragraph all about?" Reverse the procedure by giving them a topic and ask for a short paragraph that captures the topic. This oral language activity gives additional support to students with special needs, ELLs, or students with other risk factors who might not otherwise master this concept. Young authors must be taught that their sentences have to go with the topic; older students must be taught that all the paragraphs in the writing project must relate to the topic.

Repeat the Question and Answer: "What is a writing topic? That's what it's all about." Repeat this question and answer each time you talk about a topic or topic sentence.

WRITING TIPS

Writing Tips: Teaching *Topic*

- Have students from other classes read their writing selections to your class and ask the group, "What is their topic?" Have them give reasons why they think so.

- Read a published short story to your class and ask them, "What is the topic?" and "What could be the central theme?"

- Write a short story on the board that doesn't stay on the topic and ask your students, "Is this story on the topic?" Ask them why or why not and, if not, how could the writer fix it?

Big Ten Vocabulary Word 4: Illustration

An illustration is simply a picture. It can be drawn by the author or an artist. Young authors may have not learned this term yet, but teach it to them because kids love to learn big words. Young children who cannot write sentences can learn about the meaning of the topic by viewing illustrations. Children who can't read will open a book and attempt to understand the story by looking at the pictures. In writing, capitalize on this natural childhood aptitude. Give young authors a topic and ask them to draw an illustration that depicts the action. They will soon learn the connection between illustrations and topics.

As for older students, drawing may not be their favorite activity; however, they must understand the role that illustrations play in writing. Have your students flip through their literacy textbooks. They will see many illustrations that enhance the text. If students don't like to draw, have them find pictures from other sources, such as magazines or the Internet, that they can include in their finished writing projects.

WRITING TIPS

Writing Tips: Teaching *Illustration*

- Show the class a variety of illustrations from books and magazines. Ask, "What could be the topic that goes along with this story?"

- Ask young authors to draw *topical illustrations*. For instance, if the topic of their story is winter and they draw a swimming pool, their illustration doesn't reflect the topic.

- Give your students a list of topics and ask them to cut pictures from a magazine and create a topic collage.

Professor Write's Interactive Teaching Strategy

Illustration

Ask: "What is an illustration?"

Give a Precise Answer: "It is a picture."

Explain: Young authors must learn that illustrations go along with or enhance the meaning of writing. Many young children who can't read have already learned this lesson, because they often look at the pictures in a book and describe what will happen next merely by looking at the illustration.

Repeat the Question and Answer: "What is an illustration? It is a picture." Repeat this many times, even after your students know it by heart.

SUGGESTION:

Look at the Blueprint worksheet samples that match your level of instruction contained within the Rough Draft Writing Folders at the end of this chapter.

Big Ten Vocabulary Word 5: Blueprint

Good writers plan what they are going to write before they begin. Children need to be taught this concept too. Some people use outlines; others use graphic organizers. With the BEW process we

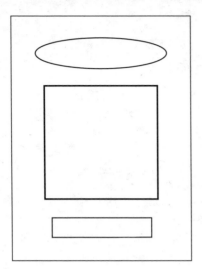

FIGURE 1.3

Mini Blueprint

recommend using our Blueprint Graphic Organizer, which provides a visual cue to help students across all genres (see Figure 1.3). Think of a blueprint that is used in construction. It is a scaled representation, including dimensions, that correlates to the size and shape of real rooms. Our Blueprint has exactly the same purpose in writing. This graphic organizer, called a *Blueprint*, is used to organize and build student writing selections. We have prepared a Blueprint for each level of writer, starting with those writing simple sentences and drawing a picture, to those who can write multiple paragraphs (see all levels of Blueprints at the end of this chapter in the Rough Draft Writing Folders). To teach the Blueprint concept to your class, use the following strategy.

 Professor Write's Interactive Teaching Strategy

Blueprint

Ask: "What is a Blueprint?"

Give a Precise Answer: "It is the plan that helps us organize and build our writing."

Explain: Use the following explanation: "How does a builder know how to build a house? He has a blueprint drawing that shows him where each room will be built (like the bedrooms and kitchen) and it tells us the exact dimensions of each room as well. In writing we can use a blueprint too. It is a plan that helps us organize and build our writing. Here is what the Blueprint that we will be using looks like. You will use this Blueprint to help you build writing project."

Repeat the Question and Answer: "What is a Blueprint? It is the plan that helps us organize and build our writing." Repeat this question as often as you need to at the beginning of your instruction for each genre. The more you repeat it, the more concrete this concept becomes for your neediest students.

Big Ten Vocabulary Word 6: Rough Draft

Do your students rush through their writing assignments, turn in their first draft, and believe they are finished? If so, you're not alone. Most school-age students feel that once they've written an assignment, it's never to be looked at again. Consequently, students don't produce quality writing assignments that reflect their true potential. This problem can be solved by teaching your students they must complete a rough draft and that it will be refined several times before they write their final copy. By doing this, students will begin to understand writing as a recursive process. A *recursive writing process* is one in which changes are made repeatedly to the writing selection by revisiting, editing, and rewriting. In order for your students to internalize this concept, they must be taught that their best work is achieved through writing many drafts.

Professor Write's Interactive Teaching Strategy

Rough Draft

Ask: "What is a rough draft?"

Give a Precise Answer: "It is the learning copy."

Explain: Tell your students that it's OK to make mistakes on their rough draft. Tell them that this is where they will practice their writing before they get it just the way they want it. By teaching this principle, students learn that writing is a recursive process. In other words, it is a process through which their writing is continually improved.

Repeat the Question and Answer: "What is a rough draft? It is the learning copy." Repeat this question and answer often.

Do your students lose their writing assignments? When it's time to write their rough draft do they search for their notes hopelessly in their desks? Tell your students to put all their writing material in their Rough Draft Writing Folders and the problem will be eliminated.

Big Ten Vocabulary Word 7: Editing

Many instructional writing programs separate revising and editing into two consecutive steps. The BEW process eliminates most writing errors that require major revisions because it forces students to follow a structured writing path that prevents errors as part of the writing process. The strategies in BEW provide a structure for genre writing. Because writing errors that would require mandatory revisions, such as veering off the topic, are corrected with BEW's Prewriting Strategies, we have combined the two traditional steps of revising and editing into one and refer to both as *editing*.

With the BEW process we address three editing steps: self-editing, peer editing, and teacher conferencing. Each of these three steps gives students the opportunity to learn and to correct their

WRITING TIPS

Writing Tips: Teaching *Editing*

- Think of a time when you made an error in writing, and tell your students about it. This could be in a letter sent home to parents or in a school calendar of events.

- Make an intentional writing error on the board and see if your class catches it. Give the class credit for doing so!

- Save newspaper articles with mistakes to use as examples of "editing gone bad" for your class.

mistakes. Initially, a class rubric is developed. This rubric is then used by each student to evaluate their own writing and to make changes as appropriate. Next the students use the rubric to evaluate a peer's writing. Mistakes are talked about among the students and further changes are made. Using the same rubric, the teacher and the student evaluate the writing selection together, and their changes are incorporated into the writing selection. You will be correcting papers after students have had three opportunities to fix their errors!

 Professor Write's Interactive Teaching Strategy

Editing

Ask: "What is editing?"

Give a Precise Answer: "It is fixing our mistakes."

- "What is self-editing? Fixing our own mistakes."
- "What is peer editing? Helping our friends fix their mistakes."
- "What is teacher conferencing? Fixing our mistakes with the teacher's help."

Explain: Use the following explanation: "After we write our sentences and paragraphs, we need to go back over our writing to see if it makes sense. We check to see if it sounds right when we read it aloud, and we fix our spelling and punctuation mistakes. This is called *editing*. We will develop an editing rubric for each writing selection that we do, and we will use it to help us edit. It is important to edit with this rubric several times to be sure each writing selection is the best that it can be. It's good to get other people's opinions about our writing to help us see things we missed on our own. So we'll edit and fix our mistakes, then we'll have a classmate edit and fix those mistakes, and then we'll have a conference with the teacher to help us edit our writing one more time and fix those mistakes. The final paper will then be our best work!"

Repeat the Question and Answer: "What is editing? It is fixing our mistakes." Repeat this question and answer each time you talk about editing.

Big Ten Vocabulary Word 8: Final Copy

Next we define and teach *final copy* as our finished assignment—our best work. Most students feel this is the easy part! They now incorporate all the editing corrections from the rough draft into their finished product.

Professor Write's Interactive Teaching Strategy

Final Copy

Ask: "What is the final copy?"

Give a Precise Answer: "It is our finished assignment—our best work."

Explain: Help the students see that they have done all the hard work, forming their ideas, putting them in order, writing them into sentences and paragraphs, and fixing their mistakes. Now they get to write the final copy—their finished assignment—their best work.

Repeat the Question and Answer: "What is the final copy? It is the finished assignment—our best work." Repeat this question and answer as often as you teach the concept.

WRITING TIPS

Writing Tips: Teaching *Final Copy*

- For young authors, instead of writing their final copies in the usual way, use a handwriting worksheet for penmanship practice and give two grades—one for penmanship and the other for writing content.

- Let students with special needs, ELLs, or students with other risk factors use the computer to complete their finished writing selection.

- Provide specialty paper or templates for students to decorate their final copies.

No complaints from Shannon as she eagerly types her final writing selection on a laptop!

Big Ten Vocabulary Word 9: Publishing

Students need to understand that writing is purposeful. This understanding eliminates a writing assignment that is, for example, taken out of a student's pocket, smoothed out, and then handed in. Students must know from the beginning that their work will be published. *Publishing* means sharing their work with others. This may include speeches, peer readings, readings to different grade levels, grade-level presentations, bulletin board displays, or any other creative way you choose to share finished selections.

Professor Write's Interactive Teaching Strategy

Publishing

Ask: "What is publishing?"

Give a Precise Answer: "It is sharing your work with others."

Explain: Tell your students that we write for a purpose, and this purpose needs to be defined before you start. This way, your students will have a goal for sharing their writing with others. Remind your students who they are writing for as they work on their projects and who they will be sharing their stories with.

Repeat the Question and Answer: "What is publishing? It is sharing your work with others." Repeat this question and answer, reminding your students that they will publish the genre they are writing about now, and each genre that you teach during the school year.

WRITING TIPS

Writing Tips: Teaching *Publishing*

- Have a parent publishing committee assigned to type and bind student stories, and assemble them into books to be placed in a special corner of the school library.

- Display stories on bulletin boards.

- Look in Chapter 5 to find many more ideas!

Big Ten Vocabulary Word 10: Student Portfolio

A student portfolio is a collection of your students' writing selections, including the teacher's rubric used for evaluation. This portfolio can be kept in a large envelope for young authors or in folders for older authors. Always keep these portfolios available for students to review, which will help them improve future writing assignments. You will find that your students will then go back and reread their writing selection for fun and will also review the assessment. Often they will be surprised by recognizing their own writing growth. Students tell us, "I was only writing two paragraphs in September and now I'm writing two pages!"

Step 2: Conventions and Grammar

The four major conventions and grammar concepts appropriate for grades K through 8 are:

1. *Complete Sentences* (especially for young authors): sentences with a complete subject and predicate

2. *Paragraphs:* sentences that relate to one topic

3. *Topic Sentences:* sentences that introduce that topic and serve as a hook to draw the audience into the story

4. *Transition Sentences:* sentences that connect one paragraph to another

Conventions and grammar may bring to mind the use of workbooks or worksheets. Stop! Don't go there yet! With the BEW process, this step is interactive and authentic. Teaching conventions and grammar vocabulary authentically is achieved by first using examples in spoken language. For example, instead of doing a workbook page on how to write a complete sentence, write a sentence on the board using one of your students' names and something they like to do. This automatically engages your students and the result is concept understanding. What you'll hear from your students is: "Can I make up a sentence now?" These examples should come from your students' backgrounds and not from workbooks. Teach them interactively. To bring power to these concepts well before writing, they must be embedded in the students' own words first by speaking. Connect concepts, such as story topics, to your students' own real-life experiences.

This is *vital:* Students must first use these concepts correctly in their oral language before you can expect success when teaching conventions and grammar in writing. Therefore, we recommend that when teaching authentic vocabulary for conventions and grammar, teachers should first work with students' spoken words and *then* with their written words. When taught interactively through two-way, meaningful conversations between teacher and student, lessons on conventions and grammar transfer more readily to their writing selections. This may be the only successful method for teaching conventions and grammar effectively to students with special needs, ELLs, or students with other risk factors. Using this method, students internalize these principles far more effectively than by doing workbook exercises. In addition, students use more complex phrases in their first draft—a distinct advantage when taking high-stakes state proficiency tests.

We present suggestions for teaching many grade-level conventions and grammar vocabulary in Section III. Teaching these vocabulary words spirals across grade levels. Some of the same concepts appear at each grade level, but with added vocabulary each year. Even so, there are four main concepts in conventions and grammar that we suggest be taught at each grade level.

Complete Sentences

Many young authors have a difficult time with the formulation of complete sentences. Are your students writing phrases instead of complete sentences? Do they write run-on sentences? It seems that students at every age can use a refresher on sentence writing! We like to use a strategy that looks like a math problem—and it works too!

WRITING TIPS

Writing Tips: Teaching Sentence Writing

- Try writing student names with actions in it directly under the sentence equation, like this:

  Who or What + A Doing = A Sentence
  Jessica + eats lunch at school.

- Ask your students, "Who's the Who?" and they will respond with, "Jessica." Then ask, "What's the Doing?" and they'll respond with "eats lunch at school." Repeat this activity with the names of various students and different activities.

- Read sentences to students and play the game "Is it a sentence or not?" Read a fragment to your students and ask them if it's a sentence or not. They'll say, "Not." Then ask them, "What's missing? The Who or What, or the Doing?" Have them identify what's missing and write it on the board. All young authors will learn to write full sentences from this vocabulary activity.

- As for older students, use the same teaching method but complete the activity by doing a basic sentence diagram including subject and predicate. Like this:

  Subject / predicate
  All students / enjoy a hot summer day.

Professor Write's Interactive Teaching Strategy

Sentence

Ask: "What is a sentence?"

Give a Precise Answer: "Who or What plus A Doing equals a sentence."

Explain: For young authors, use a sentence strip to teach the parts of a sentence. Our suggestion is to write it like a math problem: Who/What + A Doing = A Sentence. We find that students can connect with the math sentence before they understand a word sentence. Both parts, "Who or What" as well as "A Doing" must be present to be a sentence.

Repeat the Question and Answer: "What is a sentence? Who or What plus A Doing equals a sentence." Repeat this every time you are teaching what makes a sentence.

Paragraphs

Many students, especially young authors, have a hard time writing paragraphs. In our BEW strategies we outline an interactive plan for teaching paragraph writing. The first principle is teaching the importance of writing three sentences on one topic. Advanced students fully understand that a paragraph may have from one to many sentences, but to teach the principle of paragraphing to young students, it's best to use this rule.

Professor Write's Interactive Teaching Strategy

Paragraph

Ask: "What's a paragraph?"

Give a Precise Answer: "It's at least three sentences on one topic." Model and ask students to put up three fingers and then one finger, matching the words of the sentence. A shortened version is *three on one.*

Explain: Teach that a paragraph must be at least three sentences on one topic. Tell students to repeat the phrase and hand action *three on one* to remember this concept. Provide both oral and written examples of paragraphs for which you demonstrate three sentences that *are* on one topic and three sentences that are *not* on one topic. Use your students' names and real-life narrative examples when teaching to your class.

Repeat: "What's a paragraph? It's at least three sentences on one topic." Say this using the hand actions. Repeat this question and answer each time you talk about a paragraph.

Do your students have trouble formatting paragraphs? Frequently, young authors tend to write their sentences in a list fashion, like a spelling test, with each sentence on its own line rather than in true paragraph form. It is important to teach these young students to begin each sentence in a paragraph right after the punctuation mark of the sentence before it. This idea of writing that goes from side to side to make one paragraph is called *word wrapping* in the BEW process. Demonstrate this visually on the board by running your hand across it from side to side, and tell students to do the *word-wrap dance.* This motion is just like one that a computer makes when it automatically moves to the next line as you type. Students swing their hand right to left in front of their body chanting, "We write side to side, side to side." This jingle and the hand action quickly teach all students paragraph formatting.

Professor Write's Interactive Teaching Strategy

Paragraph Word Wrap

Ask: "How do we write a paragraph?"

Give a Precise Answer: "From side to side; from side to side." Model moving your hand from side to side and ask your students to do it too.

Explain: Run your hand across some sentences, showing the students that paragraphs are written across the paper in a side-to-side fashion. Turn this into a hand jive and call it the word-wrap dance. Show your students that paragraphs are written side to side and that words wrap across the page just like a computer writes them. Your hand motions will visually show students how to write a paragraph in the correct form.

Repeat: "How do we write a paragraph? From side to side; from side to side." Say this using the hand action. Repeat this question and answer, if needed, before students write their rough draft or final copy. Have your students tell their neighbor too.

Topic Sentences

Do your students begin their essays without a topic sentence or with boring topic sentences? Remember that *topic* was taught as a vocabulary word in the previous step. Now we are showing students how to use this topic when writing paragraphs. We believe it is appropriate to teach topic sentence writing as a concrete skill by starting a paragraph with a topic sentence and teaching specific methods on how to do this. We know that as students become accustomed to the purpose of this type of sentence, they will automatically try more creative choices.

18

No matter what the genre, your students need direct instruction and modeling on the ins and outs of writing catchy topic sentences regardless of the grade you teach. Read examples to your class from books, magazines, or even your own writing. Make it clear to your students that an interesting topic sentence makes your audience want to read more no matter what the genre. This is sometimes called a *hook* in expressive writing programs.

Professor Write's Interactive Teaching Strategy

Topic Sentence

Review: "What is a topic?"

Students Recite the Precise Answer: Sing, "That's what it's all about" with arms outstretched.

Ask: "What is a topic sentence?"

Give a Precise Answer: "It's a sentence that introduces the topic of the paragraph. That's what it's all about! [sung with arms outstretched]."

Explain: Explain that a topic sentence tells the reader what the paragraph is all about. Read some sample paragraphs but with-

out reading the topic sentence. Ask, "What is this about? Who can give a good topic sentence for this?" Put a topic sentence on the board and ask students to give sentences that go with the topic sentence and then give those that don't.

Repeat This Question and Answer: "What's a topic sentence? It's a sentence that tells about the paragraph. That's what it's all about!" Frequent repetitions and oral responses help your students remember and recall this important concept while having fun with the song at the same time. Students with special needs, ELLs, and students with other risk factors will remember this tune.

When instructing this skill, remind students about writing three sentences on one topic. Then start by teaching four enjoyable and effective strategies to write their topic sentence. With BEW, we use those strategies defined as *best practices* in teaching.

Topic Sentence Strategy 1: Ask a Question

The first and most popular method with students is to have them ask a question. Questions capture the reader's attention and get them to start thinking about the writer's topic. One of our young second-grade authors wrote a personal narrative about her dog's birthday. She began her first paragraph with a creative topic sentence in a question format asking, "Have you ever seen a cocker spaniel blow out birthday candles or eat birthday cake?" She included a photo of her dog eating birthday cake. One of our third-grade students wrote an informational essay on China and began with, "How much do you know about China?" Using a question as a topic sentence provides a visual image for the reader and makes the reader want to continue reading the story.

Topic Sentence Strategy 2: Tell An Interesting Fact

A second way to start a paragraph with a catchy topic sentence is to tell an interesting fact. Yet another one of our second-grade students wrote a fact about his dog saying, "Dusty is ten years old in human years, which is really seventy years old in dog years." Telling a fact about the topic creates an interest level for the reader.

Topic Sentence Strategy 3: Begin with a Riddle

Another method for writing an interesting topic sentence is to begin with a riddle. Beginning a writing selection with a riddle draws the audience into your writing and creates an interest or desire for them to want to know more. One of our eighth-grade students began his persuasive writing selection with this topic sentence riddle: "What's smaller than a bread box, necessary in all homes, and something you can't live without?" His riddle actually got his audience thinking, "What could this item be?" Continuing on, he described his mystery product (a can opener) and used it to develop his persuasive genre selection.

Topic Sentence Strategy 4: Use Imagery

A final method for teaching creative topic sentence writing is through the use of imagery. The key component in this type of effective topic sentence writing is the utilization of great expressive vocabulary. Tell your students to be specific. For example: "If you're writing about being cold on the ski slopes, I want you to make me feel cold and to help me envision the scene that you actually saw when you were there." One of our sixth-grade students used this method to write her topic sentence about skiing. She wrote, "As I was sitting on the ski lift, soft snowflakes fell, tickling my nose, and the sound of silence was around as all I could hear was the crunching of the squirrel's footsteps far below as I headed for the mountaintop and the first ski run of the day." This is a great image, although it is a bit long! During the editing phase you would help her rework it into two sentences or take just a feature of it as the topic sentence. When you provide specific strategy ideas, students have a concept or formula to experiment with as they develop their ideas for writing something unique.

Transition Sentences

It is important to teach students about writing good paragraphs that have a topic sentence and stay on topic. After this is learned, you can begin to teach students to add transition sentences when they are writing their rough drafts. Yes, as early as first or second grade, good writers are ready to learn about the importance of including a transition sentence in their

WRITING TIPS

Writing Tips:
Teaching Topic Sentence Writing

- Create a chart with prewritten sentence starters in each of the four teaching categories and keep them posted in the classroom.

- Write an example of a starter topic sentence on the board and ask students to identify which type of topic sentence it is.

paragraphs. Check with your state standards and reading series to determine whether these transition sentences should be placed as a final sentence in a paragraph or as the first sentence in the next paragraph (the placement can vary). A common writing error of both young and experienced authors is not having a connection or transition between paragraphs. This can be remedied by giving instruction on how to create transition sentences. Using the BEW approach, we believe it is important to teach this as a specific skill and ask students to use it when moving between paragraphs. It will become more subtle as students gain writing experience.

Professor Write's Interactive Teaching Strategy

Transition Sentence

Ask: "What is a transition sentence?"

Give a Precise Answer: "It is a sentence that moves us from one paragraph to the next."

Explain: Use the following explanation: "A transition sentence helps you connect what you said in one paragraph to what you want to say in the next one. Transition means *to move,* so this sentence helps to move the reader from one topic or idea to the next one."

Repeat This Question and Answer: "What's a transition sentence? It's a sentence that moves us from one paragraph to the next." Repeat this interaction when you are reviewing this skill when writing the rough draft.

Step 3: General Vocabulary

With our BEW process we provide a vocabulary graphic organizer called the Web of Words. As you see in Figure 1.4, this graphic organizer has a square in the center with lines that extend out from it and a square at the end of each line. The Web of Words is used to explore vocabulary related to the central theme or topic and to develop analogies or to find creative imagery words. Put the central theme (such as *courage*) in the center square, and work with students to expand this into expressions. In this example, you could use *courageous as a lion* or *brave as a knight*. Or you could use our topic idea depicted in Figure 1.4—*laughed hard*—and develop vocabulary images such as *laughed until I cried* or *laughed so much my face hurt*. This tool allows your students to expand their vocabulary verbally and to build new and creative ways to express their thoughts.

FIGURE 1.4

Web of Words

Key: Because writing is taught across the curriculum, our Web of Words teaching strategy can be used to teach subject-specific vocabulary as well. Use the Web of Words strategy to teach science, social studies, and other core subject vocabulary to your students.

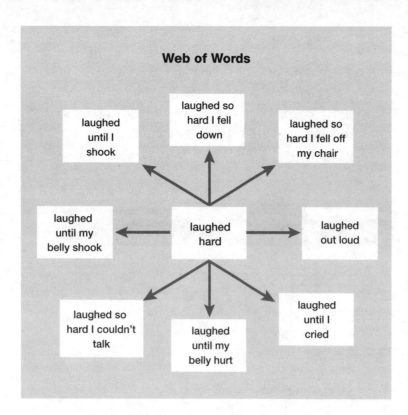

Web of Words

- laughed until I shook
- laughed so hard I fell down
- laughed so hard I fell off my chair
- laughed until my belly shook
- laughed hard
- laughed out loud
- laughed so hard I couldn't talk
- laughed until my belly hurt
- laughed until I cried

The Web of Words is best used by drawing the graphic organizer onto large art roll paper and posting it on a wall or blackboard in your classroom for the duration of your instruction on that theme or genre. This way, as you work with the class to develop creative vocabulary, the Web of Words should remain on display to provide reminders and spelling assistance for students who may need it. You may have two or three Web of Words posters for a genre. It is important to teach this concept to your students. (See student Worksheet 1.1 for individual Web of Words worksheets.)

WRITING TIPS

Writing Tips: Teaching Web of Words

- Write your Web of Words on art roll paper that can be taken down, put away, and then brought out again for the next writing session.

- Have students use the *Scholastic Book of Idioms* (Terban, 1996) to come up with phrases that are new and interesting.

- Aim for having many completed Web of Words sheets on display for a single writing assignment. Having these on display supports students' memories for recalling their ideas as well as the spelling of key words.

- Create a topic dictionary. During the general vocabulary teaching sessions, students can record the words in a notebook that are specific to a topic. Use only words that are associated with the specific topic or subject. Then, together as a class, write the meanings of these words on the board. Draw an interesting cover for the dictionary and make a book by having your students staple the cover on the pages that contain the words and their definitions. These dictionaries are not very large, so students will use them frequently.

Professor Write's Interactive Teaching Strategy

Web of Words

Write: Write a word in the center square of the web.

Lead a Discussion: Ask students to help you rephrase that word. Write the students' ideas in the web boxes at the end of each line. Continue until there are many different ideas listed. Variations include the following:

- Help students think of words to say that are *similar* and *different* in a variety of ways so that they don't sound repetitive in their writing.

- Help students increase adjective and adverb usage or use a variety of verbs to add power to their own writing.

- Write a word in the middle of the square and have students write phrases that form a visual image about the word (as in our "laughed hard" example).

Do: Leave the Webs of Words in a visible place in your room to support your students with special needs, ELLs, or students with other risk factors, so they can review the list periodically and see the correct spelling of some words as well.

ELL–BEWCONNECTION

ELL students lack sufficient vocabulary development. Expand their vocabulary with the Web of Words activity.

In Summary: Authentic Vocabulary Phase

We outlined three key steps for teaching the vocabulary of written expression as the starting point for your instruction for each genre in your writing curriculum. The Big Ten expressive writing vocabulary words and the four conventions and grammar concepts should be taught across all grades. Additional conventions and grammar vocabulary are taught following grade-level expectations. We offer specific definitions that students can repeat during an interactive exchange. The definitions are designed to ensure that students will understand the meaning of these words. If you incorporate this new writing vocabulary into your daily lessons, your students will use it in their daily speaking and writing activities as well. Frequent review of these words and their associated jingles and hand jive movements will be particularly effective for your students with special needs, ELLs, and students with other risk factors.

Student Worksheet 1.1

Name _____ Topic _____ Date _____

Web of Words

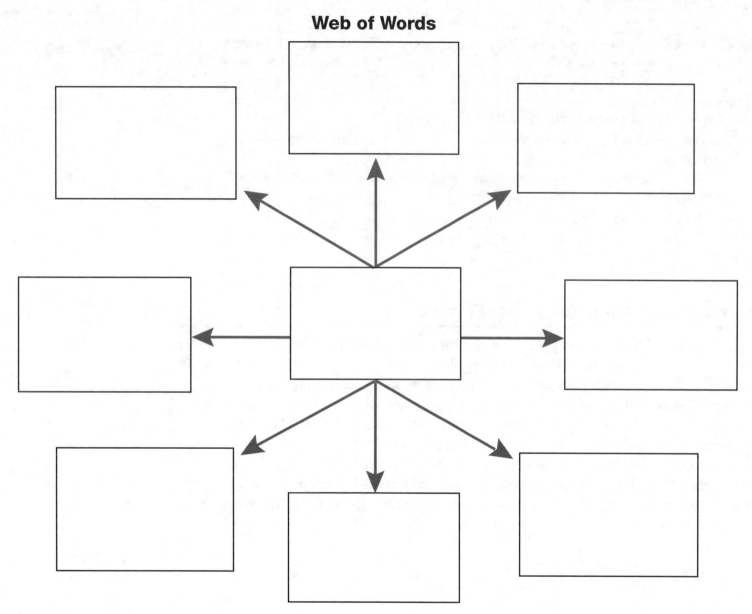

Name _____

Rough Draft Writing Folder

Genre _____

Theme _____

Topic _____

Date Started _____ **Date Finished** _____

Student Worksheet 1.3 Rough Draft Writing Folder: Blueprint for Early Elementary Students

Name _____ Paragraph Number _____

BLUEPRINT

1. Topic

1. _____

little illustration

2. Detail

2. _____

little illustration

3. Detail

3. _____

little illustration

Name _____

Date Started _____ Date Finished _____

Rough Draft Writing Folder

Genre _____

Theme _____

Topic _____

Section I

ROUGH DRAFT WRITING FOLDER BLUEPRINT

BLUEPRINT

Introduction or Beginning

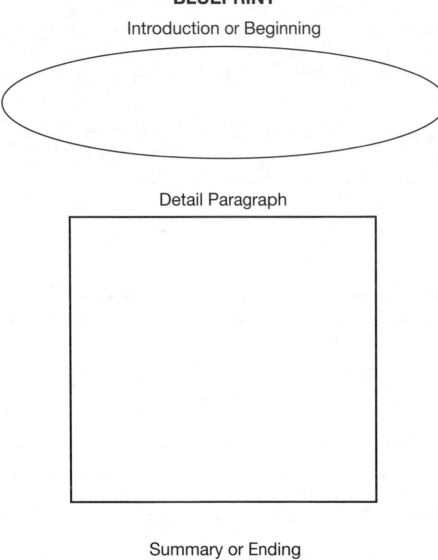

Detail Paragraph

Summary or Ending

Title

Name _____ Class _____

Date Started _____ Date Finished _____

Rough Draft Writing Folder

△ **Genre** _____

△ **Theme** _____

△ **Topic** _____

BLUEPRINT

Introduction or Beginning

Topic sentence idea

Transition ideas!

Detail Paragraph

Topic sentence idea

Transition ideas!

Summary or Ending

Topic sentence idea

Title

Our prewriting activities stimulate oral language and give students a means to connect their writing topic with a real-life knowledge base.

Phase II: Teaching Prewriting Strategies

Once students know the necessary vocabulary words such as *genre, theme,* and *topic*, it is vital for them to spend time thinking and talking about their ideas before writing begins. This is especially true for students with little background or vocabulary on the topic. BEW strategies provide five steps in this phase, which when added to the vocabulary phase, establish the foundation upon which your students can build their writing skills.

These students in Dr. Fontenot's resource room easily discover their own personal writing topics through the lesson on the Wheel of Thought.

Key: If your students can speak it, they can write it! Students must be given opportunities to speak about their ideas before writing.

It's no secret that your students come to you with varying backgrounds, experiences, and language skills with which to address the central theme of the genre you are teaching. You need strategies to stimulate thoughts and language to help you *scaffold* your teaching to the level that each student needs. Scaffolding is just what it sounds like—building a structure of experiences that helps each student own the topic.

This allows them to talk about it more fluently using firsthand information. If students can experience the topic and talk about it in logical and sequential ways, then they will be able to record their thoughts more successfully. Writing will be so much easier for your students. They will be eager to get started instead of rolling their eyes when they hear the word *essay*.

Just before you begin the prewriting strategies included in the BEW process, you must select a writing topic within the assignment theme. Use this topic to write an essay of your own in front of your class as an example for each unit you teach. Don't panic. Just follow our steps. You will be modeling every step within every phase of the BEW process—from Prewriting to Publishing. This is critical to success in using BEW teaching strategies, because students learn best through example. Your students will follow your lead.

Five Steps in Phase II: Prewriting

BEW has five prewriting steps (see Figure 2.1) to ensure that your students have something to say on their topics. Each step is defined fully in this chapter.

Step 1: Multisensory Experiences: activities related to the students' senses

Step 2: Wheel of Thought: a specific graphic organizer to stimulate student thought on a topic

Step 3: Genre Format and Voice: the specific format followed for the genre writing plan

Step 4: Blueprint Note Taking: writing ideas as fragments or notes on the Blueprint

Step 5: Talking Paragraphs: speaking one's notes in full sentences and paragraphs

Your students will have an opportunity to work in small groups during each of the five steps. Here you can help your students to build a stronger background on their topic through multisensory experiences, to find their own writing topic, and to develop their own voice to respond to the genre. Some groups won't need much guidance and some will need more; this is how you scaffold to meet the needs of each of your students. They will learn to use a Blueprint to outline their thoughts and then speak those thoughts aloud to hear what they have to say.

Through participation in these classroom exercises, your students will develop not only a richer background and vocabulary on a topic, but a shared comfort level with classmates. This builds a successful *writing community*, which leads to creative expression both verbally and in writing. The key to what makes BEW strategies different than other approaches is this *front-end loading*. This means spending a great deal of time helping students understand the topic and personalizing it so it becomes uniquely their own well before the actual writing process begins. Students love to talk, to communicate, and to write and share ideas, but they must have a starting point. Front-end loading using our prewriting strategies helps each and every student find a starting point from which they can develop and organize the ideas that ultimately lead to the end product: their written selection. All students have a story to tell and a *voice* to make that story uniquely their own.

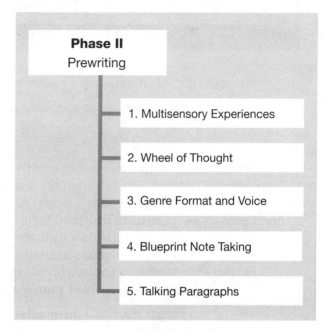

FIGURE 2.1
Master Plan Steps for Prewriting Phase

Step 1: Multisensory Experiences

This first prewriting step involves probing student backgrounds and connecting their backgrounds to the writing assignment. The variety of backgrounds in any classroom can be quite diverse, but they can be supplemented and enhanced by use of class discussions, DVDs, and special activities like cyber trips and literacy bags or boxes. Cyber trips are online field trips to explore places or topics that may not be a part of their background. Literacy bags are plastic bags filled with items that provide ways for students to see, hear, taste, touch, or smell in relation to your theme. Literacy boxes contain similar items as those included in a literacy bag, but on an entire classroom basis. Multisensory

ELL–BEWCONNECTION

Appealing to the senses is a great way for ELL students to connect to the world around them. These multisensory experiences promote language for their writing.

WRITING TIPS

Writing Tips: Multisensory Experiences—Cyber Trips

- Do research first. Sit down at your desktop computer and run a Web search on your curriculum topic. Save these Web addresses in your computer. Make sure these websites are kid friendly (most school computers have filters that will not allow you to visit inappropriate websites). Then select the best pictures or videos that show your topic.

- Use a computer lab that has a lead computer that feeds to individual computers. Have students view the pictures or videos on their individual monitors. Conduct and lead a question-and-discussion session.

activities allow students to learn through their senses by participating in sensory-based lessons that have been designed by you with the aid of our helpful suggestions.

Use your imagination in this area. Many of the students that we work with just don't have the life experiences to be able to talk about topics, let alone write about them. We can't make up for the lack of these experiences, but we can help our students grasp a deeper meaning of life experiences vicariously by using multisensory activities.

In Depth: Cyber Trips

A good cyber trip uses computer technology to enhance students' knowledge about places, traditions, events, or concepts without actually being there. Although we may not be able to take real field trips, a class can go anywhere in the world we choose with a class cyber trip! Cyber trips should expand the horizons of students who have not had real-life experiences that your literacy program introduces. Think of these experiences as being kid-friendly documentaries.

Professor Write's Interactive Teaching Strategy

Cyber Trips

Set Up: Find a computer picture or website that is related to your topic, for all to see. *Example:* Miami Beach.

Ask: "What do you see? Where are we going today?" *Example:* "We're going to the beach!"

Discuss: Begin a class discussion using computer images to stimulate thought, generate concepts, add new vocabulary, and allow students to have personal experiences with this topic. Provide time for students to talk about this cyber trip and develop their own unique insights. Have fun with this; it will help your students have something to say! *Example:* Allow students to watch surfboarding, building of sand castles, scenes of people on the beach.

In Depth: Literacy Bags or Boxes

Beyond learning about topics from cyber trips, students benefit from firsthand opportunities to see, touch, taste, smell, and hear things related to your topics. You can accommodate this by creating literacy bags (small items related to your topic that can be distributed to each student) and literacy boxes (bigger items, class objects, and materials that students can enjoy). When students experience a topic in this way, they begin to speak their thoughts aloud, build experiences, and engage in dialogue that will help them prepare for the writing activity. This levels the playing field for students with relatively few background experiences.

For example, you might have a topic related to the beach. Ask your students what they know about going to the beach. Ask them to think about what they would hear, see, smell, taste, and touch. (It is always important to have students relate to their senses.) In your literacy box you might have a CD with wave sounds, pictures of children playing on the beach, a beach towel, a bottle of suntan lotion, a pair of sunglasses, a bottle of water, and a piece of artwork with a big sun on it. These sensory items will trigger student responses such as, "I hear waves splashing on the shore," "I see children playing on the beach," "I remember playing with a beach ball," "I'll get thirsty with the sun shining on me all day." When it's time to write about the central theme of the beach, set the scene for your students by playing wave music on a CD player when they enter the room. Have sunglasses on each student's desk and a cotton ball with suntan lotion on it. As your students enter the class, tell them to stop, listen to the sounds, then go to their desk and smell the cotton ball on their desk and put on the sunglasses. Ask them what they think the writing topic might be today. Your students will remember this writing project and have better written essays and more fun writing than if you simply entered into your classroom and stated, "We're writing about the beach today."

Professor Write's Interactive Teaching Strategy

Literacy Bags or Boxes

Set Up: Set out literacy boxes or bags for students to explore that are related to your central theme or topic.

Ask: "What's in your literacy bag or box? What do you know about these things?"

Discuss: Begin a class discussion using the items in the bags or boxes to stimulate thought, generate concepts, add new vocabulary, and allow students to have personal experiences with this topic. Provide time for students to talk about these items and develop their own unique insights. Have fun with this; it will help your students have something to say. You can even begin to write down some of the vocabulary words the students are saying so that they can use them as visual reminders for when they begin to write.

WRITING TIPS

Writing Tips: Multisensory Experiences—Literacy Bags or Boxes

- Get several large boxes (we prefer to use large, clear plastic storage containers) and label them using titles related to your curriculum writing topics.

- Have teachers, parents, and students work together to contribute items that they have accumulated while on vacation and during shopping trips, and from other life experiences. Put these items in the appropriate container, where you can store them and add to them from time to time.

- Store the literacy boxes in the library and have a return and checkout policy just like other library materials. Use them year after year; they will grow and become richer as time goes on.

- The best literacy boxes are inexpensive to create and keep; this is meant to be a simple activity.

- Literacy bags are just small, resealable bags that contain small items that relate to the topic. Students can have on them on their desks to stimulate their thoughts and words.

Step 2: Wheel of Thought

Central Theme

After you have spent time exploring a central theme or potential topic with multisensory experiences, you probably won't hear the complaints you used to hear, such as, "I don't know what to write about" or "I don't know where to start." Students will have some thoughts on the topic. However, these thoughts need to be developed. Using a Wheel of Thought graphic organizer with your class will help students discover their own ideas on any selected theme. The Wheel of Thought is designed with a circle in the center and has many rays extending from the circle, like the spokes of a wheel.

We recommend that you keep the Wheel of Thought (usually created on a large piece of art roll paper) displayed in the classroom throughout the writing process on that topic. It will help to keep the children focused on their topic by providing a visual reminder for topic and subtopics (for example, detail paragraphs) as well as spelling. We recommend that

WRITING TIPS

Writing Tips: Wheel of Thought

- Use art roll paper to construct your Wheel of Thought so that it may be saved and displayed throughout the entire writing process.

- Always use the same title for the Wheel of Thought and do it in the same manner so that students learn to associate the term with the process.

- Younger children can draw pictures on sticky notes instead of writing words to share their ideas for the Wheel of Thought.

you use a Wheel of Thought across all genres for generating student topics. If you follow this suggestion, when your students hear the term *Wheel of Thought*, they will automatically associate this activity with thinking of their own topic. This will give them a cue to begin their own thought process and to begin gathering topic ideas. (See Student Worksheet 2.1 for an individual Wheel of Thought. If your students need more rays for ideas, have them draw more rays extending from the circle.)

Professor Write's Interactive Teaching Strategy

Wheel of Thought

Set Up: Draw a Wheel of Thought on art roll paper. Write the central theme for your genre in the center circle. *Example:* Courage.

Model: Say, "Our central theme is _____. If I were writing on this theme, my own personal narrative [or other genre] would be about the time I . . . ." It is important to model each step of the writing process for your students, and sharing personal examples is a powerful way to do this. *Example:* "My personal narrative will be about the time I had to show courage when I got lost on my vacation."

Ask: "Can you think of a time when you . . . ?" Write down each student's response on the rays that extend from the circle in the Wheel of Thought, or have students come forward and write their own ideas on the class-displayed Wheel of Thought. Listing many ideas will help students know where and when to start. *Example:* "Can you think of a time when you showed courage?"

Discuss: Ask questions to stimulate thought about student topics, such as "Where did this happen?" or "Who else was there?" or "When did this happen?" or "How did you feel while this was going on?" or "Why do you think this happened?" The class discussion of student topics will help the students who are having a difficult time generating their own ideas.

Repeat and Review: Ask students to turn and tell a neighbor their topic. You will soon see that every student has been able to get a good idea on selecting their topic.

Student Topic

Now that your students have a thorough understanding of the central theme and ideas about their topic, it's time to narrow their focus and begin a list of story details in chronological order. You accomplish this by giving each student his or her own Wheel of Thought and model this process for them.

Wheel of Thought

Set Up: Draw a Wheel of Thought on art roll paper to model your personal topic in front of your class. Distribute a Wheel of Thought graphic organizer to each of your students. Write your personal topic on the class-displayed Wheel of Thought. Tell your students to do the same on their own Wheel of Thought with the topic they've selected. Your example might be getting lost on vacation. One of your students might write about showing courage when he or she heard a scary sound.

Model: Say, "My topic is. . . . If I were writing on this topic, my own personal narrative [or other genre] would be on the time I. . . ." It is important to model each step of the writing process for your students. Students will enjoy this even more if you share your own examples. *Example:* "My personal narrative will be on the time I had to show courage when I got lost on my vacation."

Ask: "What happened when . . . ?" Write down notes about your story in chronological order on the rays that extend from the circle, with one event per ray. *Example:* "First, everyone wanted

to hike." Write TAKE A HIKE (ray 1). "Then, we began to get thirsty." Write, GOT THIRSTY (ray 2). "Suddenly, the trail seemed to disappear." Write, TRAIL DISAPPEARED (ray 3). "It started to rain." Write, RAIN CAME (ray 4). Continue writing the story sequence on each subsequent ray in note form until the story line is completed. List as many details as possible to help your students learn to sequence their stories.

Teach: Ask students to write the story sequence for their own topic on their personal Wheel of Thought in the same way that you did. Ask questions that stimulate their thoughts about the story events, such as, "What happened first?" "How did you get into this situation?" "Who was on this adventure with you?" "Tell us what happened on this adventure from start to finish." "How did you feel while this was going on?" "What did you learn from this whole adventure?" These types of questions will help your students complete their personal Wheel of Thought. Questions generate ideas and students will answer them based on their own experiences.

Definition: Genre is a kind of writing. It communicates a purpose to a specific audience.

Step 3: Genre Format and Voice

Genre can be a hard concept to teach students. We make it simple and say it's a kind of writing. Some typical examples of genre include narrative, persuasive, research, and poetry; there are about thirty-three types in all. If students know who the audience will be and the differences between the genres taught at their grade level, they will better understand what language to use and how to organize their thoughts. You will know which genre to teach based on your grade level, and your district and state standards and benchmarks. We provide some helpful information on four key genre types as well as "Response to Reading" in Section II.

Professor Write's Interactive Teaching Strategy

Genre Concept

Review: Review the vocabulary that you used to teach genre with your students. Ask, "What is genre?" Give them a precise answer: "Genre is a kind of writing." Repeat this definition to warm up your students and set the stage for beginning a new genre.

Scaffold: Genres are categories for writing. Give examples of the importance of categorizing in other areas to which students can relate. *Example:* Say, "How many of you have seen an iPod? You can listen to different music on your iPod. Have you ever looked at the menu of an iPod?" (Show them a menu on an iPod using a document camera and real iPod. They'll love it!) "What would genre mean related to music?" Students might respond, "The kind of music, like rap, country, or rock." Tell them, "Just as there many different genres in music, there are also many different genres in writing. Different writing genres sound different, and use a different language and different purposes, just like the music genres on an iPod."

Genre

After your students thoroughly understand the concept of genre, use the Blueprint to teach specific genre principles or *genre format*. This is taught in connection with the Blueprint graphic organizer (Figure 2.2). By using the same Blueprint for all grade levels, students learn that writing begins with an introduction or beginning, followed by text development in detail paragraphs in the middle, and finishes with a summary or ending paragraph.

When teaching genre format, it may be helpful to bring an actual building blueprint to class. Let your students examine the blueprint. Ask your students what a blueprint is used for. They will usually say something like, "It's used for constructing buildings." Make sure your students recognize that according to a blueprint, each room has a certain measurement and purpose. Connect the purpose of this construction blueprint to the Blueprint graphic organizer. Make the connection with your students: "If blueprints are used in the real world to build homes, what do you suppose we will build with our Blueprint?" Your students should respond with, "Our writing assignments."

We use the Blueprint as an organization format to teach all genres. The format of the Blueprint does not change—only the specific building blocks change for each genre. The Blueprint is made up of three basic shapes: a medium-size oval, large square(s), and a small

FIGURE 2.2

Mini Blueprint

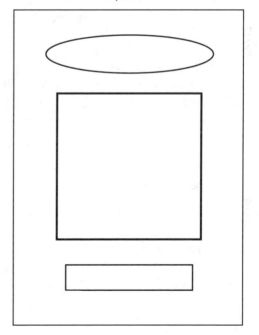

rectangle. Students will use this Blueprint to take notes and organize their thoughts about their selections. Each shape corresponds with a specific paragraph type required in genre writing. That's why it's called the Blueprint!

Professor Write's Interactive Teaching Strategy

Teaching the Blueprint

Scaffold: Before you start, either draw a Blueprint on art roll paper or use an overhead projector to display a Blueprint for class demonstration purposes. Compare a real blueprint with our Blueprint. Show how the purpose of both is to help build a final product. Tell the students that their Blueprint will be used for all their writing projects. Highlight the different shapes used in the Blueprint. Explain how each shape has a different purpose and size, just as each room drawn on a blueprint has a special purpose and size.

Teach: Point to the oval shape on the Blueprint and have a discussion similar to the following: "What's this shape?"

"Yes, it's an oval."

Then say, "The oval shape represents the introduction or beginning paragraph. The introduction or beginning paragraph introduces your topic and sets the scene. It is of medium size [demonstrate with your hands]. We put our notes for the introduction or beginning paragraph in the oval shape on the Blueprint."

Ask: "What paragraph does the oval represent?"

Give and Practice a Precise Answer: "The introduction or beginning paragraph."

Ask: "What is the job or purpose of the introduction beginning paragraph?"

Give and Practice a Precise Answer: "A paragraph that introduces the topic and sets the scene [depending on the writing genre]."

Explain: "Yes, you will put your notes for the introduction or beginning paragraph here. Your notes will then help you write your first paragraph. How big is an introduction or beginning paragraph? Medium size" [and ask students to show you medium size with their hands].

Repeat: Say, "Tell your neighbor the job or purpose of the oval shape in our Blueprint." Repeat this exercise several times and give examples.

Teach: Point to the square on the Blueprint and ask, "What's this shape? Yes, it's a square. It is large." Then say, "The square shape represents the detail or middle paragraphs of your story. The square shape is where you write the notes for the detail or middle paragraphs in your story. It is the largest part of your story because it has all the details."

Ask: "What does the square represent?"

Give and Practice a Precise Answer: "The detail paragraphs or the middle of your writing project. You put your notes for the details or middle paragraphs in the square."

Ask: "How big are the detail paragraphs?"

Give and Practice a Precise Answer: "Large [and ask students to show you with their hands]."

Repeat: Say, "Ask your neighbor, what is the job or purpose of the square in our Blueprint?" Repeat this exercise several times and give examples (see Figure 2.3).

Teach: Point to the rectangle and ask, "What's this shape?" "Yes, it's a rectangle. It is small." Then say, "The rectangle represents the summary or ending paragraph. The summary or ending paragraph summarizes or finishes the story. It is small [demonstrate with your hands]. We put our notes for the summary or ending paragraph in the rectangle."

Ask: "What paragraph does the rectangle represent?"

Give and Practice a Precise Answer: "The summary or ending."

Ask: "What is the job or purpose of the summary or ending paragraph?"

Give and Practice a Precise Answer: "A paragraph that ends or finishes the story [depending on the genre]. We put our notes for the summary or ending here."

Ask: "How big is an ending or summary paragraph?"

Give and Practice a Precise Answer: "Small [and ask students to show you with their hands]."

Repeat: Say, "Ask your neighbor the job or purpose of the rectangle in our Blueprint." Repeat this exercise several times and give examples.

Review: Point to each shape once again on the class-exhibited Blueprint. Review all its shapes, emphasizing their size and purpose. Do this frequently for each genre you teach.

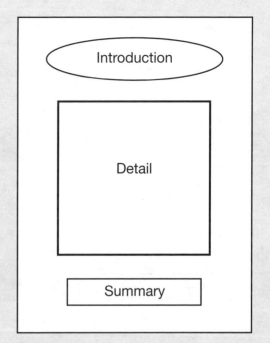

FIGURE 2.3
Mini Blueprint with Labels

We also recommend color coding the shapes of the Blueprint for young students. This strategy links the color and shape for each section of the Blueprint to support students who need this structure. Because our sample is in black and white, you could trace the shapes in color for your students who need this (or let your students do it). Trace the oval shape with a green marker to represent note taking for the introductory or beginning paragraph across all genres. Keep the square used for detail paragraph note taking black. Trace the rectangle with a red marker as a color code for note taking for the summary or ending paragraph. Have the students keep their Blueprint on the left side of their Rough Draft Writing Folder. Within this folder there should be corresponding writing paper that has lines for each of the paragraph shapes. If you're using a color-coded Blueprint, code the corresponding writing lines to match: green for the introductory paragraph, black for the detail paragraphs, and red for the summary. For an added feature, your students could use colored pencils or pens to match the color-coded shapes and lines (see Figure 2.4).

ELL–BEWCONNECTION

ELL students need graphic organizers to format and organize their thoughts prior to writing their selections. Use the Blueprint to help them get organized.

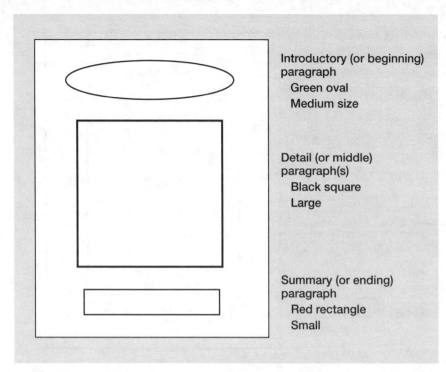

Introductory (or beginning) paragraph
  Green oval
  Medium size

Detail (or middle) paragraph(s)
  Black square
  Large

Summary (or ending) paragraph
  Red rectangle
  Small

FIGURE 2.4

Blueprint with Colors and Shapes

Believe it or not, even kindergartners can learn to write a good paragraph. By consistently using the Rough Draft Writing Folder, students of any age learn the pattern of writing in a concrete way. The Blueprint concept can be expanded to suit any type of writing at any grade level.

Voice

Voice is a student's personality or character in written form. It's their style of writing. The amount of voice that a student uses in any given writing selection will depend upon the genre. For example, little voice is used in research papers whereas a great deal of voice is expected in personal narratives.

So, are you wondering: Exactly what is voice? Voice is a critical writing element, particularly in the personal narratives your children will be writing. If you erased all the names from your students' papers, could you identify which paper belongs to which student? Voice is the way in which a person speaks. It is also reflected in the style in which they write. This is why the BEW approach uses so much oral language at first, so students hear their own voices aloud. Even kindergartners can learn to write with voice (see Section III for additional activities on teaching *voice*).

WRITING TIPS

Writing Tips: Voice

- Take time to ask your students the following: "If we erased all the names off your papers and read them together, could we pick out whose paper is whose?" This exercise will get your students thinking about voice. They will begin to think: What makes my writing my own?

- Create a bulletin board full of posters with dialogue boxes. Record the phrases of famous people on each dialogue box, and write the name of the speaker on the back. Ask your students, "Who can correctly identify the greatest number of these phrases?" Again, students will then start to understand the concept of voice in written expression.

Step 4: Blueprint Note Taking

Often, teachers are anxious to have their students begin to write at this point. But wait! We find that the next two steps are critical in helping students prepare well-thought-out and well-planned compositions. We find that if students learn to write notes in their Blueprints and have a chance to put them in order and talk about them out loud before writing, the writing process is easier and their success is greater.

At this stage we ask students to write their notes on the Blueprint in the shapes that represent the proper paragraph type. *And* we ask them to put their thoughts in the correct order. First, it's important for students to understand how to take notes. This is achieved by you modeling how to do just that.

Professor Write's Interactive Teaching Strategy

Note Taking

Scaffold: Help your students understand the concept of note taking by connecting it to something they already know. *Example:* Ask your students, "When you go to the grocery store, do you write out sentences like, I must buy potato chips, I must buy milk, and I must buy ice cream?" Your students will answer, "No. I just write POTATO CHIPS, MILK, and ICE CREAM." Then say, "You're right! Why don't you write out the entire sentence?" They will tell you, "I don't need to. All I need to do is remember the stuff I need to get from the store." Relate this concept to the skill of note taking. Tell your students, "Just like you remember what to buy from looking at your short grocery list you will remember your story by listing a few key words, in the right order, about your topic."

Model: Demonstrate how to write a few words to remind you of each of your thoughts so that your students can see how this is done. Use the topic and thoughts that you wrote on your Wheel of Thought in chronological order. Model the notes you would write in the introduction or beginning oval, the detail paragraph square in the middle, and the summary or ending in the rectangle for your own writing project.

Choose the Proper Blueprint Graphic Organizer

We provide three different Blueprints to accommodate three different levels of writers. Our youngest authors are only able to write simple sentences (see Figure 2.5), so their Blueprint allows room for drawing a picture followed by a few words. The basic Blueprint (the three-component Blueprint with introduction or beginning, detail or middle, and summary or ending paragraphs) can be used from first through eighth grade (and beyond). Using this format, students of all ages and abilities are

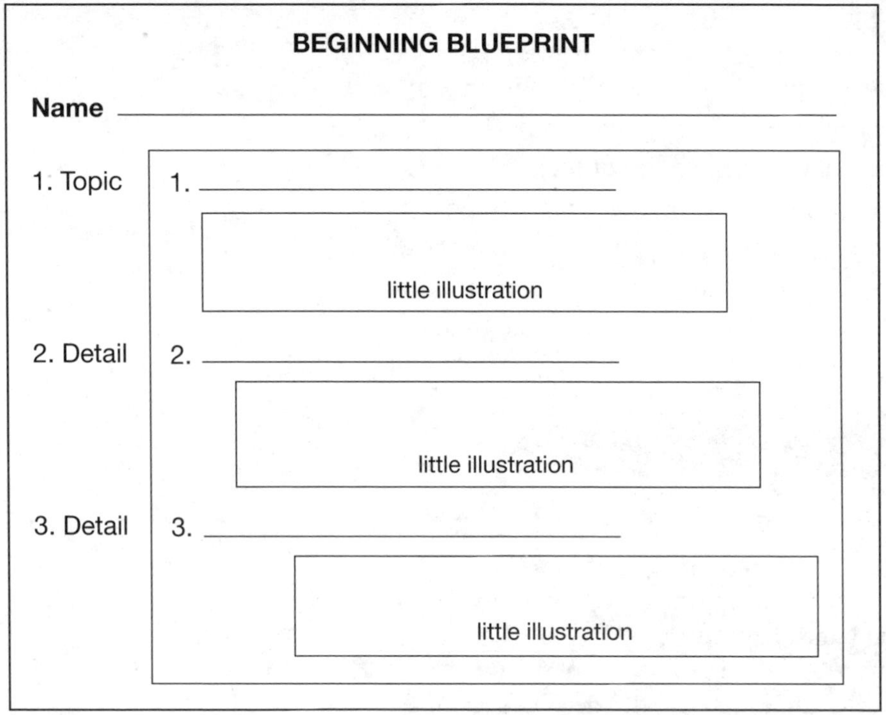

BEGINNING BLUEPRINT

Name _____

1: Topic   1. _____

little illustration

2. Detail   2. _____

little illustration

3. Detail   3. _____

little illustration

FIGURE 2.5

Beginning Blueprint: Add
Additional Beginning Blueprints
for Each Young Author's New
Paragraph

reminded of the purpose of each component, which helps them know what to think about and write down as notes in that area. The final Blueprint form allows for multiple detail paragraphs to be inserted between the introductory or beginning paragraph and the summary or ending.

As long as you stick to the purpose of each of the three components you can highlight or expand a component to meet the needs of your grade level. For example, you might want to teach first graders how to write a simple topic sentence with two detail-supporting sentences as their first simple paragraph. In this case you might pull out the format for the detail paragraph square and make a Blueprint using that shape alone (see Figure 2.5).

At a higher grade level you might ask students to write three detail paragraphs to answer a complex question. In that case you might pull out the detail paragraph square and make a Blueprint with three squares, knowing that they are writing three detail paragraphs (see Figure 2.6). By teaching the three-shape Blueprint and demonstrating how any writing that students do fit into this pattern, you can teach great writing skills at any age. Merely tell your students to write an answer in a detailed format, and students will know to use detail paragraphs in their answer (see Figure 2.6 or Student Worksheet 2.2). If you tell your students to write an essay for any genre-specific selection (for example, a personal narrative or a persuasive argument), they know to write an introduction or beginning, a detail or middle, and a summary or ending, because you have repeated this so often throughout the school year.

Differentiation

We have designed our Blueprint to support students at various ability levels of learning. As students begin to understand the purposes and expectations of the different paragraphs in the Blueprint, they will not need to depend upon the structure of the Blueprint to make notes and organize their thoughts. Some of our sixth-grade students have told us, "The Blueprint is in my head, I know the introduction, details, and the summary." Your response should be, "Great!" because they have learned the lesson and feel comfortable with the writing process. Even though students come to understand the process, some may still want to use the Blueprint to help them get their thoughts down in proper order. As the teacher, you have the opportunity to provide support at various levels until students feel they are ready to do this step independently.

Step 5: Talking Paragraphs

After students have recorded their ideas sequentially on the Blueprint, they are now ready to speak their thoughts aloud in complete sentences and paragraphs. It is our belief that if students can speak it, they can write it, because writing is simply thoughts that are written down. One young author told us, "I don't know what to write 'til I hear what I gotta say." We agree. Even as we are typing this, we feel like we are talking. Do you talk to yourself as you write at the computer? We often tell our students, "When we type and write, we talk either out loud or quietly to ourselves."

Therefore, our final step in the prewriting phase is called *talking paragraphs*. While looking at their Blueprint notes, students tell their stories to each other or to the class. When doing this exercise, a student may have written down the note No GIVING UP. But when he

Blueprint with Just Squares for Details Only

Student Topic —————————

Paragraph #1
Details

Paragraph #2
Details

Paragraph #3
Details

FIGURE 2.6

Blueprint with Just Squares

Jordan proudly tells his class a talking paragraph. *His story is based on one that he read and brought to class to share.*

is doing the talking paragraph, he should say it as a full thought: "I knew I couldn't give up." By teaching your students to be good listeners and to focus on whether their story makes sense and stays on the topic, students can make changes in their notes before they write their rough drafts. This step needs to be taught and then modeled for your students so that they thoroughly benefit from this activity.

Professor Write's Interactive Teaching Strategy

Talking Paragraphs

Review: Say to your students, "We have learned about our topic and have written our notes for what we have to say on our Blueprint. What are the three paragraphs that need to be in all of our stories? Yes, introduction [or beginning], detail [or middle], and summary [or ending] paragraphs. Now we want to use our notes and just tell our story so that it makes sense. When we hear what we have to say, it will be easier to write it in sentences. Listen to see if you can hear the introduction [beginning], detail [middle] paragraphs, and summary [ending] when we do our talking paragraphs."

Model: By this point you will have modeled writing your thoughts onto a Blueprint graphic organizer. Now you need to *talk out* those notes from your personal writing example so that students begin to understand how you use notes and yet speak complete thoughts. Place your Blueprint on an overhead projec-

tor or a document camera so your students can watch you point to your notes and listen to your whole sentences. Model what to do if you see that you wrote your notes in the wrong order in one of the paragraphs and how you fix it when you hear what you say in your talking paragraph.

Practice: Now ask if there are any students who would be willing to do their talking paragraphs in front of the class. Teach the class how to support the speaker, to give compliments and talk about strengths, to say whether it makes sense, to suggest a better order, or to ask questions that could help the student add something that seems to be missing. Clap for the speakers when they finish, because they are taking a risk in front of the class. Next, let students sit in pairs and practice talking out their paragraphs. Walk around and help each group—both the speaker and the listeners.

ELL–BEWCONNECTION

Oral language development is critical for ELL students. Talking paragraphs are essential for language development.

You will notice that students will self-correct and revise their Blueprint notes as they go through this phase. Students will change concepts, add ideas, and resequence events well before the assignment has been written in rough draft form. It isn't necessary for each and every student to demonstrate a talking paragraph to the class, but it is important that each student complete a talking paragraph to someone in the class. By practicing speaking sentences out loud in the proper order [introduction (beginning), details (middle), and summary (ending)], students are rehearsing what they will be writing during the next step. We *know* that our students like to talk, and they do have a voice and want to be heard. This step lets them do just that!

WRITING TIPS

Writing Tips: Talking Paragraphs

- Modeling is the key to success in this process. Teachers must model their talking paragraphs to the class.

- During talking paragraphs, it is beneficial to ask students questions about their story and to ask them what happened next.

- If students can't formulate a thought verbally, chances are they won't be able to write it down.

- Prepare a podium or speaker's area, and ask students to come to the podium and "talk out" their notes from the Blueprint.

- Use *wh* questions, such as: *Who* is this about? *What* else happened? *Where* did you go? *When* did you do that? Also ask: *How* did it happen? Then allow students to add notes to their Blueprint.

In Summary: Prewriting Phase

All efforts put into the Prewriting Phase will result in more proficient student products during the Writing Phase and will also reduce the time you spend editing student work. Spend time frontloading the writing process; it will pay off. Students will produce high-quality writing assignments and you won't have to spend hours at home checking and writing corrections on student assignments.

Wheel of Thought

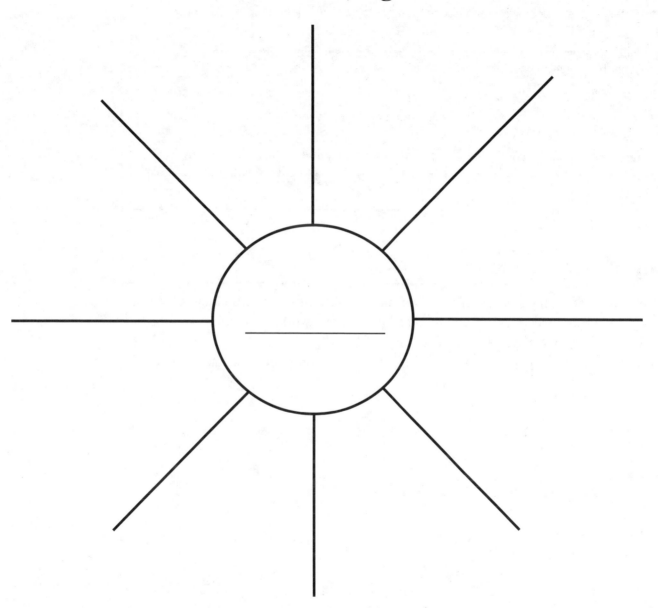

Blueprint with Just Squares for Details Only

Student Topic _____

Paragraph #1
Details

Paragraph #2
Details

Paragraph #3
Details

Students are now ready to write the first draft. Display all visual materials like your Webs of Words and Wheels of Thought to give your students the help they need to develop well-written essays.

Phase III: Teaching Writing

Do your students have difficulty getting started writing their first drafts? Have you heard the words, "I just don't know where to start writing?" Fortunately, by the time students reach the actual Writing Phase in the BEW process, they have practiced the vocabulary and concepts of their topic so that they know what they want to say. They also understand their writing purpose and to whom they are writ-

Sylvanus is concentrating on writing his final selection!

ing—their audience. They have their notes organized using their Blueprint and have, in fact, talked out their paragraphs. This leads them directly to the next phase: *writing*. As you will begin to see during this phase, students will complete their rough drafts quickly and easily.

During the Writing Phase, students take out their Rough Draft Writing Folders and use the notes they have written on their Blueprint as an organizational tool. These notes are transformed into complete sentences that are assembled into full paragraphs. As in all process writing models, students are taught that a rough draft will be revised and restructured as often as needed to capture what they want to say. Students often have the notion that a completed first draft finishes their writing assignment. It is at this point, right at the beginning of the writing process, when students need to be reminded that it takes practice to get their papers ready to be published. They will be revising several times before their best work is completed—their final copy.

Two Steps in Phase III: Writing

Students usually dislike writing because they don't have a thorough understanding of where to start or how to formulate paragraphs on different genres. The steps in BEW prepare your students for writing the draft so that the writing process seems effortless. The steps of Phase III are as follows:

Step 1. Draft Writing: assembling sentences and paragraphs from Blueprint notes

Step 2. Title Writing: writing an interesting title that reflects the essence of the drafted writing selection (see Figure 3.1)

As students begin to write their rough drafts, you must teach or review how students should use the Blueprint so they can build their notes into interesting sentences and paragraphs. Don't say, "OK, now use your notes and write your sentences," unless your whole class is able to do this independently and at grade level. This is the time to use whole-class instruction to review key concepts one by one and to bring the class along step by step. You need to review topic sentences, the size and

ELL–BEWCONNECTION

ELL students require a step-by-step instructional process for mastering writing. BEW steps in each phase lead students to writing the draft.

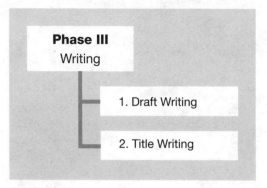

Phase III
Writing

1. Draft Writing

2. Title Writing

FIGURE 3.1

Master Plan

purpose of each type of paragraph, transition sentences, and writing titles. Students will become more and more independent as you repeat each step for each genre.

Step 1: Draft Writing

As you move your students into the Writing Phase, it is important to review the correct Genre Format and Voice for their assignment. By doing this you will teach the important elements needed for a proficient writing selection. This is done quickly to help students recall all the prewriting activities that your class completed on your current genre selection.

Professor Write's Interactive Teaching Strategy

Review Genre Format and Voice

1. The introduction or beginning paragraph

Ask: Point to the oval on the Blueprint and ask, "What paragraph does the oval represent and what is its job?"

Give a Precise Answer: "The oval represents the first paragraph called the *introduction*. Its job is to introduce the topic and set the scene for the story." If you are teaching personal narrative, you would say, "This is the introduction or beginning of your story. It's how your story starts."

Say: "We will begin writing by looking at our Blueprints and taking our notes from the oval and writing them into complete sentences in our first paragraph. Remember, the introduction paragraph should be medium size in relation to your entire writing selection."

2. Reviewing the topic sentence

Ask: "What type of special sentence must be written in the introduction paragraph?"

Give a Precise Answer: "A topic sentence."

Ask: "What is a topic sentence?"

Explain: "A topic sentence tells the reader what your paragraph is all about." Remind students of the recommended strategies:

"You can ask a question, tell an interesting fact, begin with a riddle, or use imagery to begin your topic sentences. Let's try using these strategies with our own paragraphs."

Model: Using one of the strategies you have taught, model a topic sentence for your own story. Write it out for your students to see. Then ask them if anyone can use that same strategy to develop a similar topic sentence to go with their own topic. Ask for volunteers to share their ideas aloud. Repeat this process for each of the four topic sentence teaching strategies.

Background: Model and give examples of topic sentences to your class using the BEW teaching strategies for writing topic sentences (see Chapter 1, Step 2: Conventions and Grammar step). It's important to model your own topic sentence to your class on the writing assignment that you're developing with them. Students love to see that you are writing a story too, and showing them all the steps. Don't be surprised if some of your students actually use one of your topic sentences as a template for their own writing. As they gain knowledge and experience, they will be more confident in writing their own creative topic sentences.

For inexperienced authors, you may want to have your students write their introduction directly following your teaching strategies. In this way, all the information from the story introduction will be fresh in your students' minds. If your students are older and more experienced writers, continue reviewing and modeling the next section of writing the detail paragraph(s).

Along with a good topic sentence at the beginning, a paragraph needs a good transition sentence or phrase before introducing a new topic in the next paragraph. This concept is one that you should teach to students after they have some experience in writing paragraphs. This can be as early as first or second grade for advanced writers, but many children don't truly grasp the concept until third grade or later.

Professor Write's Interactive Teaching Strategy

Transition Sentences

Say: "This step involves adding a transition sentence to paragraphs to set the stage for the next topic. There are two ways that transition sentences can be taught. One way is as a *hook* to catch the reader at the end of the preceding paragraph. The other way is as a phrase at the beginning of the next paragraph to connect to the topic you are starting."

Background: Because understanding transition sentences can be difficult, we suggest teaching students that transition means "to move." Thus, transition sentences are used when the writer moves from one paragraph to the next.

Teach: We find that some students need a more vivid picture of why we use transition sentences. Try either of these ideas. First, you can relate it to a movie trailer (those little clips that lure you to wanting to see a new movie). Just like a movie trailer leads the audience to the movie, you can tell your students that a transition sentence must lead your audience to the next paragraph. Hopefully the transition sentence will entice the reader with a desire to want to know what's coming next. Movie trailers often end with, COMING SOON TO A MOVIE THEATER NEAR YOU. Your students can learn to write words, phrases, or sentences that create this same feeling or emotion, such as, "You'll never guess what happened next" or " What happened next is unbelievable." Our second strategy to help teach this concept involves showing students a pair of glasses that have self-darkening lenses when you go outdoors. Transition sentences are like self-darkening lenses, which change color when you move from inside to outside. When we use transition sentences, we can move more easily from one paragraph to the next. Be sure to check with your state standards and reading series for direction regarding how they recommend this should be done. Transition sentences are taught using the same format used to teach topic sentences.

After you've taught the vocabulary concept of transitioning, it's your turn to model your own transition sentence for your students. Then ask if anyone can think of a transition sentence that they might use in their writing selection. Have those volunteers recite their transition sentences to the class. Your class can then comment on these ideas to help each student build a better sentence. Lastly, have your students write their own transition sentences leading to the detail paragraph(s).

Professor Write's Interactive Teaching Strategy

Detail Paragraph(s)

Ask: Point to the square on the Blueprint and ask, "What paragraph does the square shape represent and what is its job?"

Give a Precise Answer: "The square represents the detail paragraph(s) and its job is to tell the story." If you are teaching the personal narrative genre, you would say, "The second paragraph tells the plot of your story—the details of what happened."

Ask: "How big is a detail paragraph?"

Give a Precise Answer: "The detail paragraphs are the biggest [show the relative size with your hands one above the other]."

Background: Upper elementary and middle school students will learn to use multiple detail paragraphs. Each detail paragraph will relate directly to the writing selection topic but must have its own unique topic sentence. Teach your students our rule for starting new detail paragraphs. Say, "I start a new detail paragraph when there is a new place, new person, or a new event." Ask more experienced writers, "Does each paragraph have a catchy topic and transition sentence?"

Reinforce the concept of a detail paragraph by writing and then reading your own detail paragraph(s) to your class. Only after your class has heard and seen your example should you ask them to write this paragraph for their own topic. Allow enough time for your students to complete this section of their writing assignment. Because students finish at varying rates, ask those students who have finished this section to assist other students who need help until all students have finished. When the class has completed writing their detail paragraphs, ask for student volunteers to read these paragraphs to the class. Encourage the class to comment on these paragraphs for the reader. The audience should ask themselves

- Is there an interesting topic sentence?

- Did the student stay on the topic?

- Do the paragraphs make sense?

- Is there a smooth transition sentence?

This may help the writers make changes in their rough drafts based on class comments. In addition, it strengthens the listening and speaking skills of your students.

Again, for young authors you may want to have them write the detail paragraphs before moving to the next part of the story. The number of detail paragraphs the students write depends on the genre and their grade level. Younger authors will write one detail paragraph whereas upper elementary and middle school students will write multiple detail paragraphs.

The last section to model for your students is the summary or ending paragraph.

Professor Write's Interactive Teaching Strategy

Summary or Ending Paragraph

Ask: Point to the rectangle on the Blueprint and ask, "What paragraph does the rectangle represent and what is its job? What is the name of the last paragraph?"

Give a Precise Answer: "The last paragraph is the summary. Its job is to tell what the story is about in a few words. If your genre is a personal narrative, it should have a statement relating to your emotions at the end."

Ask: "How big is a summary paragraph?"

Give a Precise Answer: "The summary paragraph is small [show the relative size with your hands one above the other]."

Say: "We will read our notes from our Blueprints and expand these notes into full sentences. These sentences must fit together and become your summary or ending paragraph."

Background: The purpose or manner in which the student's summary is written depends upon the genre that is being taught. Each genre has a specific format and purpose to follow. The important point to remember is to model this summary by speaking it and writing it in front of your class.

Younger authors will write their summary paragraphs at this point. More experienced authors will write their entire writing selection.

Writing Tips: Draft Writing

- Prepare a Rough Draft Writing Folder for each student.

- Remind students that there will be several more steps to finishing their writing, and that getting the ideas into paragraph form is just the beginning.

- Help students with spelling and word choice. The goal during this phase is word flow, not spelling.

Step 2: Title Writing

We suggest that you save the process of title writing until the very end of the Writing Phase. You may be thinking, Why write a title last? Shouldn't the title be written first? The answer to these questions is simple. Writing the title last gives the writer an opportunity to create a more interesting title that better suits the actual details of the writing selection. For instance, if you've given your class the assignment of writing a personal narrative on their summer vacation and you have twenty-five students in your class, what do you think the twenty-five titles will be? You've guessed it: *My Summer Vacation*. Students tend to use the central theme as their title. This limits their writing creativity. Tell your students that you get bored reading twenty-five of the same titles. You want them to be more creative and write titles that don't parrot back the central theme. You are hoping for interesting titles that relate to the content of each student's writing.

We also believe that students write titles in unimaginative ways because they really don't know how to write interesting titles. With the BEW process we suggest a variety of strategies for writing an interesting title. Explain to your students that as their writing selection develops, more details will crop up that will make their writing more interesting. Their titles should uniquely represent their selection, regardless of the genre. The following strategies will help.

Title-Writing Strategy 1: Titles of Songs, Movies, or TV Shows

The first BEW title-writing strategy invites your students to consider using the names of songs, movies, or television programs that might match their own writing selection. For instance, Jessica, a second-grade student, wrote a narrative about her pet dog who is constantly trying to escape from her

WRITING TIPS

Enhance the Writing Process

- During the Writing Phase, post your students' Web of Words sheets on the classroom walls to help them with spelling and vocabulary development.

- Create pre-made, open-ended sentence starters to help students get going on their writing, such as "I remember when . . . ," "I felt . . . ," "Have you ever . . ." Leave these sentences up around the classroom for your students to copy and use.

- Have a number of copies of the *Scholastic Book of Idioms* (Terban, 1996) available for your students to look up their favorite idioms to increase writing vocabulary.

- Create small topical vocabulary dictionaries for different student themes.

- Set a timer in the classroom to help students finish within a designated time frame.

backyard. If her title were written before she wrote her story, it might be *My Pet* or *My Dog*. However, when using the BEW strategy of relating a current song to her story line, the title Jessica selected was, "Who Let the Dogs Out?"—a song that she heard on the radio. Ask your students to think of a song, television program, or movie that describes their writing selection. Tell them it is OK to use these ideas as titles for their stories. Now model this technique by coming up with a title for your own story. Then ask your students if they can think of a title for their writing selection by using this technique. If so, have them share it with the class. Students have fun with this title-writing method. Let their imaginations flow!

Title-Writing Strategy 2: Catchy Phrase

Another technique to use when teaching title writing is to create an interesting image by writing a catchy phrase that relates to your story. Model how to use this method by giving an example of a title you might write for your own selection. One of our third-grade students thought about this strategy as he was looking for a title for his writing selection on his hockey skills. After a little thought Jacob raised his hand and said, "My title will be *Razor's Edge*." When asked to explain to the class why he selected this title he responded, "Well, my hockey skates are really sharp and that's why I can skate so good and my story is about what a great hockey player I am!" Students can write very creative titles when given a strategy to consider.

TIP: Have a number of copies of the *Scholastic Rhyming Dictionary* (Young, 2006) in your classroom for students to use. This is a dictionary of rhyming words!

Title-Writing Strategy 3: Rhyming Words

Students' titles can be written by thinking of rhyming words that pertain to their writing selections. Model this title-writing technique to your class by changing your title yet again on your own writing selection that you are using for the class demonstration. One of our sixth-grade students used this strategy to write a creative title for his writing selection about a problem that he solved quickly. His title was *Rick's Fix.* Ask your students to think of an example of this title-writing strategy for their selection. Call on volunteers to share their rhyming titles. Students love to write rhyming words. This is a fun exercise that teaches them one more strategy for writing a title.

Model all these teaching strategies for your class as they begin writing creative titles. You will see more interesting titles written by your students than ever before.

In Summary: Writing Phase

The Writing Phase will go more smoothly than ever before in your classroom. Your students can't help but be successful, because you have spent your time teaching vocabulary, stimulating language, and providing experiences with prewriting activities before you've even asked your students to begin writing. By modeling and giving direct instructional examples for each part of their draft writing, you will be amazed to see them write more easily and with better quality than ever before.

We believe that true learning regarding the entire writing process begins during the Authentic Editing Phase. During this phase, students learn to recognize independently the elements of genre format and voice. They begin to analyze their work critically to determine whether their selections meet genre-specific requirements of fluency, consistency, structure, and form that have been taught to them. Self-correcting all these inconsistencies leads to student mastery of writing. This is what we mean when we say, "True learning begins during the Authentic Editing Phase."

Phase IV: Teaching Authentic Editing

We believe that editing is the most important phase of the BEW process. True student learning about the writing process as a whole begins here. This is because Authentic Editing isn't just an exercise in finding errors in conventions and grammar. This phase involves critically evaluating the overall quality of the writing selection. Positive change in student writing is possible only if students are able

Terrell is very happy to confer with his teacher about his writing selection so that he can fix all his mistakes and finish the final product.

to find and correct their own errors. By repeatedly analyzing their own work, your students become self-directed in improving future writing assignments.

Although editing is one of the most important student learning experiences, it seems to be the phase of writing that teachers and students struggle with the most. Nearly every teacher who instructs writing openly admits that their students are not comfortable editing their work or the work of other students. We find that the support and repetition provided in the first three steps of BEW editing strategies can help students overcome this reluctance. Based upon your teaching of grade-level writing curricula, students learn the concepts and get multiple opportunities to practice using the skills to check their writing. By repeating this phase for every writing genre that you teach in a school year, you help your students build their skills so that their final writing selections will amaze you in quality and proficiency. It will truly be their best work!

ELL–BEWCONNECTION

ELL students must learn to apply the concepts of editing to their own work. Using BEW allows three opportunities for students to review and revise their work using a class-generated rubric, providing lots of practice on these skills.

Five Steps in Phase IV: Authentic Editing

BEW strategies give students skills that allow them to edit their own work and the work of other students more easily. We call it *authentic editing*. To have a more thorough understanding of authentic editing, think back to how you may have been taught writing. In the past, a teacher might have given directions for a writing assignment, specified a timeline for its completion, and then collected the writing selections. These were taken home over the weekend, edited with a red pen to correct your mistakes (remember the red writing all over your paper?), and finally given back to you in class with a score or grade. In other words, your teachers probably only gave you directions to do a writing assignment and then edited the selection themselves. There was not much instruction on how to write the assignment, nor was there the opportunity to get support in fixing your mistakes before you turned it in. Your teacher did the editing. When you finally received your writing selection back from the teacher and your assignment was covered with a great deal of red ink pointing out your mistakes, you probably didn't feel very good about it. Did you learn from these corrections and incorporate them into future writing assignments? Probably not. Consequently, what could have been a learning experience was missed.

It is through the learning experience of finding and correcting mistakes via Authentic Editing that these same mistakes are eliminated from future writing selections. Authentic Editing consists of five important steps (see Figure 4.1):

Step 1. Self-editing: Students edit their own work.

Step 2. Peer Editing: Students edit each other's work.

Step 3. Teacher Conference: Students meet with the teacher individually or in a small group to edit writing selections.

Step 4. Final Copy Writing: After the editing steps, students write their best work.

Step 5. Teacher Assessment: The teacher evaluates the students' best work and gives them a grade.

To accomplish any of the authentic editing steps, you must develop an editing rubric. This rubric is class generated and becomes the tool used in steps 1 through 3 of the Authentic Editing Phase.

Section I

Phase IV
Authentic Editing

1. Self-editing

2. Peer Editing

3. Teacher Conference

4. Final Copy Writing

5. Teacher Assessment

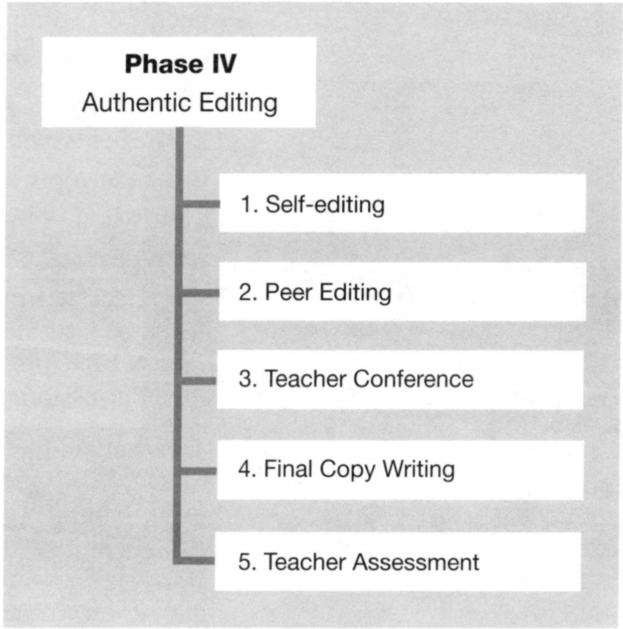

FIGURE 4.1
Master Plan

Creating the Assessment Rubric

An important tool during this phase of writing is the writing rubric. This rubric is an assessment tool that allows students to record and then check key points before submitting their final writing selections. Oftentimes teachers use a pre-made rubric based on their language arts curriculum or state proficiency standards. Once completed, they use the same writing rubric for the entire school year for every writing assignment based on the same genre. *Stop!* We have a different idea.

We suggest you try this. Create a writing rubric for each and every writing assignment by drawing out suggestions from your class. By using this approach with your students, their involvement will automatically help them buy into the assessment method of the rubric because they assisted in developing it. You will receive fewer arguments over the assessment criteria because your students actually proposed them. You will also know whether students have internalized your lessons, because they will only suggest ideas for the rubric that they understand and remember.

This is an important strategy in the BEW process. Don't put a concept into the writing rubric if the students don't propose the idea or respond to a prompt. Often, your students won't come up with all the correct rubric questions. Don't worry if they don't tell you all the rules that you feel you have taught them. What makes this process *authentic* is that the students give you feedback on what they have learned. If they leave something out, this is your signal that you need to reteach that concept later. For example, we taught the concepts of adjectives and adverbs for two weeks in our second-grade classroom. When it came time to develop the student-generated editing rubric, not a single child proposed any rules about adjectives or adverbs—even after prompting them. We immediately knew that we must reteach the *adjectives* and *adverbs* concepts in the near future. We did not include these concepts in the writing rubric for the current week because the students did not offer the idea even when prompted. During this phase of BEW, your class will teach *you* what they have learned from past lessons. This makes these rubrics a valuable learning tool for both you and your students.

Each writing rubric should include three areas of assessment:

1. **Genre Format and Voice:** specific format and voice usage applied to different genres (an in-depth discussion is given in Section II)

2. **Vocabulary Development and Word Usage:** student word choice and vocabulary development

3. **Grammar and Conventions:** universal grammar and convention rules

Your class-created rubric needs to be organized to include these three categories by inserting specific criteria that students remember as important under each heading. You may be thinking: How do I create a student-generated writing rubric with my class? It's very easy to do one category at a time.

Professor Write's Interactive Teaching Strategy

Writing Rubric—Genre Format and Voice

Ask: "What should you be checking your writing selections for in the areas of Genre Format and Voice?"

Students Answer: "Did I follow the Blueprint by having introduction, detail, and summary paragraphs [or beginning, middle, and end]?"

Background: Remember that as you use this system to create a rubric for each writing selection, students will become accustomed to the questions and answers. For your first selection or two each year, you may need to remind them what the terms Genre Format and Voice mean (see Chapter 2). Review the Blueprint style needed for the genre plus how much of the student's voice or personality needs to be incorporated. Also, your students may need a verbal prompt to trigger their memory about a specific technique taught. Make sure that you follow up with prompts, but don't give away the answer.

Teach: "Great, yes, you need to check to see if you have all three types of paragraphs. Let's write that on our rubric under the Genre Format and Voice heading. We'll write, 'Do I have all three types of paragraphs?' Then we'll write a way for you to evaluate yourself on how well you did."

Background: You will find it valuable to add scoring points for each criterion on your rubric such as a 0-to-3-point scale or 0-to-5-point scale. Students can assess themselves after they do each editing step, which helps them become critical thinkers of their work. Giving students a range of scores allows them to determine whether improvement is possible or necessary.

Ask: "Now let's look at each of these paragraphs. What specific areas or criteria should the introduction include?"

Student Feedback: At this point, your students will answer your questions with the concepts taught during previous lessons. You may hear your own words coming back to you here, which is great. They may say things such as, "Did the introduction have a catchy topic sentence that makes my audience want to read more? Does the introduction do its job [depending on the genre]?" Remember to add these questions to the rubric and add the corresponding evaluation scale.

Ask: "What about the last sentence of the introduction?"

Students Answer: "Oh yeah, did I write a creative transition sentence?"

Ask: "What things should we be looking for in the detail paragraph?"

Students Answer: "Did I have a good topic sentence for each detail paragraph? Did I use an effective transition sentence?" Because you have taught the concept of paragraphing earlier, your students will also tell you, "Did I add additional paragraphs correctly by starting a new paragraph each time I wrote about a new event, described a new place, or discussed a new person?"

Ask: "What things should we be looking for in the summary?"

Students Answer: "Did I write a summary? Did the summary do the job it was supposed to according to the genre?"

Key: Young children benefit by using a rubric to correct their work by putting their finger on their paper, item by item, and check each point as the teacher reads it aloud.

Over time, students will respond with questions you have asked them and modeled for them during the Prewriting and Writing Phases. They will have internalized these important writing strategies through repetition. For example, depending on the genre you've selected, your students may respond, "Did I follow the writing prompt directions?" or "Did I have a story line (if the story is a personal narrative)?" To your surprise they might also say, "Did I use the correct amount of voice for the genre?" It is important to write these concepts down exactly as your students tell them to you, using their own language and in the format of students asking the questions (for example, "Did I . . . "). If they don't give you a key concept you feel you have taught even after you have prompted them, just reteach that concept.

The next concept to include in your class writing rubric is *vocabulary and word usage*. Write that heading on your rubric and continue creating your checklist for student editing.

Professor Write's Interactive Teaching Strategy

Writing Rubric—Vocabulary and Word Usage

Ask: "What should we be looking for in vocabulary and word usage to make our rubric?" (Remember, over time, these words will have meaning for your students. At first, prompt them with questions about the words they are using to build their writing selections.)

Students Answer: "Did I use powerful verbs? Did I create visual images through my words? Did I make the audience feel like they were really there with me?" Students will parrot back vocabulary suggestions you have given them during the previous weeks.

Ask: "What writing techniques help to create visual images?"

Students Answer: "Did I use words about my five senses? Did I use similes, analogies, and metaphors?" Student answers will vary, depending upon your genre and instruction.

Ask: "What should we be looking for in word usage?"

Students Answer: "Did I use complex sentences? Did I use a variety of words to express myself without using the same word again and again?"

As your students express their thoughts and ideas to you for this category, continue to record them on your assessment rubric in question format using the evaluation scale. Many state proficiency tests are very critical of the low level of student vocabulary usage. This assessment technique will help students internalize proper and advanced word usage.

The final section of the student-created rubric assessment is *Grammar and Conventions*. Here you will follow your current lessons in grammar and conventions according to your grade level and your district language arts series. During this phase of rubric development, you interact with your students by questioning their knowledge of the rules they should know based upon conventions, grammar, and genre from previous lessons.

Professor Write's Interactive Teaching Strategy

Writing Rubric—Grammar and Conventions

Ask: "What should we be looking for in the area of Grammar and Conventions for our rubric?"

Students Answer: "Did I have the right noun–verb agreement? Did I use adverbs correctly? Did I use the correct verb tense in my writing?"

Under the category of Grammar and Conventions, your student writing rubric will change according to your weekly grammar lessons. Your state benchmarks will determine these skills by grade level.

Now that the rubric has been created, it's time for students to use it to edit their writing selections. You'll need multiple copies of this rubric for your students to use as they self-edit. You will need additional copies when they edit their peers' selections. Lastly, one more copy of the writing rubric is needed when you sit down with each individual student during the teacher–student writing conference.

Step 1: Self-editing

Now that the editing rubric has been collaboratively completed, students are ready to edit their own writing selections. Because they have helped to develop this rubric, they have ownership and an understanding of how to edit and correct their own writing.

Professor Write's Interactive Teaching Strategy

Self-editing

Ask: "How did you do in writing your rough draft?"

Say: "It's now time to find out how well you did by editing your writing assignments using our class rubric. Use a highlighter to mark editing corrections [or have them use proofreading editing symbols that are taught in conjunction with many literacy programs]. Find and then fix your mistakes."

Support: If needed for young or at-risk learners, follow the same process but read each rubric question to the students aloud and have them answer each editing question together as it pertains to their own assignment. In this way, nobody gets left behind and all students will finish editing their assignments together. Circulate around the classroom to answer editing questions. Allow students to use different color highlighters to mark their mistakes.

After your class has finished editing their assignments, give them time to make the corrections that they have noted. At this time, assist your students with materials such as a dictionary or thesaurus. Give them a designated time period to finish before they move on to the next step.

Step 2: Peer Editing

Usually, writers don't catch all their own mistakes. Let's say, for example, you write an important letter to a company or individual. Do you ever then ask a friend or colleague to proofread that letter before you print a final copy and mail it? They probably found several errors that you overlooked. You're not alone. We have found that most writers miss many of their own mistakes. This is because what we see looks perfectly good to us. It takes somebody else to ask the question: What do you mean by this? Children are no different. Many students may not find their own mistakes because their selection sounds and looks correct to them. Peer editing can be a powerful tool for all authors, experienced and inexperienced, to help improve their work.

To begin, select peer editing partners for each student in your class. Take the same writing rubric that was used for the students' self-editing step and modify the rubric by adding a space for the author's name and the editor's name at the top. Make copies of this peer editing rubric and give one to each student in your class. Teach your students the social skills involved in being helpful peer editors. A good strategy is to teach your peer editors to start and end by giving compliments to the writer, sandwiching their editing suggestions in the middle.

Darren and Autumn are peer editing each other's writing selections by giving positive comments and suggestions for improvement.

Professor Write's Interactive Teaching Strategy

Peer Editing

Say: "It's time to peer edit our papers. Sit next to your editing partner. Now switch papers and complete the editing rubric for your peer partner and write your name in the designated space. You have fifteen minutes to complete this peer editing project."

Background: Always set a time limit for this editing process. Make sure the time limit is age appropriate and that students can actually finish the editing process in the given time allotment. *Hint:* Give a time limit that is a minute or two less than you might think they need. This helps them to stay on task and get right to work.

Support: Circulate around your classroom and answer any questions that your students may have about the editing process. At the end of the fifteen-minute peer editing period, ask your students to return to their seats with their writing assignments and their peer editing rubric.

Ask: "How did your peer editor help you? What mistakes did they find?" Let the class share these ideas through a teacher-directed discussion. Doing this reinforces the concepts that have previously been taught in class.

TIP: Conduct an editor's drawing! Ask students who felt they had good editors to put their editor's name in a box. Then draw five names from the box. Give the winners a new highlighter!

Step 3: Teacher Conference

This final editing step—the teacher conference—is one that can actually be completed rather quickly because you have been hearing and following the development of your students' writing assignments all along. Teacher conferencing is done by meeting with each student individually or in small groups of two or three students and then editing their writing assignments. Using the same student-generated writing rubric, review the concepts listed. Again, the purpose of this step is to help students improve their writing selections and meet your curriculum standards. This is also the time to give your students suggestions or ask them questions about their selections that are not up to curriculum standards. As you quickly read through student rough draft writing selections, ask each student questions regarding their assignment based upon the class-generated writing rubric. Compliment students for the concepts they have mastered. If you happen to see any discrepancies between the writing rubric and the student writing selection, point them out to your student at this time. For example, if you feel that a student did not include a topic sentence in a detail paragraph, ask the student to read the sentences in their detail paragraph and determine the topic or to look at their Blueprint and remember the topic they wanted to talk about. This becomes a teachable moment.

ELL students require immediate feedback for correcting writing. Use this step of the BEW editing phase to give personal feedback.

You will complete and return a writing rubric for each student during these teacher conferences and then provide an opportunity for the students to edit their writing selection one final time.

During the first writing assignment of the year, you may want to meet with each student individually in a writing conference. But don't feel that this is necessary for each and every student on all assignments. For the students who have acquired more substantial writing skills, teacher–student conferencing may not be needed for each writing selection. We find this desirable because on many state proficiency exams, students need to write and edit their own work without teacher input.

Step 4: Final Copy Writing

It is only after completing self-editing, peer editing, and teacher–student conferencing that the final copies of the writing selections are written. Students have had the opportunity and direction to improve their writing selections. Now the time has come to write their final copy. We recommend that older students use a computer and a printer to produce the final copies for assessment. This makes finishing the assignment less tedious. What you'll find is that your classes' assignments are much longer than they have ever been before, and typing them will speed up the process of completing the final copy. As for younger authors, using a computer for typing may not be an option. In this case, you can cover two academic areas with one assignment: writing and handwriting. Why not practice handwriting for a few days by rewriting student stories rather than by asking students to write in a handwriting workbook?

Given the preparation and class experiences students have received on their writing selections, don't be surprised if you can hear a pin drop in your classroom as they begin to prepare their final copies. They are approaching the time when they will be sharing their work with their audiences (the purpose of their writing), and they are confident that what they have prepared will be successful. Be sure you give them a reasonable time limit to complete their assignments in class.

Step 5: Teacher Assessment

Assessment is an essential part of the writing process. During this step, students are given their grades for their writing selections based upon your student-generated rubric. Because you base your instruction for each genre and writing selection on the grade-level expectations tied to your curriculum and state standards, your grades on these papers should coordinate with curriculum expectations. Using our BEW strategies (Phases I–IV), you will have enhanced your instruction yet not interfered with teaching the critical elements you are expected to cover at your grade level. It's at this time that you will compare your students' final work with the state's high-stakes testing rubric and curriculum assessment for each grade level. This allows you to estimate your students' current performance compared with where they need to be and to plan for future assignments.

After you collect the final copies of your student writing assignments, we promise that it will not take you as long to assess these assignments as it has in the past. The scoring system on the student-generated writing rubric (0–3 points, 0–4, points, or 0–5 points) that you asked your students to use can now be used for your final grading. Simply add up the maximum number of points associated with each question in the rubric as the highest possible score a student could earn for the writing selection. Then, read each assignment and score it according to the rubric. Total the score the student earned, and divide by the maximum number of possible points, which gives a percentage score. That percentage becomes the student grade for the assignment.

Beyond assigning the grade, it is important to note any recurring mistakes that show up in the writing assignments. For example, if one of your students wrote many sentences starting with the word *then*, you could write a note at the bottom of that student's grading rubric that would highlight this problem so that student could correct it during the next writing assignment. Use the same skills you have taught your peer editors to use. Compliment each student on one or two things they have done well, then highlight one or two areas to focus on for the next writing unit.

After the grade has been given and students have prepared their best and final copy, it is time to move into the Publishing Phase!

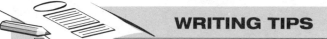

WRITING TIPS

Writing Tips: Final Copy

- Work in coordination with the computer technology teacher and request that students use their computer lab time to retype their writing selections.

- Some at-risk or special needs students may write their final copies more legibly if completed on *raised-lined paper* (paper with textured lines that students can feel as they write). Additionally, some students may need pencil grips to assist them in recording longer paragraphs more legibly.

In Summary: Editing Phase

You may be thinking that spending several days on editing student work is longer than you want to devote to this phase. This additional time will all afford your students the opportunity to internalize and practice all their newly learned editing skills. When students correct their own writing mistakes, you can be assured that they will not repeat these mistakes in future writing selections. True student learning results when students internalize the elements of writing for different genres. This is successfully accomplished by the Authentic Editing Phase in BEW.

*Set up a purpose for
student writing at the start
of each assignment so
that students know how
their work will be shared.
Will it be published in the
school library? Printed
in the local newspaper?
Delivered orally in front
of an audience? By stating
the purpose for publishing
from the beginning,
students will be highly
motivated to produce their
best work.*

Phase V: Publishing—Sharing the Purpose

Publishing is the last step in the BEW process, but one that students enjoy most. Students will take pride in their work and become much more excited about their assignments if their work is purposeful. Tell your students right from the very beginning, "Your work will be published." They will come to understand that their assignments have meaning and that what they have to write about and share is

John emphatically shares his story from the podium. Students love to share their stories in the Publishing Phase.

important. Students will be more motivated if there is an authentic reason to be writing, such as a letter to persuade their parents, an advertisement for the school store, or a reading for a school assembly. The publishing suggestions in BEW will assure students that they will get the opportunity to tell their story, which, especially for very young children, makes it all worthwhile.

We define student publishing as sharing writing selections through any method or media. Within the BEW process, there are three different ways to publish student writing selections (see Figure 5.1) with many categories under each suggestion:

Step 1. Within the School: sharing with the class, sharing across grade levels, media center sharing, student public readings, school writing assemblies, school writing contests, meetings with professional authors, school publishing websites, school blogs for writing, topical books from student interests, school newspaper, class newsletter, school storytelling programs, school plays, school write-a-thons, school letters, teacher-talk bulletin boards, and poetry slams

Step 2. For the Community: sharing by using the local newspaper, cable television presentations with student readings, community writing contests, reading at senior citizen homes and hospitals, plays given at senior citizen homes and hospitals, coordination with public library events, articles in the local paper through a "Kids Korner" section, community center coordination of events, grandparent writing pals, and community writers

Step 3. Student Portfolios and Keepsakes: video books, video portfolios, writing portfolio DVDs, and audio CDs

ELL–BEWCONNECTION

Increase your ELL students' self-esteem and motivation to write by publishing their work! It will change their attitudes about writing!

Three Steps in Phase V: Publishing

We hope that you have already set up an authentic purpose for your students' writing project as motivation to inspire your students throughout the writing project. Phase Five is offered to inspire you, the teachers, to "shoot for the stars" with your young authors.

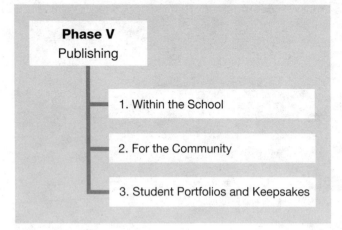

Phase V
Publishing

1. Within the School

2. For the Community

3. Student Portfolios and Keepsakes

FIGURE 5.1

Master Plan

Step 1: Within the School

Publishing is the celebration of student writing. Display students' completed writing assignments everywhere: classrooms, hallways, showcases, and the school media center. Display! Display! Display!

Idea 1: Sharing with the Class

Students love to share their stories and papers with anyone who will listen. Think about it. Don't your kids just love to talk? They talk about themselves, their families, their ideas. Why not their stories too? To promote speaking in front of the class and to provide security for speaking before an audience, we designed and built a student minipodium for young authors. Our early elementary students use this podium when they stand in front of the class and read their selections to their classmates. Our students are very excited about coming to the podium to read and, as one of our young authors said, "That's just like the podium the president stands at to talk." We readily agreed and told the student we couldn't wait to hear his story. Ask your class for student volunteers to share their writing selections. You'll notice that nearly every hand goes up. Students get to come to the podium one by one and read their writing selections to the class and then get to hear their classmates respond appropriately by applauding for the student reader. What a great way to boost students' self-esteem and create a sense of pride in writing! Realizing that not every student will choose to read aloud to the class, students can also share their stories by reading them aloud to their neighbors. This way, everybody gets into the act.

WRITING TIPS

Sharing with the Class

- Have a parent build a minipodium for young authors.

- Take pictures of your students presenting to your class throughout the year.

- Post some of these presentation pictures on your bulletin board, in the class newsletter, or on the school website.

- There are many books available that include creative templates that can be student made to display finished writing selections. Some of our favorites are found in *75 Creative Ways to Publish Students' Writing* (Sunflower, 1993).

- Have students sit in a special author's chair as they read their selections to the class.

- Let your students wear a special author's hat when they read their selections.

Idea 2: Sharing across Grade Levels

Many older authors enjoy reading their selections to younger students and, conversely, younger authors enjoy reading to older authors. We suggest that you arrange cross-grade-level readings in your school so that children of different grade levels and ages can share their writing selections. Ask students to comment on one another's writing selections during these sessions. You'll be surprised at the insight your students show when asked to critique other students' writing.

Sharing across Grade Levels

- Take pictures of younger authors reading to older authors and vice versa.
- Post these pictures in the *Kids Korner* of the library.
- Post these pictures on your school's website.

Idea 3: Media Center Sharing

Find parents in your school who would like to form a parent publishing committee. Their job is to create class books by typing the writing selections for the entire class, compiling a table of contents so each student's selection can be found easily, and then using a plastic or laminated cover to bind the student selections into a *class book*. Create a "Kids Korner" in your media center where class books can be readily displayed. For some assignments, enough class books can be prepared so that each child receives a copy. When visiting the media center you'll find your students will rush to the Kids Korner section of the library first.

Hang a small bulletin board near the Kids Korner in your school library so that students can write comments to one another about their stories. Put the small bulletin board near the displayed books with a basket of sticky notes and a few pencils. Allow students to post positive comments and questions to student authors whose books are being displayed and put the sticky notes on the bulletin board. This creates an opportunity for student dialogue about their literature. Give students time to respond to the questions and comments about their books using sticky notes that are then posted on the small media center bulletin board. You, too, can get into the act by reading, commenting, and posting notes to student authors. What a wonderful way to create student–student and student–teacher dialogue in writing.

WRITING TIPS

Media Center Sharing

- Clip local newspaper articles related to student writing in your school. Laminate and post them in the Kids Korner.
- Keep a stack of sticky notes, pens, and pencils close by the Kids Korner bulletin board.
- Purchase different types of sticky notes, animal shapes, voice callouts, hearts, and flowers to create a variety of choices for students.

WRITING TIPS

Public Readings

- Record your students sharing their readings over the PA system. Send CD copies of these readings home to parents.

- Take pictures of your students reading from the office over the PA system. Post these pictures everywhere!

- Create a school job: school announcer of the day!

Idea 4: Public Readings

Many schools conduct daily announcements in the morning before the academic school day begins. Does yours? This is a great time to have one student per day share a writing selection with the entire school. Students enjoy reading their writing selections to others, especially for a large audience like the whole school. These types of schoolwide readings can be topical or school-event specific. For example, many school districts establish March as school reading month, a perfect occasion for reading aloud on the public address (PA) system. One thing is for sure, your students will be thrilled as they read their writing selections over the PA system for all to hear!

Idea 5: School Writing Assemblies

Again, students love sharing their finished writing selections with an audience. Most schools have a variety of schoolwide assemblies throughout the year, such as holiday programs, spring concerts, and talent shows. Why not hold a schoolwide or grade-level writing assembly? The students meet in the gym or auditorium to read their writing selections to fellow students. Because it won't be possible for all students to share their work as a result of time limitations (nor will all students have the desire to share stories in a large-group format), we suggest that teachers ask for a set number of volunteers per grade level. Because most students who have been taught by BEW strategies are very comfortable with presenting to others, students look for opportunities to present their work to a large group. As one of our students recently asked us regarding his finished writing assignment, "So will this be a reading to the school or just to other classrooms? I prefer to read to the school in the gym!" After students have presented their ideas to a group and heard the group applaud, there's no stopping them.

WRITING TIPS

School Writing Assemblies

- Create grade-level writing assemblies at which students can read their selections aloud for their peers. Or choose a younger grade and have a writing assembly at which older students inspire the younger ones to write creatively.

- Ask your local mayor to give the awards for a school writing contest. Make sure your local paper is there to write a story and take pictures of the event.

Idea 6: School Writing Contests

Another activity that students enjoy is a good old-fashioned contest. Why not have a schoolwide writing contest based on a specific theme? Consider using themes associated with holidays or seasons. Print school flyers describing the contest timeline, the selected judges, and the prizes that will be offered. Distribute the flyers to the entire school. Create posters that describe the school contest and its parameters. Hang them in the school hallways and in the school media center. You may wish to have a winner or two per grade level. Announce the winners over the school PA system, have an awards presentation for the winners, and ask the winners to read their selection to the school (and parents!). Perhaps it might be in order to have a reporter from the local newspaper present during the award ceremony to make a connection between school and community. After all, who doesn't like to get their picture in the local newspaper?

Idea 7: Meetings with Professional Authors

Students learn most effectively through modeling. Why not use professional authors as models for your students? Conduct a schoolwide assembly during which professional authors of children's books tell about the art of writing in general, their own writing (and where they get their topics), and how the process of publishing works. Have these professionals read some of their short stories to the students during the assembly. You will notice that your students will begin to imitate their favorite author in their own writing style.

WRITING TIPS

Meeting with Professional Authors

- Ask a local reporter or newspaper editor to visit your school and talk about newspaper work!

- Find a local children's illustrator to hold an assembly on illustrating books.

Idea 8: School Publishing Website

Have you noticed that your students are really proficient with using computers and researching websites? You're not alone; today's students love computers. Why not capitalize on expert student computer skills and connect these skills to learning? Create a link on your school's website where student stories, poems, and illustrations can be posted for all to read and see. Use a student group or technology club to organize this link and give them appropriate student work to post each month.

WRITING TIPS

School Publishing Website

- If your school doesn't have a school technology club, establish one.

- Begin a schoolwide media center with in-house TV programs that can be used for announcements, general school communication, and student publishing.

- Always have students create schoolwide media projects.

Idea 9: School Blogs

You've probably already noticed that your students like blogs too. Go one step further than a link on a website and create a student blog where the topic is writing. You may want to try different genres and topics for different grade levels. You'll be surprised at the number of students that will write in a school blog. Be sure you get online and submit ideas and supervise student entries.

Idea 10: Topical Books from Student Interests

Create special-topic books (such as cookbooks) containing favorite student recipes by grade level. Parents love this one. One way to be successful with this type of activity is to center it on holiday cooking. For example, put together a Kid's Cookie Cookbook and include easy-to-make recipes. Moms love to get new holiday cookie recipes, and this book could also serve as a holiday present to family members. Another example (as well as a cultural learning experience) is an ethnic cookbook. Everyone likes to try new types of food. Try creating a students' cookbook centered on a specific culture, like French, Spanish, or perhaps even the students' own ethnic backgrounds.

Idea 11: School Newspaper

Before you begin writing a school newspaper, take a field trip to your local newspaper. Let the students talk to some of the reporters and the editor. When you return to school, your students will have a better understanding of how a newspaper is published and the work that goes on behind the scenes. Consider having a few special columns like "Dear Abby," "What We're Writing Now," or "Classroom News."

WRITING TIPS

School Newspaper

- Ask a reporter or two to give a student-centered class on being a journalist. We've had a lot of fun with this activity.

- Unsure of how to begin a school newspaper? Here's a free website that offers great information on the in's and out's of creating a school newspaper: www.emints.org/ethemes/resources/S00000488.shtml.

Idea 12: Create a Classroom Newsletter

A creative way for teachers to communicate with parents is through a class newsletter. The key to a successful class newsletter is to include student-written articles. This newsletter should be completely student centered. Don't forget to scan in student illustrations and class pictures. Children won't forget to take these newsletters home!

Idea 13: Professional Storytelling at School

Expose students to a professional storyteller who will capture their attention and leave them with a real-life experience that will remain with them forever. Storytelling is an ancient art that exemplifies the skills of oral tradition and the building blocks of a story. Professional storytellers travel the world gathering tales from other cultures, distant lands, seeking the yarns of the old and new. Many storytellers perform in the area of education. Professional storytellers bring to life their stories, travel, and characters, and touch the hearts of all who hear them. Your students can learn this craft from experts when your school arranges a schoolwide storytelling assembly.

Idea 14: School Storytelling Programs

Students can effectively and interactively learn about genres such as fables, folklore, and narratives from a professional storyteller. Have students tell their own stories to a group of young children, complete with sound effects and character dialogue. They will be writing special effects into their stories in no time!

WRITING TIPS

Professional Storytelling

- Contact and learn about storytellers from a national storytellers organization. Check out their website: www.storynet.org.

- Many professional storytellers sell audio stories on CDs that can be played to your class.

- Check out the website of our favorite storyteller, Dr. Debra Christian: http://hometown.aol.comDebraC4. She has stories on CDs that will capture the interest of students young and old.

- Two of our other favorite storytelling websites are: www.storyarts.org and www.storycraft.com.

Cecalie, a fourth grader, proudly shares a story with first-grade students.

Storytelling promotes many writing skills, like understanding and writing expanded descriptions, enriched vocabulary, the use of voice both vocally and in written composition, and attention to detail. So, start a school storytelling program or perhaps even a club. Older authors can tell their stories to younger authors. Students can recite their stories in the classroom and at school assemblies.

Idea 15: School Plays

Many standard reading curricula include student plays. Some of our fondest memories from elementary and middle school are participating in classroom and all-school plays. Some children really enjoy this activity. We sure did. Plays are an excellent way to improve student self-esteem and student-speaking skills, and, at the same time, the kids will have a great time. Try having students write an original play or rewrite an existing story into a play. Students are very creative and come up with clever ideas. For instance, some of our young authors rewrote the story of Cinderella. In their story, Cinderella became an elementary school teacher and they were in her class. Imagine that!

Idea 16: School Write-a-Thon

It's not unusual for schools to have schoolwide read-a-thons. During a read-a-thon, the objective is to have a contest based on high-volume reading. It's very simple: The class that collectively reads the greatest number of books wins the contest and, in our school, a class pizza

WRITING TIPS

School Plays

- Author Barry Lane produces audio CDs that have a variety of unusual fairy tale endings. Try playing Barry Lane CDs for your class. They'll love them. Check out his website at www.discover-writing.com.

party. Why not do the same thing with writing? Hold a school write-a-thon. How do you start? Perhaps create a poster with a picture of a large fountain pen for each grade level. The fountain pen should be upright and should each be labeled with a numerical scale, say, one through 500. Assign a genre or two to your students as a writing assignment. Have assigned due dates for the assignments, collect the completed writing, and draw an ink line across the picture of the fountain pen corresponding to the current number of stories collectively written by your class. Make sure the posters are prominently displayed in the hallway outside participating classrooms. The classroom with the largest number of selections written wins the contest. Don't forget to display the student writing assignments too.

Idea 17: School Letters and Student-Made Cards

There are many opportunities to send cards and letters to different organizations or groups throughout the school year. Recently, our school conducted a *writing campaign* during which students wrote letters and made cards for our servicemen and -women. It gave our students a feeling of personal satisfaction to compose and mail these letters.

Idea 18: Teacher-Talk Bulletin Boards

We feel that bulletin boards are made to be interactive. Why not place small bulletin boards outside each classroom for the purpose of creating written student–teacher dialogue and communication? Students can write notes to their teachers and others, then tack these notes to the bulletin board. Teachers can write quick responses back to their students. This is an instant method of working with dialogue in writing.

Idea 19: Poetry Slam

We remember the days of coffee houses, when college students shared their poetry. How about you? If you're not part of that generation, it's something that has been reinvented and is called a *poetry slam*. During this event, students share their poetry in a performing arts milieu by taking the stage, one at a time, and giving a short explanation of the motivation for their poetry and any other personal information that may have contributed to their work. Then they read their best poem. This type of sharing may take place at school, perhaps in a corner of the library. Encourage your students to dress to match the mood of their poetry.

Step 2: For the Community

There are numerous ways that your students can share their writing in your community. Be creative as you publicize your students' best work!

Idea 1: Publicity in Local Newspapers

Be certain to call your local newspaper for schoolwide writing assemblies. Our students love seeing their pictures in the paper, and so do their parents! Recently, our school held a writing assembly. We invited the local newspaper to take pictures and write a story about our event. Later, we saw one of our school parents buying a stack of newspapers. We jokingly said to her, "You must like to read." She responded, "My daughter's picture and interview are in the paper." Like us, we know you will beam with pride knowing that you helped your students be recognized in such a positive way by their families.

Idea 2: Cable Television Presentations

A great way to spread the word about student expressive writing talent is by having students do presentations at school board meetings. As you may know, many community members and parents watch telecasts of school board meetings on local cable television networks. Sometimes community members are astonished at the proficiency of young children in their ability to express themselves in writing as shown on local cable network programs. One time we had first graders read their Thanksgiving stories (personal narratives) to the school board. Later, a woman at the local grocery store asked us, "Did those kids really write that stuff? I mean, those first graders, did they really write those stories?" We assured her that they did indeed write those stories and we're still not certain that she believed us. One thing is for sure, parents watch school board meetings these days. Use school presentations at school board meetings as a positive vehicle to communicate interesting programs and services to community members.

Idea 3: Community Writing Contests

In our community, certain organizations (such as Breakfast Optimist and some local community businesses) sponsor elementary school writing contests. What better way to increase student self-esteem while working on writing skills than to win a contest? Perhaps even a monetary prize! Recently, one of our local jewelry stores sponsored an expressive writing contest for Mother's Day. Students were asked to write a story about why their mother deserved a diamond necklace. Can you think of a better opportunity to provide an authentic purpose and reason to write a great persuasive paper? (In case you're interested, the first-, second-, and third-place winners were from our school district! Our students love to write!)

Idea 4: Reading at Senior Citizen Homes and Hospitals

There is no audience more receptive to listening to children perform than our senior citizens. You may already visit these homes or hospitals for your music programs, but consider setting up a visit when your students can read their stories to the residents. Students love to read, show their illustrations, and perhaps even drop off a student-created greeting card. The smiles on the faces of the seniors or patients will benefit even your most reluctant students who share their work.

Idea 5: Plays Given at Senior Citizen Homes and Hospitals

This is a real treat for both the audience and the student performers. The best time to perform these types of events is around a holiday. Holiday topics are fun for our students and they provide an easy-to-write-about topic. Students can write from personal experience. One year our class created a holiday play for our community seniors. The elementary students wrote the play, created a dance, and made fifty holiday baskets to give away to the senior citizens after the play. Needless to say, it was a great success.

Let your creativity work here, matching a topic to an audience in your community. Again, the audience response will be reward enough for the hard work your students put in to their writing.

Idea 6: Coordination with Public Library Events

Many schools coordinate events with their local community library. Try something new such as coordinating a Saturday Coffee House Reading. If you're worried about attendance, advertise in your local paper and on your local cable television network. Organize student readings according to genres. Let the fun begin on an early Saturday morning.

Idea 7: Local Newspaper

Most towns have a community newspaper that is published once or twice a week that covers local events. Think about coordinating student writing activities with your local editor. Ask the newspaper editor if they would be willing to have an editorial "Kids Korner" feature. Students love this concept and it will encourage them to read the local newspaper and write letters to the editor on current issues in their community. Your class can discuss issues and write informational pieces or persuasive papers, and vote on several to be submitted to the paper. The editor would undoubtedly be pleased to publish student poetry from time to time as well.

Idea 8: Community Center Coordination of Events

Community theater programs and community music programs are just a few of the types of activities that may occur in your area on a regular basis. Form a partnership among various community organizations and your school. For instance, our local symphony holds regularly scheduled performances at the local performing arts center. At the start of each new program, the symphony narrator gives a brief speech regarding the performance that will soon be heard. We ask students to do a research paper on a musician that will be heard at the local symphony. We then coordinate this student research project with the symphony agenda and have one of our students be the historical narrator for the evening. What can you arrange with the community programs in your area? Perhaps the parent of one of your students will help you make a connection and inspire an opportunity.

Idea 9: Grandparent Writing Pals

Establishing a grandparent writing pals program in your community will thrill your students as well as the senior citizens. Students can write letters to their selected senior citizen writing pals on a scheduled basis.

Idea 10: Community Writers

Many school districts already sponsor a similar concept using *community readers* to help children with reading difficulties. The objective is for school volunteers to visit teachers and classrooms on a scheduled basis (say, twice a week) to help students with reading in a small-group or one-on-one basis. Try this same concept with student writing. Ask for community volunteers to assist students in a small group or one-on-one basis. At-risk, special needs, or ELL students could benefit from a personal editor. Let your parent organizations, your local newspaper, and even your high school know of your need. This relationship could be powerful in helping your students become better writers.

Step 3: Student Portfolios and Keepsakes

You may have your students write for activities in your class or school, or even to share with the community. However, your students will love to create special writing projects that they can keep as well.

Try to find a way to connect student writing to something memorable for your class—an heirloom they will cherish.

Idea 1: Class-Made Books

We talked about students compiling their own books during step 1 of the Publishing Phase. We talked about the books being typed and assembled by volunteers if desired and kept in the Kids Korner of your school library. You can also have students make a book that is personal that they can keep or take home. With today's technology, it's even possible to scan student illustrations quickly and then use a computer to cut and paste these illustrations within each student's own writing selection. With each new student topic or writing selection, there's an opportunity to create a student book. We've found that our students just can't wait to get their books, bring them home, and share them with everyone. Recently, one of our parents called our school and requested that we quickly publish another student book. When asked why, the parent responded with the answer, "I have this one memorized because my daughter has read it to me over one hundred times and I need some new material!" Indeed, our students cherish their published selections. We've actually had students come back to our elementary school and bring old copies of class books to show us. To our surprise, some of these former students are now juniors and seniors in college. That's right! They've saved these books all those years.

WRITING TIPS

Class Books

- Try creating a class anthology for specific genres such as poetry. Collect your student poems over an extended time, such as two semesters, and then publish them in a larger book called an *anthology.*

- Have an illustration contest for the cover illustration. Let the best, most innovative illustration be selected as the book cover!

- Create a class poster of students looking at their anthology for the media center Kids Korner.

Idea 2: Class-Made Portfolios

Kids love to see growth in their writing, and there's no better way than to have a portfolio collection. Why not a class portfolio with writing samples from different students on various genres? Make sure your student work includes illustrations too! At the end of the year, take a picture of your class and use the picture as the cover for the anthology. Have the class anthology bound, indexed in your library, and prepared for student library loans.

Idea 3: Video Books

Today, many parents and grandparents own very nice camcorders. Invite parents or volunteers who are good with video camcorders to come to your class to tape student readings. One of our fourth-grade teachers had her class do a written assignment in the biography genre. When students read their biographies to the class, they were videotaped by a talented parent. It was quite the presentation because the students were encouraged to dress up like the subjects of their biographies and to act like and affect the accents of their subjects when they did their readings. The videotape was then edited and burned into multiple DVDs. Each student received a copy of the class video-book DVD. We hope you find a way to publish student work in this fashion. Even though the first time you may need to depend on the expertise of others for the technology, it is worth it to see how much fun the students have, and even more fun when you get the feedback from families who watch the DVD.

Idea 4: Video Portfolios

Much on the same line as creating a video book, try developing a video portfolio. Again, you'll need an eager parent who is familiar with videotaping and editing. Throughout the entire school year, tape your class writing presentations, school writing assemblies, school plays that the students have written, or any other publishing activity that can be successfully videotaped. At the end of the school year, combine the shorter videotape segments into one large tape. Then create a DVD and burn multiple copies for each student. These will be treasured for years to come.

Idea 5: CDs of Student Readings

An alternative to using camcorders and making DVDs is to create a CD of students reading their selections to an audience, or even an audiotape recording. This is low tech in today's world, but can still be effective. This type of media lends itself well to poetry presentations. Your students will enjoy listening to each other's poetry or stories as they sit at the listening center in your classroom during their free time.

In Summary: Publishing Phase

The Publishing Phase is the last phase in the BEW process, but it provides the motivation that drives each writing unit. Without this motivation, students find that spending time on writing assignments becomes just one more paper that is read and graded by the teacher. They are not motivated to put in the necessary effort to make it their very best work. On the other hand, if students know the purpose for their writing, then the steps in the writing process have meaning. Be sure you develop interesting and culturally relevant topics that match your required genre and that you match these topics with purposeful publishing activities. When your students know their audience and how they will publish, they will willingly progress through the phases and prepare high-quality work.

Section II

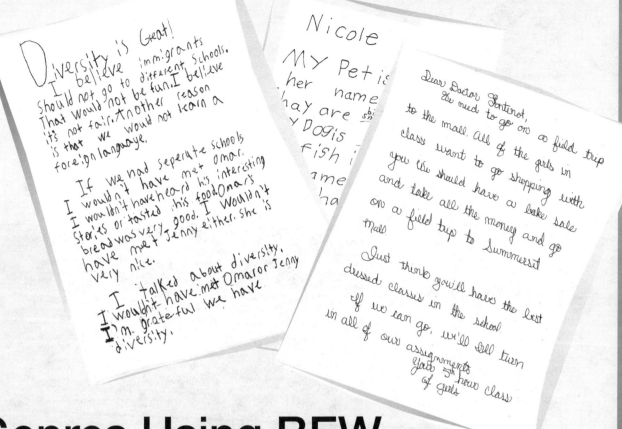

Teaching Genres Using BEW

Chapter 6 Personal Narrative Writing

Chapter 7 Persuasive Writing

Chapter 8 Research Papers

Chapter 9 Poetry Writing

Chapter 10 Response to Reading

A personal narrative tells the audience my story. This type of story must include a well-planned story line, with details that occur in chronological order, character development using dialogue, a vivid story setting, a plot that informs the audience as to what is happening, and a story conclusion or ending that tells the audience that the author has achieved problem resolution or some new level of enlightenment.

Personal Narrative Writing

What Is a Personal Narrative?

Lights! Camera! Action! It's time for a story! Narrative writing appeals to the audience's emotions. This genre usually entertains and amuses the audience while telling a story of an experience, an event, a list of recurring events, or a firsthand observable account. Elementary and middle school students usually start their writing careers with personal narratives. It's the perfect genre for beginning authors because we all know that everybody, young and old, has a story to tell!

A personal narrative may be fiction or nonfiction. It may be written as any one of the following story types: tall tales, folktales, fables, scripts, or personal narratives. It may be written about an event in your life or about being an eyewitness to some type of historical event. In any case, the personal narrative becomes a version of "*my* story."

Personal Narrative Building Blocks

If you've ever built a house or watched one being built in your neighborhood, you realize that in order for a house to withstand the test of time, it must be built correctly. Building a house requires *specific* building materials, such as wood to build the frame, bricks and mortar to cover the frame, and shingles to cover the roof. Building a house requires a carpenter to follow a blueprint or plan as well as a *sequentially* ordered building process to make sure each step is completed at the appropriate time. Everyone agrees that building a house is a process that should result in a fine product just like the one that you live in; however, it requires quality materials, good workmanship, and paying careful attention to the plan.

Writing a personal narrative can be compared with building a house. To begin, the author needs a blueprint or an organizational plan along with all the necessary *quality* materials—just like building a house. And, yes, writing a personal narrative is a process too—just like building a house; however, wood, brick, mortar, and shingles won't build you a strong personal narrative. You must still use a blueprint or organizational tool, but you also must use the specific personal narrative building material if you want to build a strong story. First, you need a way to plan or organize your story. We advocate the use of a specific graphic organizer: our Blueprint. Using your notes to complete this Blueprint results in a plan for your story. What next? Writing *my story* requires that all the building blocks of a personal narrative be carefully assembled to produce a quality story. The final product will be a personal narrative that gives authors a unique opportunity to tell an audience about their special life and learning experiences. So, you may be wondering, what exactly are the specific materials needed for building a great personal narrative?

Key: Narrative writing includes tall tales, folktales, fables, and personal narratives—to name only a few. The most commonly taught version of narrative writing in grades K through 8 is personal narrative.

ELL–BEWCONNECTION

Every culture believes in the power of storytelling. It was a primary method of relating information before written language. Allow your ELL students to share their cultural stories with the class.

Section II

Building blocks for a personal narrative must include characters, a story line with substantial detail, a vividly described setting, and a plot with a story climax or problem resolution that results in personal growth for the author. Within the story there should be substantial character development and the characters should use dialogue. The story line should have a setting and should take place over time, yet include detailed events. Also, the writer should strive to incorporate voice and interesting vocabulary. In a personal narrative, the writer should draw the reader into the story so that the reader vicariously shares the same feelings experienced by the characters.

For young authors, rather than using a plot, the story may develop a sequence of events, but the author must reach a new level of enlightenment that results in a new learning experience. In either case, whether it's a suspenseful personal narrative with a well-defined plot or a description of a real-life sequence of events leading to a lesson well learned, the author must use the building blocks required for constructing a personal narrative selection.

Following these building blocks may seem like a mighty big order for young as well as older authors. However, when you teach process writing with BEW strategies, the elements of a personal narrative are brought into focus, leading to great student writing selections. (See Table 6.1.)

Common Student Mistakes: What a Personal Narrative Is *Not*

It is important for you to know the proper building blocks needed to build a good personal narrative. However, it is equally important to know some of the stumbling blocks.

Topic Is Too Large

Not: Don't write a book!

Oh, you mean write on just one topic!

Using traditional teaching methods, students may be off target when attempting to write a personal narrative. Students tend to use stories they know from children's literature as examples. This results in narratives written on topics that are much too broad. Students also tend to include too many details or have complicated character development. In addition, they may try to include convoluted problems with many spin-offs, leading to complex problem resolutions.

While teaching this concept to our class, one of our students came up the acronym *TMI* or *too much information* to describe this problem. When students are not successful in writing personal

Table 6.1   Personal Narrative Building Blocks

Genre Purpose	Appeals to your audience's emotions, usually entertains and amuses
Building Block Features	1. Interesting characters 2. A story line with substantial detail 3. A vividly described setting 4. A plot with a story climax or a problem resolution that resulted in personal growth for the author 5. Substantial character development within the story; characters should use dialogue 6. A story line with a setting that takes place over time yet includes detailed events 7. Incorporation of voice and interesting vocabulary 8. Readers drawn into the story that they vicariously share the same feelings experienced by the characters
Genre Writing Techniques	1. *Point of View:* written in the first person is best; written in the third person is acceptable 2. *Audience Appeal:* appealing to the senses; puts your audience in the scene with you 3. *Show Don't Tell:* uses language that describes what is happening instead of merely telling the facts or listing the actions 4. *Character Development:* makes your characters come alive with dialogue; uses voice 5. *Vivid Verbs:* uses exciting, powerful verbs to describe action and events 6. *Flashbacks:* moving backward in time to describe an event that is part of the story line 7. Fast Forward: moving ahead in time to describe the story line
Genre Format and Voice	1. *Story Introduction or Beginning:* telling the student topic and providing a *hook* to get the reader to read on 2. *Detail Paragraph(s) with a Plot:* a story structured so that it has a problem that leads to a resolution and an ending 3. *Summary or Story Ending:* shows how the author was enlightened, leading to personal growth 4. *Chronological Order:* events listed in a logical sequence 5. *Setting:* well-defined setting relating to the author's senses 6. *Voice:* uses a lot of your voice and imagery

narrative selections, the primary reason is because the topics selected are too large (see Table 6.2). Remember to help your students narrow their topic focus.

Table 6.2 Comparison of Student Writing Topics

Topics That Are Too Large	Properly Narrow Topic
Our Family Trip to Cedar Point Amusement Park	My Roller-coaster Ride
My New School	First Day at a New School
My Fishing Trip	Catching the Big Fish

Story Line Written as a List of Details

Not: A story isn't a grocery list of ideas.

Oh, you mean I should explain the ideas!

When students' topics are too large, they tend to be constructed in a sequential format listing all the story events in the hope of getting everything down. You can see this problem in the notes they take on their Blueprint. The following table presents two examples of notes our students listed on their Blueprints for a single detail paragraph. The purpose of this paragraph was to create a story setting. The example on the left is for a topic that is too large. The example on the right is for an appropriately focused topic. Look what happens to this third-grade student's notes when the topic is too large (see Table 6.3).

Can you see what happened in this example? The student whose notes are on the left was attempting to get everything about her trip written down. She wanted to tell you how she got to the location, what time of day it was, and the events on the way. Consequently, the story would have become a sequential list of unimportant events. Note that in the second column, when the student topic is narrow, the author's notes become more meaningful and she actually sets the scene. When the topic is too large or, as we say in BEW, "Students are writing on the theme instead of writing on a topic," students tend lose their voice, shrink their vocabulary, and actually end up changing the genre from a personal narrative to an informational writing selection.

Table 6.3 Keep the Focus Narrow

Detail Paragraph Notes, Topic Too Large	Detail Paragraph Notes, Proper Narrow Focus
Our Family Trip to Cedar Point (setting paragraph)	*My Roller-coaster Ride* (setting paragraph)
1. We got up early and got into the car. 2. We were in the car forever. 3. We stopped for lunch. 4. Got to Cedar Point, it was dark.	1. Standing in line with my brother, Jim, he's eight years old. 2. My hands were sweating, felt like I was going to pass out. 3. Watched the roller coaster drop down the hill like a cannon going off. 4. Felt like I was going to pass out cold.

No Ending

Not: You're not still on vacation!

Oh! You mean I have to tell what happened at the end?

After reading thousands of students' personal narratives during the past thirty years, we've found that one of the most common errors students make in this genre is that they don't write an ending. They simply leave you hanging! That's right. There's no ending. There's no lesson that has been learned. Recently, one of our students wrote a personal narrative about her dream vacation. The topic she selected was *Swimming with Dolphins*—an excellent topic for a personal narrative because of its narrow scope. She told us about the great time she had in the water with the dolphins, but abruptly ended her narrative in the middle of the action. As far as the story goes, she's still swimming in the ocean. Many students do not know how to end a story. This problem is more prevalent today than it was when we first began teaching. We believe this is because today's children don't spend as much time reading books as children in former generations. Children in those days knew the structure of a story by the time they reached school. Today, quite a few children are coming to school language-, vocabulary-, and story-deprived. So, learning the building blocks of a story is new to many children. With BEW, we provide a structured format for writing personal narrative stories where all children can be successful.

Teach the Genre Using BEW Phases

We listed the building blocks needed for developing a personal narrative earlier in the table. We also discussed some of the pitfalls to be avoided. You may be wondering how to fit these ideas into the BEW process. To do this, we will now show you how to apply each of the phases of BEW on a step-by-step basis to a personal narrative writing. (Make a new student Rough Draft Writing Folder for each personal narrative writing selection.)

Three Steps in Phase I: Authentic Vocabulary

Step 1: Written Expression Vocabulary

Let's go back to phase I of BEW: teaching authentic vocabulary words. Along with reviewing the Big Ten vocabulary words in the BEW process, we recommend teaching the following genre-specific vocabulary words as they pertain to personal narrative writing.

Professor Write's Interactive Teaching Strategy

Teaching Personal Narrative Vocabulary

1. Genre

Review: Ask, "What is a personal narrative?" Students should respond, "My story," with their hand on their heart.

Say: "Today we will talk about a personal narrative. This is *your story*. You will be given a writing prompt or question as a theme for your writing selection."

2. Audience

Say: "You need to know who you are writing for, your audience. You will be writing this personal narrative for . . . [for example, another student or a younger student in the school, or to put into a classroom book]. Keep in mind how much the particular audience knows about your topic."

3. Characters

Say: "Your personal narrative will need to have interesting people. We call them *characters*."

4. Setting

Say: "You will need to tell the reader where your story takes place. This is called the *setting*."

5. Plot

Say: "The plot is the structure of the story. It is the rising and falling action of the story that leads to a problem resolution."

Step 2: Conventions and Grammar

Every genre has different conventions that are a part of its building blocks. A specific convention needed for the personal narrative genre is the *point of view* in which the selection is written.

Professor Write's Interactive Teaching Strategy

First-Person or Third-Person Point of View

Say: "When you write a personal narrative story, you have to decide on your point of view. Will you be saying, 'I did this and that'? That's called *first person*. Or will you be saying, 'He did this and that'? That's called *third person*. After you decide what's best, you have to keep writing from that point of view."

Background: Decide which perspective you want your students to use when writing their topic for their personal narratives. Make certain that your students have a clear understanding of the difference between first- and third-person writing selections.

- **First Person:** We believe that most personal narratives should be written in the first-person singular point of view. This means your students will be using the word *I* or the phrase *this happened to me.*

- **Third Person:** Some authorities believe that personal narratives should be written in the third person. This means your students will say *he, she,* or *it* when they write about their topic. Teach this phase of writing and give examples by using pronouns.

Section II

Step 3: General Vocabulary

Create class-generated Webs of Words with frequently used words relating to your theme. Post them in your room for students to use as they write!

Five Steps in Phase II: Prewriting

Step 1: Multisensory Experiences

Many students will be familiar with narrative stories, but perhaps not on the topic or theme that you've selected. Use your imagination to bring these topics to your classroom, such as having a storyteller come to your school. Consider using a cyber trip or using literacy bags or boxes.

Step 2: Wheel of Thought

As we said earlier, one major problem students encounter in writing personal narratives is that they select a topic that is too large. To help students narrow the focus, use the BEW Prewriting Strategy called the *Wheel of Thought.*

First, select a student writing prompt. It can be from your literacy series, a cross-curriculum concept, your own idea, or one featured at the end of this chapter. Put up a blank Wheel of Thought graphic organizer in front of your class and begin. Let's use this example: *Think about a time when you've solved a problem.*

> **ELL–BEW**CONNECTION
>
> ELL students need cues to connect what they already know to the newly taught concepts. Allowing them to select and write about their own experiences creates a connection between old and new concepts.

FIGURE 6.1

Second-Grade Classroom,
Broad Topic

FIGURE 6.2

Second-Grade Student,
Narrow Topic

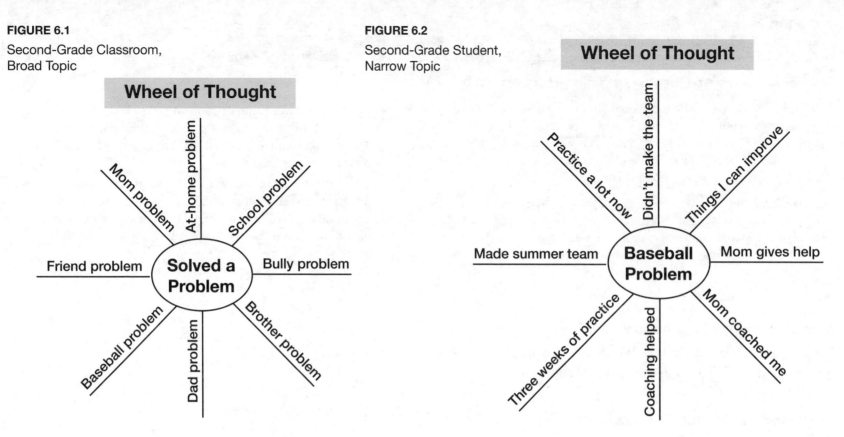

Wheel of Thought

Wheel of Thought

At-home problem
Mom problem
School problem
Friend problem
Solved a Problem
Bully problem
Baseball problem
Dad problem
Brother problem

Didn't make the team
Practice a lot now
Things I can improve
Made summer team
Baseball Problem
Mom gives help
Three weeks of practice
Coaching helped
Mom coached me

In the center of the Wheel of Thought, write *Solved a Problem*. Ask your students to begin to think about the writing prompt. As your students give you responses from events in their own lives that relate to the theme, quickly write them on the rays of the Wheel of Thought. A class example might look like the one shown in Figure 6.1.

Normally, a single class exercise using a Wheel of Thought is not sufficient to reduce the theme to a topic of manageable size. The topics in our example are still much too large. If students began to write on the topics listed on this Wheel of Thought, they would tend to list details instead of writing a personal narrative. To refine the focus, continue by giving students an individual Wheel of Thought and have them enter the topic they gave in class in the center of the wheel. Ask your students to list specific events that were part of that broader experience on their personal Wheels of Thought. Have them choose one of these events that they find most memorable (see Figure 6.2). Question them as to why this event stands out in their mind. This narrowly focused event will become the topic of their story.

ELL–BEWCONNECTION

ELL students have difficulty with the language of learning. Use the Blueprint as a visual method for teaching writing to help them learn the process.

Note taking is an important skill. Johnny carefully records his notes on his Blueprint.

Step 3: Genre Format and Voice

Each and every writing genre has different characteristics that make it a special genre. We call these characteristics *Building Blocks*. Our student writers need to incorporate the Building Blocks of the Personal Narrative genre into their writing. They can begin to do this when they write their notes in the Blueprint that is designed to help them know the correct format to use. They will also have to add the right amount of voice. It's time to start teaching your students the Building Blocks of a Personal Narrative. To do this we use a personal narrative Blueprint (Figure 6.3).

Student Topic _____

Introduction or Beginning

_____ | _____

_____ | _____

Middle or Detail Paragraphs

_____

_____

_____

_____

_____

_____

_____

_____

_____

_____

_____

_____

_____

_____

_____

Ending or Summary

_____ _____ _____

FIGURE 6.3

Blueprint for Personal Narrative

Teaching Genre Format and Voice

1. The purpose of the introduction paragraph

Ask: "What shape is this? [while pointing to the oval shape on a class Blueprint]."

The students will answer, "It's the oval."

"What type of paragraph does the oval represent?"

The students will answer, "The introduction or beginning."

"What is the job of the introduction or beginning in a personal narrative writing selection?"

"It introduces your topic and sets the scene for your story."

"To follow our writing Blueprint correctly, we must also look at the size or how long our introduction or beginning will be in comparison with the rest of the story. How big is an introduction or beginning? Medium size [and ask students to show you with their hands]."

2. The topic sentence

Ask: "What type of sentence should the introduction or beginning paragraph start with?" "A topic sentence" will be their response.

Teach: Topic sentences are very important because they act as a hook to draw the reader into the story. A great topic sentence is essential in a personal narrative. Teach the strategies outlined in the BEW writing process for creating a great topic sentence (Chapter 4).

3. The story setting

Ask: "What is a story setting? It's where the story takes place. How should you describe the setting? It should be related to your senses, because it makes your audience feel as if they are there with you."

Teach: One of the ways that personal narratives come alive is through the author's description of the setting. This takes practice! Tell your students to think about your story and the sights, sounds, and smells that trigger your memory about their story.

Do: Pass out the Writing Sensory Details worksheet (see Student Worksheet 6.1 at the end of this chapter). Tell your students to write about special sights, sounds, or other characteristics that they remember from their experience. As students begin to record these items, their memories of the experience will be enhanced. Give them some examples from your own personal story too. Students should put their completed worksheet in their Rough Draft Writing Folders.

4. Character development: Character sketches

Say: "Your personal narrative will need to have interesting people or characters. We will write detailed notes about our characters to help our readers see just what they look like and act like. This is called *character development*."

Teach: Stories or events don't happen in isolation. In order for a story to come alive, the writer needs people or characters. The more vividly the characters are developed, the more lifelike the personal narrative becomes. Character development can be taught by using character sketches.

Do: Tell your students to think about the characters in their story. Who are they? What do they look like? Give your students the opportunity to complete character sketches on their characters (see Student Worksheet 6.2, Character Details at the end of this chapter). This activity can be done individually, with a partner, or in a small group. Characters should be described vividly so that the audience can form a picture in their mind of that character. Students should put their character sketches in their Rough Draft Writing Folders (see Table 6.4).

(continued)

Table 6.4 Character Sketch: Sensory-based Examples

Character	Character's Looks	Character's Feel or Touch
My eight-year-old little brother	Red hair like a fire engine, looked as if he'd been in a sauna	Hand felt slimy like a snake when I held it in mine

Character's Smell	Character Event Look	Your Interaction with Character at Event
Sweaty, stinky, smelled like a dead rat	Turned white, like seeing a ghost, from looking at the roller coaster	He wanted to turn back, he was chicken to go on the ride

5. Character development: Character dialogue

Say: "When we write our personal narratives, it is more interesting if our characters are talking to each other. We should write the exact words that they would say. This is called *dialogue*. Be sure to add dialogue to your story."

Teach: Dialogue simply means the characters of the stories are talking directly to each other, just as though they were standing in front of you. A great way to show students what character dialogue looks like is to show them a comic strip. Students can see the words that each cartoon character says as they read through the strip. Great personal narratives include characters that speak in their own words to each other. This is the time to make sure students understand the proper use of quotation marks. Be sure to teach quotation marks even to young authors.

6. The purpose of the detail or middle paragraph

Ask: While pointing to one of the squares on the personal narrative Blueprint, ask your students, "What shape is this?"

The students will answer, "It's a square."

Then ask, "What type of paragraph do the squares in our Blueprint represent?"

They will tell you, "The detail or middle paragraph(s)."

"Yes, we'll put the notes for our story details in the Blueprint squares. How big are the detail or middle paragraphs? Large [and ask students to show you with their hands]. The detail paragraphs section of your writing will be the largest section because it contains the plot of your story and your whole story line. Your personal narrative writing will have at least three detail paragraphs with a topic sentence in each."

Background: A personal narrative written as a sequence of events by younger authors may not have three paragraphs. They may include this information in a single, well-written paragraph.

7. The plot (taught with age-appropriate terms)

Teach: The detail middle paragraph is where you describe the plot of your story. Your students might ask, "So what's a plot?" Here is a very simplistic way to explain a plot. First, all stories begin in a perfectly normal way, but then things happen that cause trouble. Next, the trouble gets worse and worse until there is a big problem. Finally, this problem must be solved or you're really, really stuck. Solving the problem is a sequence of events that makes the problem get better and better. Then the problem is gone! This may seem like a lot to teach young children, but keep in mind they do learn this sequence in childhood fables, fairy tales, and most children's television programs. Your personal narrative Blueprint has three detail squares for this reason.

8. Show, don't tell, the action

Say: "It is important in this section of your story to show and not to tell your audience all the events of your story. This means using words that make the actions of your story come alive."

Teach: The concepts of showing the audience about the story, not telling them, will expand your students' vocabulary. This skill will take practice. This is a skill expected of later

Table 6.5 Show Don't Tell

Telling a Place (Describing the Place)	Showing a Place, Not Telling (Putting the Audience There)
It was a hot day at the carnival.	The day was hot and sticky and the air was filled with the sweet smell of cotton candy.
The fabric was rough.	My pants felt like sandpaper rubbing against my blistering sunburn.
He jumped across the playground.	He leaped across the playground like a frog jumping from lily pad to lily pad.

elementary and middle school students. Show your students an example, such as the one presented in Table 6.5.

Do: Write a basic sentence on the board, one similar to the left side of the previous table. Work together with your class to develop that specific sentence into a sentence that shows and doesn't tell an event. Repeat this activity several times. Encourage your students to use this type of action in their stories when it comes time to write their story lines.

9. The purpose of the summary or ending paragraph

Ask: While pointing to the rectangle on a Blueprint, ask your students, "What shape is this?"

The students will answer, "It's a rectangle."

Then ask, "What type of paragraph does the rectangle in our Blueprint represent?"

They will tell you, "The summary or ending."

"Yes. We'll put our notes for the story ending in the Blueprint rectangle. How big is the summary or ending paragraph? Small [and ask students to show you with their hands]. The summary or ending section of your writing will be the smallest section because it contains just your story ending."

Teach: The summary or story ending paragraph(s) must be taught as just that—the end of your story. Remind your students that every story has a lesson to be learned: What did you learn from this experience? Did you learn something about yourself? Will you do something differently if you encounter this experience again? This important point must be included in the summary or ending of a personal narrative.

10. Transitions

Say: "In between each paragraph, the ideas must move smoothly. Your paragraphs must flow into each other. This is called a *transition*. Make sure your story flows."

Step 4: Blueprint Note Taking

At this point your students are ready to begin filling out their Blueprint. Demonstrate or model this to your class by writing your own notes on a Blueprint for all your students to see. As you begin modeling for your students the process of note taking on the Blueprint, make sure you use all the student worksheets as references. Students should have all the worksheets in their Rough Draft Writing Folders. You will find some students have already internalized these concepts from the previous teaching activities (such as character sketches, dialogue worksheets, and sensory worksheets).

ELL–BEWCONNECTION

ELL students have difficulty working independently. Road maps for learning are needed. Have them use the Blueprint as their road map.

Section II

As you make notes on your Blueprint, tell the students what you are writing. Remember to include all the building blocks necessary for a well-written personal narrative.

Leave your recently modeled teacher Blueprint visible for your students to see as they write notes on their own Blueprint. The key here is to model, model, model. Your students will follow your lead when writing their notes on the Blueprint (see Student Worksheet 6.3 at the end of this chapter).

Step 5: Talking Paragraphs

To begin this step, model the concept to your students by pointing to your notes in the Blueprint shapes and telling your story, using your notes in order but speaking them in full sentences. After your students have finished taking notes on their Blueprint, it's time to speak their own paragraphs out loud. Ask for student volunteers to model "talking" out their notes from their Blueprints. Students should use their notes to assist them in talking out their selections in complete sentences and paragraphs. Of course, time will limit the number of students that can speak in front of the class, so they can also do this with a partner or in small groups. Students are encouraged to listen to each other's stories for appropriate chronological story order, character development, and showing (not telling) the audience. Students should then easily revise or add editing changes to their Blueprint notes.

Two Steps in Phase III: Writing

Step 1: Draft Writing

ELL–BEWCONNECTION

ELL students require modeling of new concepts for mastery. Model your story for your students the BEW way.

Students now have their personal narratives embedded in their thinking and it's time for them to write their first draft. Remember to make available all the class Webs of Words and other supporting material as students write their selections. This will provide spelling support for students with special needs, ELL students, or students with other risk factors, as well as vocabulary enhancement. Remember the importance of modeling the steps in writing by using your own story. Take your own Blueprint notes and demonstrate how to write the first draft.

Step 2: Title Writing

Using the BEW process, we emphasize that titles are written last. It's now time to review the strategies for good title writing with your class (see Chapter 3). Give students the opportunity to write titles for their selections. Read these titles aloud for all to hear and share. You'll find that your class will write much better titles after completing their rough drafts.

Five Steps in Phase IV: Authentic Editing

Steps 1 through 3: Editing Steps

At this stage we'd like to remind you again that editing following the BEW process is done somewhat differently than you might be used to doing. We believe that students should give their teachers feedback regarding what should be included in the *editing rubric* used in all three steps of editing: self-editing, peer editing, and teacher conferencing. With the BEW process there are three important areas for writing rubric assessment:

1. Genre Format and Voice
2. Vocabulary and Word Usage
3. Spelling and Grammar

By using these three categories as a guide, a thorough student and teacher editing review can be completed. Your class writing rubric will change as your class progresses over time and grammar lessons for the week change. What follows are samples of authentic writing rubrics created with our classes at different grade levels for the personal narrative genre. They are not designed to be used with your classes, but merely serve as a model to help you understand this concept. Now you may be thinking: What does an authentic rubric created by an early elementary class look like for a personal narrative? Table 6.6 is a sample of an authentic rubric written with a second-grade class.

Yes, your second-grade students will be able to construct an authentic writing rubric for their personal narrative writing assignments just like the sixth graders! Notice that this second-grade class did not use a rating scale to score editing points, but rather used a simple yes-or-no response. Young authors should first become aware of the presence of these writing principles before they can begin to improve upon them. It is not unusual for students instructed from kindergarten and first grade in BEW strategies to use a numerical measure of quality by the second grade. If you look carefully at part C, Spelling and Grammar, of the second-grade rubric, you'll notice it is quite extensive. Young authors are just beginning to learn

Concentration is critical when writing a story. Justin is deep in thought as he edits his personal narrative.

Table 6.6 Authentic Editing Rubric, Second Grade

A. Genre Format and Voice

1. Did I have an introduction paragraph?	Yes	No
2. Did I have a good topic sentence?	Yes	No
3. Is it medium size?	Yes	No
4. Did I have a detailed paragraph?	Yes	No
5. Is it the largest paragraph?	Yes	No
6. Does it have a topic sentence?	Yes	No
7. Do all of the sentences go with the topic sentence?	Yes	No
8. Did I tell the story in the right order?	Yes	No
9. Do I have a short ending paragraph?	Yes	No
10. Did I tell what I learned from my story?	Yes	No

B. Vocabulary and Word Usage

1. Did I use detail words?	Yes	No
2. Did I use different words?	Yes	No

C. Spelling and Grammar

1. Did you start your sentences with capital letters?	Yes	No
2. Did you word wrap your paragraphs?	Yes	No
3. Did you write your title in capital letters?	Yes	No
4. Are all of your words spelled correctly?	Yes	No

the mechanics of written language, and these concepts are fresh in their minds. Now let's look at an unedited example from a fifth-grade class (Table 6.7).

Our fifth-grade class created an authentic editing rubric that focused on the building blocks of a personal narrative. It is evident that they can identify all the elements that are needed to build this genre.

In our final sample rubric (Table 6.8), notice that our middle school class has learned very well the lessons of exactly what a personal narrative should look like. They have learned all the

Table 6.7 Authentic Editing Rubric, Fifth Grade

A. Personal Narrative Genre Format and Voice	Least to Best
1. Do you have an introduction paragraph?	0 1 2 3
2. Do you have a topic sentence in your introduction that makes the reader want to know more?	0 1 2 3
3. Does your introduction paragraph introduce your personal topic?	0 1 2 3
4. Does your introduction paragraph vividly describe the story setting?	0 1 2 3
5. Does your introduction paragraph begin to develop your story characters?	0 1 2 3
6. Did you write the story in chronological order with story details with a plot?	0 1 2 3
7. Did you begin a new detail paragraph when you describe the details of the plot?	0 1 2 3
8. Is your story line narrow enough?	0 1 2 3
9. Do your characters dialogue back and forth in your story?	0 1 2 3
10. Did you develop a plot or climax that is interesting to your audience?	0 1 2 3
11. Is there a summary paragraph?	0 1 2 3
12. Does the summary paragraph do the job it's supposed to do by ending the story?	0 1 2 3
13. Does your story have a clear beginning?	0 1 2 3
14. Does your story have a clear middle section with details?	0 1 2 3
15. Does your story have a clear ending with a story resolution?	0 1 2 3
16. Did you tell a story rather than just list facts?	0 1 2 3
17. Did you fully develop your characters so that your audience has a visual image of them?	0 1 2 3
18. Is your own voice identifiable in your story?	0 1 2 3
19. Did your title reflect your story line?	0 1 2 3

B. Vocabulary and Word Usage	Least to Best
20. Did you show and not tell with your words?	0 1 2 3
21. Did you create visual images for your audience through metaphors and similes?	0 1 2 3
22. Did you write your personal narrative from a first-person point of view?	0 1 2 3
23. Did you use the correct kind of vocabulary for your audience?	0 1 2 3
24. Did you create the sense of a plot, problem, resolution, or story climax with the words that you've used?	0 1 2 3
25. Did you use techniques like reverse or fast forward in your words to create more story line details?	0 1 2 3
26. Did you use words that relate to the audience's senses to communicate details?	0 1 2 3
27. Did you use powerful verbs?	0 1 2 3
28. Did you use descriptive language?	0 1 2 3

C. Grammar and Spelling	Least to Best
29. Did you use "I" in the story for a first-person point of view?	0 1 2 3
30. Did you use the right subject–verb agreement?	0 1 2 3
31. Did you use the correct verb tense?	0 1 2 3
32. Did you use different types of sentences?	0 1 2 3
33. Did you use quotation marks correctly?	0 1 2 3
34. Did you spell words correctly?	0 1 2 3

Table 6.8 Middle School Authentic Editing Rubric

A. Genre Format and Voice	Least to Best
1. Did you write an introduction paragraph?	0 1 2 3
2. Did you write a topic sentence telling about your personal story?	0 1 2 3
3. Did you tell about the characters that are in your story?	0 1 2 3
4. Did you tell where the story is taking place, the story setting?	0 1 2 3
5. Did you write detail paragraphs telling your story?	0 1 2 3
6. Did you write about the story events in the order that they happened?	0 1 2 3
7. Did you write about a story problem in your detail paragraphs?	0 1 2 3
8. Did you avoid writing a list of facts?	0 1 2 3
9. Is your personal topic small enough?	0 1 2 3
10. Does your story have a summary paragraph?	0 1 2 3
11. Does your personal narrative have a story beginning?	0 1 2 3
12. Does your story have a middle part with details?	0 1 2 3
13. Does your story have an ending?	0 1 2 3
14. Did you solve the problem at the end of the story?	0 1 2 3
15. Did you use quotes from your characters?	0 1 2 3
16. Can you hear your voice in your story?	0 1 2 3
17. Do you have an interesting title?	0 1 2 3
18. Do you have transition sentences?	0 1 2 3

B. Vocabulary and Word Usage	Least to Best
19. Did you use describing words?	0 1 2 3
20. Did you use interesting verbs?	0 1 2 3
21. Did you use different kinds of sentences?	0 1 2 3
22. Did you use character quotes?	0 1 2 3
23. Did you use many different detail words?	0 1 2 3

C. Spelling and Grammar	Least to Best
24. Did you start your sentences with capital letters?	0 1 2 3
25. Did you end your sentences with punctuation marks?	0 1 2 3
26. Did you write proper nouns in capital letters?	0 1 2 3
27. Did you use quotation marks when your character talks?	0 1 2 3
28. Did you indent your paragraphs?	0 1 2 3
29. Did you word wrap your paragraphs?	0 1 2 3
30. Did you write your title in capital letters?	0 1 2 3
31. Do all of your sentences have a subject and a predicate?	0 1 2 3
32. Are all of your words spelled correctly?	0 1 2 3

important elements identifying a personal narrative writing selection and have repeated them back to us, enabling us to create an authentic writing rubric for this genre. Our middle school students have used a scale from 0 through 3 points to evaluate their writing efforts. On their rubric, 3 points is the best possible score and 0 points means that the item has been left out. Many of our students score themselves with 2 points and then go back to their rough drafts and rewrite certain sections to make them better. This type of scoring rubric gives your students room to improve.

Step 4: Final Copy Writing

You will find your students ready to take their edited rough drafts and use them to develop their final copy—their best work. They are now confident that they have written a good personal narrative. They are also anticipating publication, so they will want to write or type their best copy for their audience.

Step 5: Teacher Assessment

By now you're probably wondering what actual personal narrative writing selections look like as written by students at various grade levels. Here are some samples for your review. We provide you with both well-written and nonproficient examples, because we want you to understand the elements that make good personal narratives. Proficient examples are those that incorporate all the personal narrative building blocks reflected in the editing rubric. Nonproficient student examples lack one or more of the building blocks. This will help you to assess them appropriately. We also want you to understand that a story might be well written in terms of spelling and grammar, but may fail as a personal narrative because the required genre format and the associated building blocks have not been included.

Elementary Examples of Personal Narratives   The first sample was written by a second-grade student. The student used the idea of *Our Pets* as a central theme. Students were asked to write about their pet and one of their pet's bad habits. Our second-grade student chose her pet hamster as her topic. Refer to her unedited personal narrative on page 108.

Another one of our second-grade students wrote on the same theme and topic. His unedited personal narrative is also included (see page 108).

Can you see the difference between these two writing samples? The first one tells an interesting story about a pet escape artist. It describes the story events chronologically, leading to a story climax, and uses well-defined characters in a well-defined setting. On the other hand, although the second sample includes outstanding vocabulary, it just doesn't quite fit the bill of a personal narrative. It doesn't tell a story; it merely lists a number of the pet's bad habits. What kind of stories are your students writing? Those similar to the first or to the second writing sample?

Good Pet Gone Bad

Well Hamy hamster was my favorite all time pet. I just loved Hamy but she had one really bad habit.

It all started when my mom made me clean her cage. Mom said, it's smelly, clean that thing." So you see I had to. But to clean Hamy's cage I had to take her out of it and put her somewhere else. So, I put her in a shoe box and taped the top on while I cleaned her cage. But that didn't work.

After I cleaned the cage, I went to get Hamy from the shoe box and she was GONE!! I looked all over for her. I yelled, "Hamy come out from where ever you are." But she didn't come out. I looked under the sofa, under my bed I even looked in mom's shoes. No Hamy anywhere. I told my mom and brother, "Hamy has escaped. She's a really bad hamster today. Will you help me look for her?" My mom said, "We'll form a search party." So, we split up and looked for Hamy everywhere. We looked everywhere, even in the closets. I was really sad that Hamy had escaped.

My dad was coming home from work and came in the house looking for me. He said, "look who I found outside the door." You'll never guess who it was." Yep, Hamy!

You probably know that Hamy's bad habit was that she liked to run away from home. She's back now but I don't think that I'll clean her cage any time soon. I think it's better to have a hamster in a dirty cage then no Hamy at all.

Not the Perfect Cat

My cat is great but she has a lot of bad habits. She does some nasty stuff.

First, my mom gets mad at her because she chews her shoes. Then she scratches the sofa too. She's wrecked two of my mom's pillows and that made mom really upset. The other thing she does is jump up on the table and eat our food. She really likes ham. She'll jump right up on the kitchen table and take the food right out of your plate. Dad says, "Bad cat." We have to lock her up in the basement at dinner time or she'll drive us crazy. When she gets mad at us she scratches us. That makes me made. I went to school with scratches on my face because Patches scratched me. It really hurts when she does that.

Upper Elementary Examples of Personal Narrative If you're working with upper elementary students, we have two writing samples for you to read at this level. The first selection is a proficient fifth-grade sample. The second sample is nonproficient. The central theme for these fifth-grade students was *solving a problem*. Each student wrote about a problem that had to be solved. Compare the unedited writing samples of these two fifth graders.

Fifth-Grade Personal Narrative Writing Sample: Proficient

Science Survival

I was walking home from school as usual, it was a bright sunny day, it was finally warm outside and I was depressed.

My brother Sam, was walking along side me, he's only in second grade and he was saying, "I'm going to go outside and play when we get home." Then he said something that made me so mad I could have hit him, he said, "I don't have any homework!" I thought man I sure do. Not only that but I had a big problem.

When I got home from school I unpacked all of my school books and my mom said, "Do you have any homework?" I didn't know if I should tell her or not. I said, "Well a little bit." She said and "what does that mean," as she had her hands on her waist and glared at me. I thought if I told her I'd be grounded for life but if I didn't I probably wouldn't pass the fifth grade. So, I just said it really, really fast, "Well, my science project is due tomorrow and it's half of my science grade, I forgot. . . ." Her face got as red as an apple and she screamed, "WHAT!!" I said, "I didn't mean to forget."

Then the two of us sat down at the kitchen table and I thought yea, I have a big, big problem. There was nothing I could say, What was I going to do??

Just then the phone rang and my mom called me into the other room. She was talking to my Uncle Bob. She said, "You're really lucky your uncle will be over tonight to help you with that science project. Man, was I relieved because my uncle's an engineer and I knew he could help me. My mom told me to call him and he'd stop off at work and get any materials that we needed for our project. I called him right away and we thought about a topic. After thinking about many different topics we settled on volcano made from modeling clay. So, he brought clay, a large board and paint over to our house.

We went out into the garage and started molding the clay on the board. The clay was so hard it hurt my hands. It took forever to mold that stuff. Then came the painting. The paint smelled like rotten eggs. I thought that I was going to get sick from the smell. I was gagging. It took all night to finish that thing. My uncle wasn't happy either. We finished about 1:00 in the morning. Finally I got to go to sleep.

My Mom gave me a ride to school the next day because my science project was so big. I thought that was an awful night doing that project that way. My mom and uncle helped solve my huge problem. I think that next time I'd better keep a planner to write down my big projects so I don't have to do this again!

Brother Mania

Every time that I turn around he's there! Every step that I take he's right there. It's like he's my shadow. What is this all about? What am I going to do?

It's my brother. He just won't leave me alone. I walk to school and he's with me. I go to the lunch room and he sits beside me. I try to play with my friends and he's in my face. Finally, I just screamed at him, "GO AWAY!" Then you know what he did? He laughed at me. I think that I'm just gonna hit him. He's like piece of Velcro that just sticks to you and you can't get off.

I decided enough is enough. I told my mom that she had to do something. And you know what she did. She laughed at me. Man what is this world coming to? He's just a big problem. A third-grade problem. I just want him to go away.

What's the difference between the two selections? If you've said that the first one describes a problem, develops a story plot that comes to an end with a problem resolution, you're correct. The second selection doesn't solve anything.

Middle School Examples of Personal Narratives Lastly, let's take a look at middle school authors. These examples were written by two middle school students. As before we provide a well-written example as well as a nonproficient example.

The first personal narrative was written by one of our special needs middle school students. This student came to our school district as a transfer student in late fall. We weren't aware of his skill level because he wouldn't perform academically for us. Over time, the BEW teaching strategies gave him the motivation to use a personal narrative to express himself in a very emotionally moving way. Writing can be a powerful tool of expression for students in difficult life circumstances. His unedited personal narrative on the theme of courage is on page 111.

In this writing selection our middle school student used BEW writing strategies to develop his student topic quite effectively, even through he has a very significant learning disability. When it came time to publish his story by reading it at an assembly, the entire audience was moved to tears! You could hear a pin drop in the room.

Tanya's Last Day on Earth

When my mom passed away, it's a pain that will never go away!

Let me tell you about that day. "Oh my gosh," I didn't know if it was true or a dream. It all started when I came home early that day from school. My mom didn't look so good to me. I said to her, "mom come and lay down." So she did. It seemed as though hours went by. I went to lay down with her and about 15 minutes past. All of a sudden she started shaking and foaming at the mouth. Quickly I called 911 and said, "My mom's acting crazy and she just stopped breathing, help me please!!" Just a little while later I called my brother and he arrived just before the ambulance.

The fireman ran into our house and did CPR on my mom but it didn't work. By that time I knew that she was gone. The fireman said she was "flat-lining" and the next thing I knew we were on our way to the hospital.

We were all together at the hospital and my brother and me were crying. Just then the doctor came in the room and asked, "Are you the ___ family?" We said, "Yes, why?" He looked at us and said, "Well, she passed away on arrival," and I passed out. A few minutes later I got up crying uncontrollably and they asked me, if I wanted to see her before I left? And I said, "Yes." So I went into the room and said to her, "Why did you leave me alone?" I started shaking and shaking her but she didn't respond and I asked God to help me through this moment. Then they said, "Times up," and I said, "I'm not leaving my mother. I won't leave." My brother picked me up and carried me to the car.

That night I went to my sister's house. I asked her, "What am I suppose to do?" She said "Well you will have to live with me." She said, "Tomorrow morning we will get all of your stuff." All of the time I was so scared. What was going to happen? Where would I live?

I learned that I do have courage. I was able to call 911 for my mother and am keeping it together. I learned that we will all die some day. The people around us will have to show courage and keep it together like I am. Everyone I will tell each other, like my sister told me, "It will be ok, and it will."

Section II

The second example we included (see page 112) is also one written by a middle school student but who has not been identified with a disability, as in our previous example. The central theme for the writing selection is also courage. This example was written by a student who was not instructed using BEW teaching strategies. His personal narrative has many good points and you might think he deserves a good grade, but his writing doesn't contain the building blocks of a personal narrative. It is important for you to determine why this selection is a nonproficient example.

This second student's personal narrative uses great vocabulary, grammar, and conventions. Yet it isn't truly a personal narrative because it only lists and describes events. He began the selection very

Last Kid Standing

As I started to walk home from school I felt the beads of sweat building up on my forehead. I didn't know if I'd actually make it home in one piece!

As I grew closer and closer to the park that I had to pass on the way, I thought to myself, "You're in trouble." I was certainly right. Just as I walked pass the park it happened. There they all were waiting for me. I most certainly didn't feel very courageous. Yep, it happened they jumped me.

The next day at school my mom demanded that I tell the principal what happened. I anxiously waited for the bell to ring and went into the principal's office. We discussed what happened. Then she sent me back to class. I went to my math, Spanish and gym classes. I couldn't wait for lunch! I was absolutely starving, trying to stay brave throughout the day made me really, really hungry. When lunch finally arrived I felt like I could eat a house! I ate two lunches! Well, my next class was English.

I really didn't want the last school bell for the day to ring because I was afraid I'd have an instant replay of yesterday.

well, but didn't develop the story. He included details that weren't significant and the reader never really knows what happened to him. Which story do you find most interesting—the first or the second? Now that you can see the difference between a proficient personal narrative and one that does not include the building blocks, what type of personal narrative writing selections are your students writing? By teaching the genre elements as we've described, your students will become the proficient writers you hope for!

Three Steps in Phase V: Publishing

Personal narratives provide a great genre for student publishing. Students love sharing stories with everyone they can. Select one or more of our student publishing ideas from Chapter 5 or create one of your own!

In Summary: Personal Narrative

Indeed, each and every one of us has a story to tell! Personal narratives are certainly fun to write. More than likely this will be your students' favorite writing genre. You will teach personal narrative units many times throughout the school year and you will be amazed at your students' progress! Try these BEW differential teaching strategies by following the two-week lesson plan outlined for writing Personal Narrative selections.

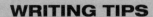

WRITING TIPS

Writing Tips: Personal Narrative

- Read different types of narrative writing selections to your students so that they can easily hear the elements of this genre.

- It's important to model the elements involved in writing a personal narrative. All students profit from this, but especially your special needs, ELL, and at-risk learners.

- Ask students to bring their favorite narrative to class and share it.

Two-Week Teaching Schedule of Personal Narrative

	Monday	Tuesday	Wednesday	Thursday	Friday
Week 1	Vocabulary	Vocabulary Review	Vocabulary Review	Vocabulary Review	Vocabulary Review
	Prewriting Activities 1. Multisensory Activities 2. Wheel of Thought	Prewriting Activities 1. Genre Format and Voice	Prewriting Activities 1. Genre Format and Voice	Prewriting Activities 1. Genre Format and Voice	Prewriting Activities 1. Blueprint Note Taking 2. Talking Paragraphs

	Monday	Tuesday	Wednesday	Thursday	Friday
Week 2	Vocabulary Review	Vocabulary Review	Vocabulary Review	Vocabulary Review	Vocabulary Review
	Writing Activities 1. Writing the Draft	Writing Activities 1. Writing the Draft 2. Title Writing	Editing 1. Self-editing 2. Peer Editing	Editing 1. Teacher Conferencing 2. Writing the Final Copy 3. Teacher Assessment	Publishing

Do you need ideas for a prompt? We've included a number of them for you. Teach these genre elements and follow the BEW plan. What will result are students who enjoy writing and who compose interesting, thought-provoking personal narratives. You will see the difference when you assess their writing. No longer will your students use the old listing-of-events style of writing. Instead, your students will develop rich and exciting stories.

Personal Narrative Prompts for the Here and Now

Many of our state writing prompts (for high-stakes testing) ask students to write on different life experiences. To prepare your students better for these high-stakes state-level exams, try any one of the following writing prompts. Make up some of your own writing prompts too!

1. Everybody loves a party and we all go to parties or have had parties given for us. Write about or describe the best birthday party that you've ever had in your life. What makes this party special or unique? Why is it so memorable? Be sure to include details that support your ideas.

2. Vacations are great! At some point in our lives we all have the privilege of taking one. Write about or describe the best vacation that you've ever taken in your life. Who went on this vacation with you? What makes you remember it so well? Be sure to include details that support your ideas.

3. Everyone needs somebody to lean on. Write about or describe a time when you were able to help others in a trying situation. Why do you remember this time? Be sure to include details that support your ideas.

4. Sometimes we're unsuccessful in our attempts to do something, but the experience can have a positive impact on us. Write or describe a time in your life when you've experienced a failure. How did this failure positively

impact your life? Be sure to include details to support your ideas.

5. Life has many disappointments. These feelings can include losses in your life. Write about or describe a time when you experienced a loss in your life. Why do you remember it and how did it change your life? Be sure to include details that support your ideas.

6. Everyone has the ability to make something. Write about or describe a time when you've been creative. What did you create or make and why do you remember it? Be sure to include details that support your ideas.

7. We encounter problems daily. Write or describe a time when you've solved a problem. Did it help others or just yourself? Why do you remember this time? Be sure to include details that support your ideas.

8. Write or describe a memorable day at school. Why do you remember it so well? Be sure to include details that support your ideas.

9. Have you ever been really afraid? Write about or describe the most frightening time that you've ever experienced. Be sure to include details that support your ideas.

10. What is it that you've done lately? Write about or describe your most significant accomplishment. Did it help just you or others too? Be sure to include details that support your ideas.

11. Have you climbed the highest mountain in your life? Write or describe a time in your life when you've overcome a difficult task or situation. Be sure to include details that support your ideas.

12. Write or describe a time in your life when you were very nervous. Why were you nervous and did you overcome it? How? Be sure to include details that support your ideas.

13. Did you earn your Red Badge of Courage? Write or describe a time in your life when you demonstrated courage. Were you successful? Be sure to include details that support your ideas.

14. Do you have a memory that will stay with you forever? Write or describe a time in your life that was precious to you. Why was this a precious moment and why do you remember it so well? Be sure to include details that support your ideas.

15. Everyone loves a clown! Write about or describe the funniest experience that you have ever had. Why was it so memorable? Be sure to include details that support your ideas.

16. Has there been a time or an event in your life when you just couldn't get somewhere soon enough? Write about or describe a time in your life when you were very excited about an event. Why were you so excited? Be sure to include details that support your ideas.

17. Do you learn from your lessons? Write about or describe a time in your life when you learned a lesson. What lesson did you learn? Be sure to include details that support your ideas.

18. Write about or describe your favorite place. What do you get to do in your favorite place? Why is it so special to you? Be sure to include details that support your ideas.

19. Let it snow! Write about or describe a time when you've had a snow day off from school. What did you do? Why do you remember this snow day? Be sure to include details that support your ideas.

20. Write about or describe a time when the weather created your mood. How did the weather affect what you did and how you felt for the day? Be sure to include details that support your ideas.

21. Friends! Write about or describe a friend that has affected your life. Why was this friend so important to you? Be sure to include details that support your ideas.

22. Have you read Mark Twain? Write about or describe a time when you've had a special adventure in your life, like Tom Sawyer or Huckleberry Finn. What was it? Why was it so memorable? Be sure to include details that support your ideas.

23. Sunshine, warm weather, and school is out for the summer. These summertime experiences bring new activities into our lives. Write about or describe a summer activity. Why was it so special and memorable? Be sure to include details that support your ideas.

24. Snow on the ground, frozen ponds, and cold weather brings a season called *winter* into our lives. Write about or describe a winter activity that was meaningful to you. Be sure to include details that support your ideas.

25. Changing leaves and back-to-school are fall-time events. Write about or describe a fall activity that was memorable to you. Be sure to include details that support your ideas.

26. Yes, the snow has melted and warm weather is on its way! Write about or describe a spring activity that stands out in your mind. Be sure to include details that support your ideas.

27. Write about or describe an important person in your life. Write about or describe how that person has affected or changed your life. Be sure to include details that support your ideas.

28. Write about or describe a time when you were a role model for someone else. Be sure to include details that support your ideas.

29. Write about a time when you have been unprepared for an event. What did you feel like? Be sure to include details that support your ideas.

30. There is an old movie called *The Good, The Bad, and The Ugly*. Have you experienced a bad time recently? Write about a time in your life when the bad turned to good. Be sure to include details that support your ideas.

31. Everybody can be a teacher! Write about a time in your life when you've taught somebody else to do something. Be sure to include details that support your ideas.

32. Do you believe in Superman? Write about a time in your life when you've been somebody's hero. Be sure to include details that support your ideas.

33. Tradition! Tradition! Tradition! Write about or describe a family tradition that's important to your family. Be sure to include details that support your ideas.

34. I protest! Write about or describe a time when you've disagreed with a decision that has been made. This decision could be at home, school, or any other environment. Be sure to include details that support your ideas.

35. So, what is it? Write about or describe a time when you received an unusual gift. How did this gift affect you? Be sure to include details that support your ideas.

36. What to do? Write about or describe a time when an emergency brought out the best or worst in you. Be sure to include details that support your ideas.

37. Whew, just made it! Write about or describe a time when you had a narrow escape. Be sure to include details that support your ideas.

38. I want to be just like . . . him or her. Write about or describe your role model. Why would you like to be like him or her? Be sure to include details that support your ideas.

39. Write about or describe the first night that you spent away from home. It could be with a grandparent, sleepover, or anywhere else. Be sure to include details that support your ideas.

40. Power's out! Write about or describe a time when you lost electricity for any reason. How did that loss change your life? Be sure to include details that support your ideas.

Genre: Personal Narrative

Student Name _____   **Writing Topic** _____

Notes for Planning the Sensory Details of Your Story

See	**Hear**

Smell

Taste	**Feel**

Genre: Personal Narrative

Student's Name _____ **Writing Topic** _____

Writing interesting details in the boxes!

Character

Character's Looks	Character's Smells
How Character Looked during an Event	**Your Interaction with Character at an Event**

Student Worksheet 6.3 Blueprint Personal Narrative

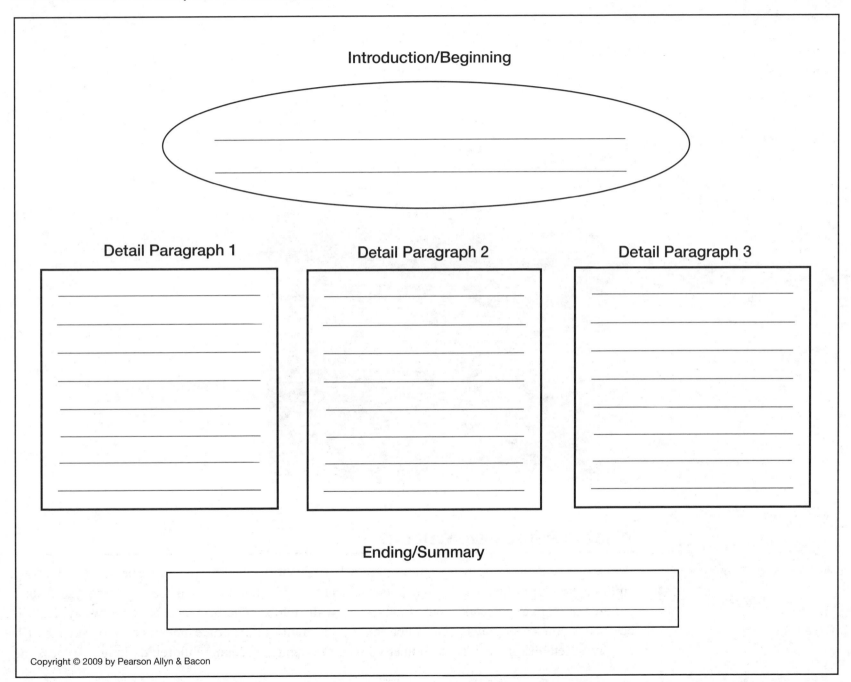

Introduction/Beginning

Detail Paragraph 1

Detail Paragraph 2

Detail Paragraph 3

Ending/Summary

Section II

BLUEPRINT PERSOANAL NARRATIVE

119

Persuasive writing is fun for students because they get to use their best arguments to convince their audience to change their minds while also informing them. These types of writings are on a single issue and authors select a stand or position. This type of writing includes a thesis or an opinion clearly stated, sound reasoning supported by strong evidence, recognition of counterarguments, and strong conclusions.

Persuasive Writing

What Is Persuasive Writing?

Persuasive selections are part of Informational (Expository) genres. If you've been around young children, you know that they learn to persuade adults to do what they want at a very early age. Young children attempt to persuade their parents to allow them to stay up past their bedtime by saying, "I'll be good if you let me stay up and watch this TV program," or negotiate an extra treat by saying, "I'll eat my vegetables if I can have another cookie." Yes, indeed, young children definitely possess the

Nina confidently presents her persuasive argument to her class and teacher.

power of persuasion. All we need to do is harness this natural ability. Young authors as well as older, more proficient authors possess the ability to think, organize, write, and present great persuasive arguments.

Using the BEW approach, the persuasive writing genre is defined as a kind of writing that attempts to change someone's mind. The question that the audience will be asking the student author is: Can you convince me to believe in your topic?

The author must know the purpose of a persuasive writing selection to lay the correct foundation for building it. There are two purposes for writing a persuasive writing selection. The first purpose is to influence the audience. The second purpose is to inform your audience.

Many types of writing can be found under the large umbrella of persuasive writing. These include editorials, advertisements and commercials, pamphlets, petitions, political propaganda, and persuasive letters—to name only a few. As you can see, not only is persuasive writing a genre in itself, but it also overlaps with several other genres. Just as in personal narrative writing, there are basic *building blocks* for this genre that provide the necessary material for your students to complete a persuasive writing selection successfully.

> **Key:** Persuasive writing includes research papers, editorials, advertisements, commercials, pamphlets, petitions, political propaganda, and persuasive letters—to name a few.

Persuasive Writing Building Blocks

So what are the Building Blocks for a persuasive writing selection? What elements will help your students write a proficient student selection in this genre? First the author must select an issue or topic that has meaning to them. They must take a stand on this issue or topic. Of course, the stand must be logical and based upon researched facts. Yes, the author must research the topic and provide supporting evidence. Even young students are capable of recording simple research facts. The author must include three factual points supporting a stand based on student research. The author can't forget to identify the opposing point of view too. The key is to explain why your viewpoint succeeds and all other viewpoints fail. The author needs to use *audience appeal* and a *voice of authority* to write an

ELL–BEWCONNECTION

Select a persuasive topic that ELL students can relate to, such as having more recess time. This real-life example will assist students in learning this genre.

outstanding persuasive argument. Using BEW teaching strategies outlined in this chapter, your students will develop the skills to write well-organized, informative, effective persuasive writing selections (see Table 7.1).

Table 7.1 Persuasive Writing Building Blocks

Genre Purpose	Use arguments convincing your audience you're correct while informing them too
Building Block Features	1. *Topic:* Must be important to you 2. *Stand:* Take a stand 3. *Reasons:* State three good reasons
Genre Writing Techniques	1. *Point of View:* First person is best, because it is your opinion 2. *Audience Appeal:* You are appealing to the audience's sense of emotions, urgency, or logic 3. *Use Expert Opinions:* Tell the audience that experts in the field agree with your stand and give examples 4. *Present Research:* Use charts, graphs or other research information to validate your stand
Genre Format and Voice	1. *Introduction or Beginning:* Write your position on the topic with general information 2. *Three Detail Paragraphs:* Give three reasons that support your position from your research (young authors may not be ready to write three whole paragraphs; three ideas should be given and recorded), tell the opposing viewpoint, and relate why your position is better 3. *Summary or Ending:* Restate your position and end your writing with a strong opinion 4. *Order of Argument:* Save your best argument for last 5. *Research Material:* Use facts to support your ideas 6. *Voice:* Use a voice of authority (style) with your own words, such as the voice of a lawyer, teacher, or any other expert in your topic field

The author must have an organizational tool just like that of a carpenter or builder—a Blueprint, of course. Your students will lay the foundation for building their persuasive writing selections with the BEW-furnished Blueprint (Figure 7.1). Once again, this organizational tool provides an easy method for students to organize their thoughts and keep their notes before actually writing their selection.

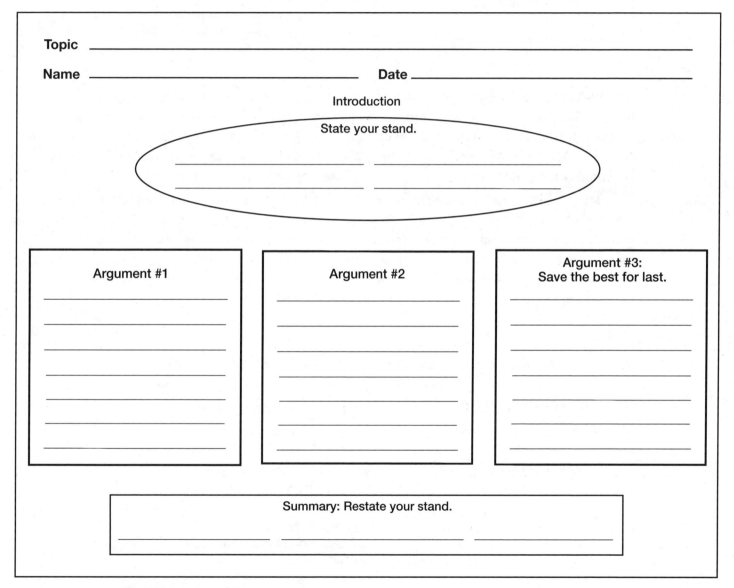

FIGURE 7.1 Persuasive Writing Blueprint

Common Student Mistakes: What Persuasive Writing Is *Not*

Topic Is Too Large

> *Not:* Don't try and write an entire book!

> *No, I'm not trying to write a whole book!*

The most common student mistake in a persuasive writing selection is choosing a topic that is just too broad. As with a personal narrative, a persuasive writing selection must also have a narrow focus. Remember the TMI observation that we discussed earlier as it applied to personal narrative writing? TMI means *too much information*, which holds true for persuasive writing as well. More is definitely not better.

Table 7.2 shows some examples of student topics that are too large in the left column with more appropriate student topics in the right column. Look at the broad topics in the left column. Students could write a book on any of these topics. What happens to students' persuasive writing selections that are too broad is that they veer from the topic. The topic drifts from one notion to another because there is just too much to write about. On the other hand, in the right column, where the topics are narrowly focused, the topic ideas spell out exactly the objective of the argument.

Table 7.2   Comparison of Student Writing Topics in Persuasive Writing

Issues That Are Too Broad	Nice and Narrow Issues
Students should be able to wear anything they want to school.	Fifth-grade students should be able to wear hats to school.
Schools should have good rules.	There shouldn't be a rule giving students after-school detention if they're tardy.
My type of music is the best.	The words in hip-hop music make it the best kind of music for telling a story.

Weak Argument

Not: You haven't told me why I should.

> *I can come up with more reasons!*

The general rule for backing one's opinion is to have three supporting reasons for your argument. Oftentimes, students don't put forward three arguments to support their stand. This could be a result of not doing enough research or merely not understanding the building blocks for this genre. (Begin by making a new student Rough Draft Writing Folder for each persuasive writing assignment.)

Teach the Genre Using BEW Phases

Three Steps in Phase I: Authentic Vocabulary

Step 1: Written Expression Writing Vocabulary

Going back to phase I of BEW, Teaching Authentic Vocabulary, you must first review the Big Ten BEW vocabulary words. In addition to reviewing basic BEW vocabulary words, your students must be taught all the new vocabulary words that are directly associated with persuasive writing. Let's look at genre-specific persuasive writing vocabulary words that are a must for your students to know before they write.

Professor Write's Interactive Teaching Strategy

Teaching Vocabulary for a Persuasive Writing Selection

1. Genre: Persuasive writing

Say: "Today we're going to learn a new genre called *persuasive writing*. Persuasion means you are going to change somebody's mind. You'll need to think about your topic, and determine at least three good reasons why your audience should change their mind and agree with you." Use a hand jive to teach this genre by placing three fingers at your temple while saying, "Persuasive writing uses three good reasons to change somebody's mind."

(continued)

ELL–BEWCONNECTION

Using motor activities (holding up three fingers for three good reasons) and direct instruction definitions ("three good reasons to change someone's mind") helps ELL students get meaning from abstract words.

Ask: "What is persuasive writing? It is giving three good reasons to change someone's mind [using hand jive with younger authors]."

Review: Repeat your question with your students answering using hand jive and the persuasive writing definition.

Background: Using the BEW approach, we define persuasive writing as writing that tries to change somebody's mind. Your students should be given a writing prompt or question as a subject for changing somebody's mind. At this time you need to model a persuasive writing selection that you've written (or one that somebody else has written) on the prompt so that the students can listen to an example of this genre and relate it to their own writing. Being persuaded or attempting to persuade somebody else is part of our daily routine. To understand better how frequently we attempt to persuade or are persuaded by others, you may want to do an activity that helps your students recall times they have been persuaded. This type of activity will have your students begin to think in detail about the art of persuasion.

Do: Have students complete a class activity worksheet on persuasion. Completing classwide persuasion activities, such as the student worksheet titled, The Art of Persuasion (see Student Worksheet 7.1 at the end of this chapter), will help your students understand the art of persuasion! After this worksheet has been completed tell your students to save it in their Rough Draft Writing Folders.

2. Audience

Say: "When we write our persuasive paper, we need to know who our audience will be so we'll know how to word our arguments. Some audiences will need different information than others. Are you writing for scientists to read your arguments or for your neighbors to read it? Let's decide who your audience will be for our topic."

Do: Have your students complete the Who Is My Audience? worksheet (see Student Worksheet 7.2 at the end of this chap-ter). It will help them identify their audience. Tell students to save this worksheet in their Rough Draft Writing Folder.

Ask: Begin your class discussion with the question: So who will your audience be? Often, the nature of the assignment will result in all members of your class having the same audience, such as the school, parents, or the school principal. All your students will have the same audience perspective. In this case the worksheet could be prepared as a class exercise.

Review: As you work on this unit, review with your class who their audience will be and what information they will need to speak to that audience.

Background: To develop an effective argument, the author of a persuasive writing selection must clearly have an audience in mind. For older writers, you can use the worksheet we provided. For beginning authors, instead of using the worksheet, give the children a specific directive such as, "You will be writing this selection for another student or a younger student in the school." Again, the key concept for your students to keep in mind regarding audience selection is how much the audience knows about their topic or how much information they need to know to be persuaded to accept their side of the argument. This is critical to the completion of a great persuasive argument!

3. Stand, position, or claim

Say: "When you write an argument in a persuasive writing paper, you need to decide what you want to say and then say it in a decisive way. This is called *taking a stand*. Your stand is also called your *position* or *claim*. Be aware of what your position is and don't waver from your stand."

Background: In a persuasive writing selection, these terms mean your opinion on the topic—what it is that you believe or don't believe. Remember to use our BEW strategy of modeling. Prepare your own example of a position statement. Read what you or some other author has written so your students have a thorough understanding of what these statements look like in writing and sound like when read aloud.

4. Opinion or fact

Say: "In a persuasive writing selection, the author must understand the nature of an opinion. An opinion is what you feel or believe or what you hold to be true. It is not necessarily a universal truth—a truth that everyone believes. An opinion is a matter of personal preference. A fact, on the other hand, is a universal truth. It is measurable and always holds true. It cannot be debated."

Do: Have your students complete the included Fact Versus Opinion chart (see Student Worksheet 7.3 at the end of this chapter). After completion this should be saved in the Rough Draft Writing Folder.

Background: Students must be able to recognize the difference between facts and opinions to develop successful persuasive arguments. Students can learn the difference between fact and opinion statements through class discussion on current event topics. Stimulate class discussion around opposing viewpoints on current event issues. Let your students discuss and tell each other why they feel the way that they do on a current event issue. We've provided a Current Event Opinion Inventory worksheet for your students (see Student Worksheet 7.4 at the end of this chapter). Use this worksheet with your class but if you have some pressing issues in your community or state use those. Tell your students to save this worksheet in their Rough Draft Writing Folder.

TIP: Most reading series stress the importance of identifying the difference between fact and opinion, both in the reading selection as well as students' own experiences. Capitalize on this when teaching how to write a persuasive writing paper.

Step 2: Conventions and Grammar

Each and every genre has special conventions that are essential building blocks for that genre. A specific convention necessary for persuasive writing is verb tense.

Professor Write's Interactive Teaching Strategy

Teaching Present Tense Writing

Say: "Arguments are stronger if you write them in the here and now. You don't want to argue a point as if you did it in the past. Use the present tense when you develop your persuasive arguments! Say words like, 'I think' or 'I believe' to start your sentences not 'I thought' or 'I believed.' Tell the reader in your own words what it is you want them to know. Use strong verbs, adverbs, and meaningful persuasive vocabulary words!"

Step 3: General Vocabulary Building

Develop Webs of Words with your class using commonly used words relating to the theme. Post them in your classroom during your writing lesson.

Five Steps in Phase II: Prewriting

Step 1: Multisensory Experiences

What background do your students have on the topic for their persuasive writing selection? You will need to stimulate their conversations and set up activities that will help them understand their arguments. Then they will need to research the issue so they can determine their position on the subject. Use role playing by asking students to act as if they're an expert who is trying to convince others of their position. You could watch commercials or look at advertisements that try to persuade the audience to buy a product. Be sure you provide some activities to engage your students verbally and to connect their prior experience with persuasive activities. This topic lends itself to social skills, such as sticking up for yourself or for what you believe in. Students can learn to be assertive in stating their positions.

Step 2: Wheel of Thought

A common student problem in the development of persuasive writing selections is choosing a topic to write about. You often hear students say, "I don't know what to write about or where to start." Typically, students pick topics that are just too large. The BEW Wheel of Thought process will help your students narrow their focus for persuasive writing selections.

Give your students a general theme to think about. It can be from your social studies text or reading series, or even a current event that ties in with your curriculum. If you can't find one to your liking, try one of the BEW persuasive topics featured at the end of this chapter or create your own. Draw a blank Wheel of Thought on art roll paper and put it up in the front of your class. Select a writing prompt to use as an example. For instance:

> The world that we live in is important to us. Our earth's environment can help or hurt us, keep us well or make us sick, be the cause of disasters or give us pleasure.

Now, write *our earth's environment* as the central theme in the circle of your class Wheel of Thought. Ask your students to begin to think about the earth, its environment, and its impact on them. As your students give you responses from their prior knowledge and experiences that relate to the theme, quickly write them on the rays of the Wheel of Thought. A persuasive writing selection should answer the traditionally asked questions of *who* and *how* these events occurred and *what will happen if . . .* ? A fourth-grade class example might look something like the one shown in Figure 7.2.

Section II

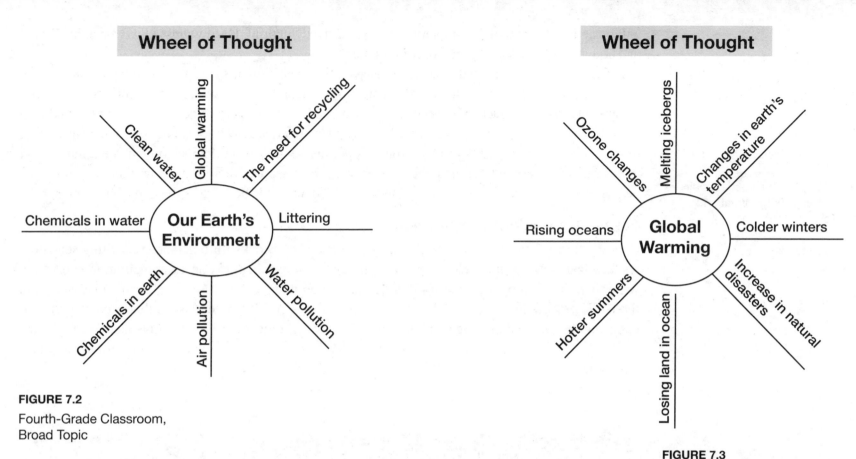

Wheel of Thought

Clean water
Global warming
The need for recycling
Chemicals in water
Our Earth's Environment
Littering
Chemicals in earth
Air pollution
Water pollution

FIGURE 7.2
Fourth-Grade Classroom,
Broad Topic

Wheel of Thought

Ozone changes
Melting icebergs
Changes in earth's temperature
Rising oceans
Global Warming
Colder winters
Hotter summers
Losing land in ocean
Increase in natural disasters

FIGURE 7.3
Fourth-Grade Student,
Narrow Topic

Notice there is a wide array of concepts listed here, from global warming to littering. What do you think would happen if your students began to fill out their Blueprint now? If you said, "Their topics would still be too broad to write about," you'd be correct. Give your students a second Wheel of Thought. Ask them to pick one of the environmental issues written on the class Wheel of Thought. Tell them to write that topic in the center of their individual second Wheel of Thought. Now model an example for the class. Draw a second large Wheel of Thought and put it up in front of the class. Select your environmental topic and state reasons why you believe your position to be true on the rays of the wheel. Model this procedure for your class. A fourth-grade individual Wheel of Thought might look like the one in Figure 7.3.

After they have finished, ask them which three arguments do they feel are the strongest or most important? Have your students highlight these three reasons. This student-created Wheel of Thought will be an important tool in completing the persuasive Blueprint. Have your students save this Wheel of Thought in their Rough Draft Writing Folder.

Once the students have three items to answer their question, it's time to research their supporting facts. Arrange a class trip to the media center for students to research their concepts. Note that not all student persuasive facts may need to be researched. For instance, students may want to conduct a school survey. In any event using the library as a place to create a school survey or collect supporting information for their argument is in order. Upper elementary or middle school students may select topics requiring research. To help them better plan their persuasive argument, let them complete the persuasive writing Personal Planning Sheet (see Student Worksheet 7.5 at the end of this chapter).

Step 3: Genre Format and Voice

Now it's time to start teaching your students the Building Blocks for a persuasive writing selection. As they learn each of these elements, your students will use them to construct their argument and to write them in the proper format for this genre. As you may have guessed, the format that we use in the BEW process involves our Blueprint graphic organizer. The three reasons that each of your students highlighted and investigated for their persuasive argument can now be translated to each of the three paragraphs in the persuasive Blueprint. Let's look at how to teach this genre format and voice in detail.

ELL–BEWCONNECTION

ELL students need graphic organizers to format and organize their thoughts prior to writing their selections.

Professor Write's Interactive Teaching Strategy

Teaching Genre Format and Voice

1. The purpose of the introduction paragraph

Ask: While pointing to the oval shape on a class persuasive Blueprint, ask your students, "What shape is this?"

The students will answer, "It's the oval."

"What type of paragraph does the oval represent?"

The students will answer, "The introduction or beginning."

"What is the job of the introduction or beginning in persuasive writing?"

"It introduces your topic, and tells your basic position."

"That's right. And in order to follow our writing Blueprint correctly, we must also look at the size or how long our introduction or beginning will be in comparison with the rest of the story. How big is an introduction or beginning? Medium size [and ask students to show you with their hands]."

Teach: The introduction paragraph of a persuasive writing selection must identify the topic and state your position. It must start with general thoughts on the topic and end with identifying your specific position.

2. The topic sentence

Ask: "What type of sentence should the introduction or beginning start with?"

"A topic sentence" will be their response.

Teach: Topic sentences are very important because they act as a *hook* to draw the reader into the argument. A great topic sentence is essential in persuasive writing. There are two interesting ways to write topic sentences. The first way is to ask a question on the writing prompt. For example, "What should happen when one student bullies another?" The second way uses a question that acts as a hook to draw your audience into your argument. For example, instead of saying, "What should happen when one student bullies another?" we could add a hook to our topic sentence by saying, "Do you know how much it hurts when someone bullies you?"

Do: Have your students complete our Topic Sentence Strategies worksheet (see Student Worksheet 7.6 at the end of this chapter) to help them develop quality topic sentences. Then tell them to save it in their Rough Draft Writing Folders.

Background: It's important to practice both topic sentence strategies for responding to a persuasive writing prompt.

3. Take a stand

Say: "Decide what the stand is that you will take on your topic."

Teach: In a persuasive writing selection, taking a stand means stating your opinion on the topic—what it is that you believe or don't believe. Remember to use our BEW strategy of modeling how to do this for your students. Prepare your own example of a position statement to model for your students. Read what you or some other author has written so your students have a thorough understanding of what these statements look like in writing and sound like when read aloud.

4. The purpose of the detail or middle paragraphs

Ask: While pointing to the square on a Blueprint, ask your students, "What shape is this?"

The students will answer, "It's a square."

Then ask, "What type of paragraph does the square in our Blueprint represent?"

They will tell you, "The detail or middle paragraph(s)."

"Yes, we'll put our notes for our persuasive writing details in the Blueprint squares. How big are the detail or middle paragraphs? Large [and ask students to show you with their hands]." The detail paragraph section of your persuasive writing will be the largest section of your paper because it contains your research and three strong arguments."

Teach: To follow the building blocks of a persuasive writing selection you will need three detail paragraphs. These detail paragraphs describe your three main arguments in a logical order with supporting details. You've already selected these three points earlier on your Wheel of Thought. There are many different ways to write or persuade an audience. The method that you select to teach will depend upon the grade level that you are teaching.

A. Voice of authority (for students of all ages)

  i. Say: "If you use your voice of authority when writing your arguments, you argue as if you were playing the role of an expert. Do you want to be a teacher, a salesman, or maybe a doctor or lawyer when you argue your case? It is important for you to sound confident when you give your three good reasons."

  ii. Do: Complete the student Voice of Authority worksheet to help your students develop their voices (see Student Worksheet 7.7 at the end of this chapter). Then have students put this worksheet in their Rough Draft Writing Folder.

B. Using your research facts (for students of all ages)

  i. Say: "Facts are always true! Is there research evidence that supports your position or claim? Use that information in your persuasive argument." Feel free to encourage your students to include graphs, charts, and statistical information that support their position or claim.

Propositions: Examples

1. School uniforms should be made mandatory in all public schools across the United States.

2. School personnel should be able to search student lockers.

3. Sports programs should never be removed from schools to save money.

FIGURE 7.4

Propositions: Examples

   ii. Do: Help students decide which research information they want to use to write in their notes. The strongest point should go last.

C. Proposition (for upper elementary and middle school students)

   i. Background: This style will probably only be taught in upper elementary and middle school writing classes because it is a more advanced term. It uses a debate format in that a proposition is written in a statement format that can then be argued for or against. Figure 7.4 shows some samples that should make it clear for your students.

D. Argument method (for upper and middle school students)

   i. Say: "There are many different ways to develop an argument. The ways that we use have special names and meanings. These ways of developing an argument will help back up your stand. Let's talk about these ways."

   ii. Students can be taught the following types of arguments:

      a. Logos: A logos argument is one that uses data, relevant facts, or just plain logic to support your claim.

      b. Pathos: We all show emotions in one way or another on one topic or another. The persuasive strategy of pathos uses emotion to appeal to your audience. Logos targets the mind whereas pathos targets the heart.

      c. Kairos: A kairos argument builds its case on urgency. You need to do something right now or there will be a catastrophe. It just can't wait!

      d. Ethos: Ethos is having a special voice of authority that gives you credibility on the topic. The term *ethos* refers to providing an argument based upon the author's credibility. In other words, "Can we believe you? Do you know enough about the topic that you're arguing? Do you have the knowledge base to give us that information?"

      e. Background: Upper elementary and middle school students should learn these methods of developing an argument. To help your students understand these terms, practice with the Types of Arguments worksheet (see Student Worksheet 7.8 at the end of the chapter).

E. Opposing position or claim

   i. Say: "To make your stand sound strong, you must recognize the other person's point of view. Then you tell why your point of view is better. This is called *recognizing the opposition.*"

   ii. Background: Students must recognize the other side's argument. They need to understand what other people are saying and feeling—what others' opinions are on the topic.

5. The purpose of the summary or ending paragraph

Ask: While pointing to the rectangle on a Blueprint, ask your students, "What shape is this?"

The students will answer, "It's a rectangle."

Then ask, "What type of paragraph does the rectangle in our Blueprint represent?"

They will tell you, "The summary or ending."

"Yes, we'll put our notes for the ending or summary of our persuasive writing selection in the Blueprint rectangle. How big is the summary or ending paragraphs? Small [and ask students to show you with their hands]. The summary or ending section of your writing will be the smallest section because it contains just your summary."

Say: "The ending or summary for a persuasive writing selection has specific points that must be included. First, you must retell or restate your stand. Then, you must write a sentence or two about each of the points that support your stand. End your summary with a strong, meaningful statement.

6. Transitions

Say: "In between each paragraph there must be smooth movement. Your paragraphs must flow into each other like a flowing river. This is called a *transition*. Make sure your paragraphs read as if they are connected."

Section II

Step 4: Blueprint Note Taking

Since your students have followed the steps for learning all the persuasive Building Blocks, it's time to put what they've learned into action. This is successfully done by using all the information from the Rough Draft Writing Folder to develop notes on the Blueprint. Your students will learn more effectively if you model how to use the Blueprint first. Therefore, write your notes on a Blueprint overhead transparency as you teach them note taking for this genre. (Check Student Worksheet 7.9 for an example of a Blueprint that has been adapted to support the persuasive genre.)

Step 5: Talking Paragraphs

After completing the Blueprint, it's time for your students to talk out their thoughts. Teachers have found this BEW strategy to be one of the most effective, if used properly. First model a *talking persuasive argument* for your class by talking from the notes you modeled in front of your class. Then, ask for a student volunteer to talk out their writing selection while looking at his or her Blueprint. Remind your class to listen closely to determine whether all the necessary elements are included in their peer's talking persuasive assignment. Is there an introduction? Are there three good arguments? Is there a summary? Have a few students demonstrate and reinforce the concepts of a true persuasive writing selection in front of the class. Then, let the remaining students perform their talking paragraph to a peer.

Your students can be trained to listen critically to each other's persuasive arguments. They can listen for a position or claim in the introduction or beginning and three sound arguments (one for each detail paragraph), with the most important being stated last. Did they hear an identifiable voice using one of the persuasive argument principles of logos, pathos, kairos, or ethos, or did they assume the character or voice of somebody else? Finally, can they identify a summary or ending paragraph, including a restatement of the author's position and a good closing? You will find your students won't gripe about making modifications or changes to their work at this point. It is much easier and quicker to revise notes on a Blueprint prior to the writing of the official first draft. This really works. Student Worksheet 7.10 at the end of this chapter, Talking Paragraphs, will help your students *listen for* categories to support each other with this step. This worksheet should also be saved in the students' Rough Draft Writing Folder.

Two Steps in Phase III: Writing

Step 1: Draft Writing

It's time for your students to write their first draft! Your students have already taken a position, organized their thoughts, taken notes, and spoken their arguments to their peers. They will now be able to write a proficient persuasive writing selection. To assist your students with vocabulary development, sentence transition, and great persuasive adverbs, display all the students' Webs of Words and other supporting materials. You'll find this to be a helpful aid to your students who are ELLs, at risk, or who have special needs. Their vocabulary will flourish.

Step 2: Title Writing

The last step in this phase of BEW is title writing. Review all the BEW title-writing strategies with your class (see Chapter 3). Think of some of your own examples. Invite your students to share insightful, creative titles with your class. Give students the opportunity to write titles for their selections. Titles written with BEW strategies will be great.

Five Steps in Phase IV: Authentic Editing

Steps 1 through 3: Editing Steps

It's now time to create an authentic editing rubric BEW style. This means asking your students to give you feedback on what they believe should be edited in their persuasive writing selections. According to the BEW differential teaching strategies, students should give their teachers feedback regarding what should be included in the editing rubric used in all three phases of editing: self-editing, peer editing, and teacher conferencing. In BEW persuasive writing editing there are three important areas scored for writing rubric assessment:

1. Genre Format and Voice
2. Vocabulary and Word Usage
3. Spelling and Grammar

It's important to remember that your class writing rubric will change as your class progresses and grammar lessons for the week change over the course of teaching multiple genre units. Although we don't recommend you use any of our rubric examples for your class, we have included some samples to give you an idea of what they could look like. You may be thinking: What does a persuasive writing selection rubric look like for younger students? In this case, there won't be quite as much detail, but young authors can master persuasive arguments too. We include a sample of our first-grade authors, persuasive writing rubric for you to review (see Table 7.3).

Table 7.3   First-Grade Authentic Editing Rubric

A. Genre Format and Voice	Least to Best
1. Did I answer the question in the first paragraph?	0 1 2 3
2. Did I give three reasons why I think so?	0 1 2 3
3. Did I say the answer to the question again at the end?	0 1 2 3

B. Vocabulary and Word Usage	Least to Best
4. Did I use words that make sense?	0 1 2 3

C. Grammar and Spelling	Least to Best
5. Did I start my sentences with a capital letter?	0 1 2 3
6. Did I put end marks at the end of my sentences?	0 1 2 3
7. Did I spell my words right?	0 1 2 3

Our first-grade students did a fine job creating their persuasive writing rubric. One thing is for sure, they understand the building blocks for this genre.

Moving along the grade continuum in an elementary school, let's now look at a rubric for persuasive writing created by a third-grade class. This rubric includes more detail than the rubric of our first-grade students (see Table 7.4).

An interesting point to make with this third-grade rubric regards the teaching lessons that occurred during that week. What part of speech do you suppose the teacher was instructing that week? Yes,

Table 7.4 Third-Grade Authentic Editing Rubric

A. Genre Format and Voice	Least to Best
1. Did I take a stand?	0 1 2 3
2. Did I write an introduction that tells about the topic?	0 1 2 3
3. Do I have three middle paragraphs with three reasons to support my stand?	0 1 2 3
4. Did I save my strongest point for last?	0 1 2 3
5. Did I restate my stand in the summary paragraph?	0 1 2 3
6. What type of argument did I use to appeal to my audience?	

B. Vocabulary and Word Usage	Least to Best
1. Did I use persuasive vocabulary words?	0 1 2 3
2. Did I use a variety of sentences?	0 1 2 3
3. Did I use our Web of Words?	0 1 2 3

C. Grammar and Spelling	Least to Best
1. Did I start my sentences with capital letters and end with punctuation marks?	0 1 2 3
2. Did I use adjectives?	0 1 2 3
3. Did I spell my words correctly?	0 1 2 3

adjectives! These third graders remembered this concept and, more than likely, incorporated it into their writing and offered it as an editing suggestion. In addition, our third-grade students have used a scale from 1 to 3 to evaluate their writing efforts. In this rubric 3 points is the best possible score and 0 points means that the element is missing.

We would expect middle school students to have the most elaborate rubric. If you are a middle school teacher, you know middle school students have great arguing skills. Let's see how they did on their editing rubric (see Table 7.5).

Table 7.5 Middle School Authentic Editing Rubric

A. Genre Format and Voice	Least to Best
1. Did I write a hook sentence to draw the reader into my paper?	0 1 2 3
2. Did I take a strong stand?	0 1 2 3
3. Did I give information from general to specific in my introduction?	0 1 2 3
4. Did I research my stand?	0 1 2 3
5. Did I write three detail paragraphs with good arguments?	0 1 2 3
6. Did I use good transitions?	0 1 2 3
7. Did I save my strongest point for last?	0 1 2 3
8. Did I restate my stand in my summary paragraph?	0 1 2 3
9. Did I write in the present tense?	0 1 2 3
10. Did I write the paper in an understandable way?	0 1 2 3
11. What method did I use to argue my stand?	

B. Vocabulary and Word Usage	Least to Best
1. Did I use a wide variety of persuasion words?	0 1 2 3
2. Did I use audience appeal words?	0 1 2 3
3. Did I use different types of sentences?	0 1 2 3

C. Grammar and Spelling	Least to Best
1. Do I have subject and verb agreement in my sentences?	0 1 2 3
2. How's my spelling?	0 1 2 3
3. How are my topic sentences?	0 1 2 3

Our middle school students have learned their lessons well! They've cited each and every important element that needs to be present in a persuasive writing selection. Our middle school students have also used a scale from 1 to 3 points to evaluate their writing efforts. Again, in this rubric 3 points is the best possible score and 0 points means that the element is missing. This type of rubric will allow your students to correct their assignments before you grade them.

Now that your students have completed the self-editing phase of BEW with their authentic rubric, they will continue on with the remaining BEW editing phases. After each editing phase, they will correct and rewrite their persuasive writing drafts until they are ready to complete the final writing selection.

Step 4: Final Copy Writing

This step of each writing genre will be easier than you think because your students are so well prepared to write their final copy. They will have talked out their arguments and edited their rough drafts three times. Be sure to help them as they write or type this best copy of their persuasive writing selection for publication. It is this final copy that you will formally assess.

Step 5: Teacher Assessment

We know that if you are just becoming familiar with the different genres, you may not know what a good example of a persuasive writing selection actually looks like. We have included an example of a well-structured writing piece as well as a nonproficient persuasive writing assignment. The first writing sample is by one of our first-grade students on the persuasive proposition: *Schools should not have a lunch recess anymore*. As you might imagine, the student who wrote the first selection has taken the stand that there should be a school lunch recess. Her persuasive writing selection is shown at the left.

Note that this first selection includes a stand in the first paragraph, three reasons for her stand, and a restatement of her position in the last paragraph. This student is proficient because she includes the building blocks of a persuasive writing assignment at a first-grade level.

First-Grade Persuasive Writing Sample: Proficient

Lunch Recess or Not

YES! YES!! YES!! I need lunch recess. I won't come to school if there's no recess.

I need to get outside and exercise at lunchtime. I need to jump rope with my friends. I do my school work and learn better if I have recess. I need to have fun with my friends at lunch time.

Yes, I need lunch time recess. Lunch time recess has to be a rule. All of the kids need it.

The next writing assignment is a nonproficient example of a first-grade persuasive writing assignment (shown at the right).

This second selection is nonproficient because it doesn't contain the proper building blocks for this genre. This student does take a stand, but then doesn't give reasons to support his stand. Which writing selection does your students' work resemble?

As students progress through the grades, they naturally become better writers. In the following examples, this third-grade student was attempting to persuade the school principal to take the entire third-grade class on a trip to Cedar Point Amusement Park. The third-grade student's unedited persuasive writing selection is shown below.

First-Grade Persuasive Writing Sample: Nonproficient

Lunch Recess

Yes I want lunch recess. It is fun. We need to have fun at lunch. I play soccer with my friends at lunch recess. I need to see and play with my friends at lunch recess. Lunch recess is the best ever.

Third-Grade Persuasive Writing Sample: Proficient

Cedar Point or Not

Mrs. Smith we need an end of the year field trip just like the fifth grade class but I want to go to Cedar Point. Our class can all take a bus trip there for the day and come back late at night.

Everybody has an end of the year trip, why not us? We deserve it too. You told us that we were the best third grade class ever. None of the third grade students have gotten in any trouble this year. Well, you know your school records show that none of the third grade kids have been suspended or gotten into ANY trouble this year at all. That deserves a reward—Cedar Point! We know that is hard to organize but our mom's and PTA have said that they will help us get it all together.

Mrs. Smith if you let us go to Cedar Point our good behavior will continue next year. We will know what a great principal that you are and we will not bully anybody and not get into any trouble in fourth grade. Kids that are rewarded for their behavior will be better kids. No trouble from us next year.

We could call the papers and have them write a article about what a great principal you are because of the trips that you let your students take. All of the parents will read the article and want to send their kids to your school. Letting us go to Cedar Point will make you a NUMBER #1 principal for everybody to see!

Yep, you're third grade kids will be off to Cedar Point soon. You know our record, how rewards make us better and that we'll make you look great. Just one question, "Are you coming with us?"

Third-Grade Persuasive Writing Sample: Nonproficient

Here We Come Cedar Point

We need to go to Cedar Point. All of the other schools are going. Why not us?

Every year all of the grades have a great field trip. It's our turn. We deserve it. We have been great students all year long.

Our parents will plan the whole thing. We will pay for everything ourselves.

We need this trip.

ELL–BEWCONNECTION

ELL students quickly learn through modeling. Allow students to hear and see the writing selections of other students. This provides excellent examples through modeling.

The student who wrote this selection was very confident about the principal's final decision. Perhaps this is because she developed a well-written persuasive argument using this genre's building blocks.

It is important to know that students can complete a literate persuasive writing assignment and yet the selection may be considered nonproficient because it does not contain the proper building blocks of this genre. The student who wrote the selection at the left wrote on the same writing prompt as the first: *Should the third-grade class go to Cedar Point for their end-of-the-year party?*

Although this student did state his case, he then fell short on using the persuasive writing building blocks in his essay. He didn't develop his stand with three arguments or restate his opinion and summarize at the end. Do your students follow the persuasive writing building blocks?

Of course, the grade-level expectations for middle school students are much greater than those of elementary students. Next you'll find an example from a student who has reached a high level of proficiency when it comes to writing persuasive arguments. His class writing prompt was: *Should students in public schools wear school uniforms*? His unedited persuasive writing assignment is shown on page 141.

The student who wrote this selection stated his stand well. In addition, he even conducted a student survey to support his stand. Yes, he did follow the building blocks for writing a good persuasive argument.

Lastly, here's an example of a typical writing sample from a middle school student who has not mastered the elements needed for a proficient persuasive writing piece. His unedited persuasive writing selection is shown on page 142.

This writing selection begins very well. The author has a nice strong stand and introduction, but then doesn't go on to develop his ideas. So, what is missing here? If you've said that he hasn't built his stand on research or survey material, you're correct! How do your students develop their persuasive writing selections? Similar to the first or second selections?

Dress for Success

How a person dresses determines what other people think of them. If a poorly dressed teen-ager with long hair and dirty clothes walks into a store a store workers are going to think differently of them than a nicely-dressed teen-ager. How you dress is who you are and it is important. As long as a teen-ager dressed nicely we should be accepted. Public schools should not make mandatory uniform requirements for students!

First, how we dress in school doesn't have anything to do with our grades. There isn't any research that shows students who wear uniforms have better grades than students who do. Isn't that why we're in school, to learn? If how we dress doesn't have a thing to do with our goal of learning, schools shouldn't worry about it. I don't wear a school uniform and I get straight A's in school. How would wearing a school uniform make me learn or do any better?

Second, the students in our middle school don't want to wear uniforms. I did a school survey of the seventh grade students and found that NOBODY wants to wear school uniforms. All of the students were against school uniforms and some students said that if uniforms were made mandatory they would find another school.

Finally, we do have a dress code and that's enough. How we dress in public at school is important. Girls shouldn't be able to wear halter tops to school, but we don't need uniforms. Dressing the way we want is a right under the Constitution. We have a freedom of expression and speech. That means we can dress the way we want as long as it's appropriate to our school dress code.

NO, uniforms in public schools I say. Uniforms have nothing to do with getting good grades in school, we don't want uniforms at school and it is our right to dress the way we want by the U.S. Constitution. Think about it, "Do teachers wear uniforms?"

Middle School Uniforms

No, middle school students shouldn't be forced to wear uniforms! The only people that wear uniforms in the world are those people that need to be recognized quickly, like policemen, fireman and doctors. Us middle school students are just part of the regular world.

Uniforms cost more money. Why spend money when we can wear our blue jeans to school. I like the way that I dress and so do my friends. We don't want to be uncomfortable in school or just look stupid. I go to a public school because I don't want to wear a uniform. If those private school kids want to wear uniforms that's fine, we don't! You know, wearing a button up shirt and a necktie everyday to school is just not comfortable. I bet you don't dress like that for work.

No, uniforms for public school students.

Three Steps in Phase V: Publishing Phase

Persuasive papers are a great way to help students see different sides of a school, family, or neighborhood issue. They can be read out loud to younger audiences, to stimulate thought, then the listeners can vote at the end for which side had the best arguments. Encourage your students to find the facts to see both sides of an issue!

In Summary: Persuasive Writing

Language can be a powerful tool and persuasive writing can help students learn to put together strong arguments to persuade someone of their position. This is an important social skill for your students to master. By following the BEW phases and teaching and modeling each step, you will be delighted

Section II

with the results. Your students will learn the building blocks and become proficient writers in this genre. Remember that even young authors can put together a strong argument. When you see this requirement in your grade-level expectations, be confident that you can teach it well!

We recommend that most genre units be taught over a two week schedule. Try teaching these BEW strategies by following the schedule suggested in Table 7.6. You will need to determine how long your students require on any particular phase so feel free to alter the schedule to match your needs. Tie your unit to your district or state curriculum. Don't forget to model by writing one yourself! Enjoy!

WRITING TIPS

Writing Tips: Persuasive Writing

- To teach the art of persuasion, conduct class discussions on current events that are important to your students.

- Try forming a debate club at your grade level to teach argumentative skills.

- Show television commercials to older students and ask them to identify which persuasive method the advertiser used to persuade the audience.

Table 7.6 Two-Week Teaching Schedule for Persuasive Writing

	Monday	Tuesday	Wednesday	Thursday	Friday
	Vocabulary	Vocabulary Review	Vocabulary Review	Vocabulary Review	Vocabulary Review
Week 1	Prewriting Activities 1. Multisensory Activities 2. Wheel of Thought	Prewriting Activities 1. Genre Format and Voice	Prewriting Activities 1. Genre Format and Voice	Prewriting Activities 1. Genre Format and Voice	Prewriting Activities 1. Blueprint Note Taking 2. Talking Paragraphs
	Monday	**Tuesday**	**Wednesday**	**Thursday**	**Friday**
	Vocabulary Review	Vocabulary Review	Vocabulary Review	Vocabulary Review	Vocabulary Review
Week 2	Writing Activities 1. Writing the Draft	Writing Activities 1. Writing the Draft 2. Title Writing	Editing 1. Self-editing 2. Peer Editing	Editing 1. Teacher Conferencing 2. Writing the Final Copy 3. Teacher Assessment	Publishing

FEATURE: Persuasive Writing Prompts

Are you unsure of what to have your students write about? The best writing prompts are those that create an emotional connection with your students. They must feel strongly about the topic to defend or attack it. What are the current hot issues in your community or school? If you can't think of any, look at the following persuasive writing prompts and select one that is age appropriate and relevant to your curriculum.

1. Our environment is important to us because it's the place that we live. It can keep us healthy or make us sick. Therefore, to save our environment everybody should be forced to recycle!

2. Letting our parents get in touch with us is important. Students should be able to have their own cell phones in school.

3. All public school students should get a free laptop computer to help them with their school assignments.

4. Body piercing is an art form. Students should be able to wear all body piercing jewelry to school.

5. Tattoos are beautiful. Students should be able to have any tattoo that they want on their bodies and show it at school.

6. All public school students should wear uniforms to school. That way there would not be any fights over clothing.

7. Being allowed to smoke is a right. High school students should have a smoking lounge in school.

8. Safety in school is important. All public schools should have metal detectors at the doors for their students and guests.

9. School cafeterias need to provide better lunches. They should hire McDonald's as a school lunch provider.

10. Books in school libraries are censored. This should stop. Censorship in school libraries is wrong.

11. Schools are looking for ways to save money. Sports programs should never be cut to save money in schools.

12. Schools are looking for ways to save money. Music programs should never be cut to save money in schools.

13. All high school students should be able to work half a day and go to school for half a day.

14. Elementary schools should stop all recess times to increase the teaching day.

15. There shouldn't be any vacation breaks in schools. Students need to attend school on a regular basis just as adults go to work each and every day.

16. We need to learn more information now more than ever. The school day should be extended to be two hours a day longer so we can learn more.

17. The public school calendar should be extended all year long. Students need to go to school in the summer to keep up with the demands of education.

18. How you dress depends on what you like or don't like. There shouldn't be any dress codes in school.

19. Students get hungry in school. Public schools should have vending machines in the hallway for students to buy food throughout the day.

20. Students get hungry in school. Teachers should let students bring food and water to class.

21. Homework is awful. Public schools should have a no-homework policy.

22. We know when we don't feel well. Students should be allowed to call in sick for themselves to school.

23. Sometimes you just can't go to school. Public schools shouldn't have a limited-absence policy.

24. Everybody has a bad hair day. Students should be allowed to wear hats to school.

25. It gets hot in school. Elementary students should be allowed to wear sandals in school.

26. It gets hot in the spring. All public schools should have air-conditioning.

27. Elementary schools should have school dances.

28. There isn't enough playground stuff for us to have fun at recess. All elementary schools should have a water slide on the playground.

29. The school day is too long. All public elementary schools should have a half day of school.

30. Everybody knows how to study. Students should be given days off from school to study for midterm and final exams.

31. All students need a computer. Our schools should give each student in the sixth grade and up a free laptop computer.

Genre: Persuasive Writing

Student Name _____

1. Think of one television commercial that has attempted to persuade you to buy its product. How did they do it?

2. Think of one magazine advertisement that has attempted to persuade you to buy its product. How did they do it?

3. How has a friend tried to persuade you to do something that you really weren't interested in doing? Were they successful?

4. How has your teacher tried to persuade you to do an activity today? Was he or she successful? Why?

5. How have your parents tried to persuade you to do an activity today? Were they successful? Why were they successful?

Genre: Persuasive Writing

Student Name _____ **Writing Topic** _____

1. Exactly who am I writing this persuasive writing selection for?

   ☐ my peers ☐ my teachers ☐ my family ☐ another group

2. My audience is _____ with my topic.

   ☐ very familiar ☐ somewhat familiar ☐ familiar ☐ not familiar

3. My vocabulary should be _____ .

   ☐ very detailed ☐ somewhat detailed ☐ not detailed

4. Is there something about my audience that I should consider when writing my selection?

   ☐ yes ☐ no

Genre: Persuasive Writing

Student Name _____ **Writing Topic** _____

Fact Statements (What truly is!)	Opinion Statements (What you think or feel!)
Red roses are the most frequently sold flowers.	Red roses are very beautiful flowers bought by a lot of people.
In Canada, public education continues one year longer than in the United States.	In Canada, children in public education learn more than in the United States.
The month of March has 31 days.	The month of March is too long.
Now you write some critical facts or opinions related to your topic:	

Section II

FACT VERSUS OPINION CHART

Genre: Persuasive Writing

Student Name _____ **Writing Topic** _____

Current Topic	Number of Students Who Answer Yes	Number of Students Who Answer No
1. Should all schools have metal detectors?		
2. Should public schools require student uniforms?		
3. Should schools hold classes all year long?		
4. Should schools give each student a laptop computer?		

Genre: Persuasive Writing

Persuasive Argument Methods Worksheet

Student Argument _____

Name _____ Date _____

What facts support your stand or position?

1.   2.

I believe . . .

3.   4.

What values are important to think about for your audience to be convinced?

What are the "hot buttons" (emotional reactions) or opposing arguments you need to consider?

List your three most important arguments. Put a star by the best/strongest one.

1.

2.

3.

Section II

PERSUASIVE ARGUMENT PLANNING WORKSHEET

Genre: Persuasive Writing

Student Name ———————————————————— **Writing Topic** ————————————————————

1. Start with a Question	
Effective Question Statements	**Ineffective Question Statements**
Is it fair that students should be mad at you if you told a teacher that someone was getting bullied?	Is telling on one of your classmates a good or bad thing?
Shouldn't schools start at about 10:00, when most students are awake?	What time should school start in the morning?
Try writing a question as the topic sentence for one of your paragraphs.	

2. Hook Your Audience	
Effective Examples	**Ineffective Examples**
One out of five kids admits to being a bully, or doing some bullying.	Being bullied isn't fun.
You can't learn if you're yawning!	It's too early to start school.
Try writing a direct appeal as the topic sentence for one of your paragraphs.	

Genre: Persuasive Writing

Student Name _____ **Writing Topic** _____

Teacher

Lawyer

Which Voice Will I Take?

1. Do I want to instruct or tell my audience information like a teacher?

yes ☐   no ☐

2. Do I want to sway my audience like a lawyer with principles based on law?

yes ☐   no ☐

3. Do I want to sell my ideas like a salesman?

yes ☐   no ☐

4. Do I want to base my ideas on research facts like a scientist?

yes ☐   no ☐

Section II

VOICE OF AUTHORITY STUDENT WORKSHEET

Genre: Persuasive Writing

Student Name _____ **Writing Topic** _____

Persuasive Argument Methods Worksheet

I believe . . .

Student Argument _____

Name _____ **Date** _____

My Strategies

Answer the persuasive question by stating your opinion.

Persuasive Argument Methods	My Example
1. Logos: data or information	
2. Kairos: has to happen right now!	
3. Pathos: appeal to emotions	
4. Ethos: are you trusted?	
5. Expert agreement: who important agrees with you?	
6. Research: statistically sound	

Section II

BLUEPRINT PERSUASIVE WRITING

Topic _____

Name _____ **Date** _____

Introduction

State your stand.

_____ _____

_____ _____

Argument #1	Argument #2	Argument #3: Save the best for last.
_____	_____	_____
_____	_____	_____
_____	_____	_____
_____	_____	_____
_____	_____	_____
_____	_____	_____

Summary: Restate your stand.

_____ _____ _____

Genre: Persuasive Writing

I believe . . .

Persuasive Argument Talking Paragraphs Worksheet

Student Argument _____

Name _____ **Date** _____

Take turns with your partner. Be a speaker and then a listener.

Speaker #1_____   Listener #1_____

Speaker #2_____   Listener #2_____

Listen for . . .

	1. A good introductory paragraph:		Topic sentence _____
			State position _____
			Transition _____

	2. Good detail paragraphs:		#1	#2	#3
		Topic sentence	___	___	___
		Explain position	___	___	___
		Support it	___	___	___
		Best for last			___

| | 3. A good summary paragraph: | | Restate position _____ |
| | | | Closing statement _____ |

What did you like about the speaker's argument?

Section II

TALKING PARAGRAPHS STUDENT WORKSHEET

Research is an informational writing selection. Research writing tells the reason for the project, the methods for gathering research, what the research actually is, and the findings and conclusions. It involves finding answers to research questions through credible procedures.

Research Papers

What Is a Research Paper?

Asking questions, making inquiries, and seeking answers about the unknown are all part of the human experience. Everybody has questions about something: how a process originated, how an invention came into being, how a discovery was made, how a battle was won or lost. The list is endless! We're certain that you don't go through an entire day without asking yourself a question of this sort. Our students are no different. Recently, we were taking our turn as appointed playground lunchtime supervisors. We happened to notice a little girl by herself completely absorbed in examining something in a far corner of the playground. She was intently focused on a small pile of sand. When we first approached her, she didn't even notice that we were there until we asked her, "So, what are you doing?"

She said, "Shhh, don't scare them off or step on them; I'm watching them."

Well, we were very curious by this time and said to her, "Watching what?"

She told us, "The ants, of course." Then she asked us, "How do they build their sand houses?"

Because neither of us have science backgrounds, we weren't able to come up with an answer for her. We suggested that she research the question: How do ants build their houses? She told us that she would and we naturally assumed that she would probably forget about our playground encounter. To our surprise, the very next day, this inquisitive third-grade student tacked an answer to her question on the small dialogue bulletin board outside our office. Although she didn't know it at the time, she had completed an analytical research project. She stated a research question and then found the answer in an online encyclopedia. Proudly, she wrote her masterpiece and presented it to us for our comments. This was a very small research project, but as you can see, research projects definitely come in all shapes and sizes. This third grader simply took our suggestion as a method of finding the answer to a question that had caught her interest.

Very simply, research involves finding information on a topic in an organized way. Research papers can include informational reports, persuasive arguments, and analytical research papers. Research involves finding information on a topic or interest. This is not a difficult concept; however, when many older students hear the words *research project,* they panic! Many college students won't attend a university that requires a master's thesis as a graduation requirement. This fear comes from misconception and misunderstanding of what a research project really is and how to plan, organize, and write one. Many older authors just don't understand the basic concepts that our third-grade student naively used in her small quest for personal satisfaction.

Writing an effective research project depends on understanding the components of a research project. There are two basic types of research projects that elementary and middle school students will be required to complete according to most curriculum standards:

1. An argumentative research project

2. An analytical research project

KEY: Research papers may include persuasive writing, book reports, biographies, and formal research projects, to name only a few.

ELL–BEWCONNECTION

Research topics should be connected to the student's interests. Suggest that ELL students research individual topics that are relevant to their culture or home.

In an argumentative research project, the author selects a topic, takes a stand, defends the stand with research, and arrives at the conclusion that the defended stand is the correct one. In elementary and middle school curricula, the argumentative research project overlaps with the persuasive writing genre. It's difficult to separate these genres because establishing a strong persuasive argument requires that the author do research. The elements of writing a persuasive selection are covered in Chapter 7.

The analytical research project seeks to answer a question. This is often called the *research question*. Here the author chooses a topic, looks for information on the topic, analyzes the information, draws conclusions, and then presents the results. Most elementary and middle school research projects will usually take the form of *analytical* research papers. Just as with other genres, students will benefit when you model the genre using your own personal examples. Share a variety of grade-appropriate research projects with your class. Lower elementary examples could relate to topics talked about in science, such as "Where do butterflies come from?" or "What's a volcano?" Upper elementary students might do research on an aspect of their state history or a type of animal (mammal, bird, and so forth). For middle school students, use your district curriculum guide for determining research topics across the curriculum. As with all other genres, the important question is: How do I teach my students to be successful writers of research papers at a grade-appropriate level? Use the teaching concepts in this chapter coupled with our BEW differential teaching strategies and this process writing approach will ensure student success.

Research Paper Building Blocks

Research papers have specific building blocks that make it a unique genre. The building blocks for a research paper begin with laying a solid foundation by selecting a topic that can be adequately researched. Selecting a topic is very important. Students must understand that completing a research project will require a large time commitment on their part, so selecting a topic that is highly interesting to them is critical. After topic selection, students must write a research question. This is an important building block because it will be the basis for the paper. Students must formulate a question to begin their search for an informed answer. The search for and documentation of information are the building blocks at the heart of the research genre. Finally, after information is gathered, it must be organized through the use of students' analytical thinking skills and then written up in research paper format (see Table 8.1).

Table 8.1   Research Paper Building Blocks

Genre Purpose	To find an answer to your question
Building Block Features	1. Selecting a topic that can be researched 2. Formulating a research question 3. Doing the research investigation 4. Gathering all the information 5. Analyzing the research
Genre Writing Techniques	1. *Point of view:* It can be first person or third person 2. *Verb tense:* Use past-tense verbs
Genre Format and Voice	1. *Introduction or beginning:* moving from general to specific and stating your research question 2. Three different detail paragraphs with supporting concepts that have been analyzed and synthesized by the author, and answer your research question 3. Summary paragraph that restates your research question and summarizes the three supporting concepts 4. An interesting title

Common Student Mistakes: What a Research Paper Is *Not*

Topics Too Large

Not: It's not an encyclopedia.

So, that's why I can't finish—too much information!

What is the most common student error found in research papers? If you guessed selecting a topic that is too large, you're correct. Our BEW student's editing acronym *TMI,* which stands for *too much information,* is again the major problem for research writing just as it was for the other genres.

Table 8.2   Common Mistakes: Topic Focus

Large Topic	Narrow Topic
Whales	Are blue whales soon to be extinct?
Deer	Are we destroying the natural habitat of deer?
Education	Do different countries have different types of schools for their kids?

Research questions that are too broad do not allow students to refine their focus. Consequently, they don't formulate first-rate research questions and they tend to lose their writing focus and clarity. Look at the teacher examples of research topics in Table 8.2. Topics that are too large are shown in the left column. Topics that would make high-quality research topics are shown in the right column.

If your students' research topics have TMI, then they will not successfully complete a research project. Help them narrow their focus.

Not Citing References

Not: Did you discover that information on your own?

Oh! I have to write down where I found that information?

The second most frequently seen problem with research papers written by elementary and middle school students is the lack of citing reference materials. Yes, all that expert information must be credited. Many students, inexperienced and experienced, forget about this critical step. Specific guidelines can be found in the Modern Language Association's (MLA's) reference manual, *MLA Handbook for Writers of Research Papers* (Gibaldi, 2003). Keep one on your bookshelf. Table 8.3 is a quick reference guide for citing books, magazines, and the Internet.

Table 8.3   Bibliography Guide (MLA Style)

Internet	Author (if it's available). Page title (written in quotation marks). Website title (underlined). Date published. Date visited. Internet address.
Books	Author (with the last name first). Title of the book (underlined). City (where it was published). Publishing company, copyright, and date.
Magazines	Author (with the last name first). Article title (underlined). Magazine title (underlined). Date of magazine. Page numbers (of the article).

Teach the Genre Using BEW Phases

Three Steps in Phase I: Authentic Vocabulary

Step 1: Written Expression Vocabulary

Phase I of BEW describes teaching authentic vocabulary words. Along with reviewing the Big Ten vocabulary in the generic BEW process (see Chapter 1), we recommend teaching the following genre-specific vocabulary words. (Have your students make a new Rough Draft Writing Folder for each research project.)

Professor Write's Interactive Teaching Strategy

Teaching Research Vocabulary Words

1. Genre

Say: "Today we will talk about a research paper. A research paper is a writing selection that answers one of your questions. You find answers to your questions by looking up information in books or other sources." While you are giving this definition to your students, do a hand jive for research writing at the same time. Begin with your hands in front of you, palms together, and then move your hands as if you were opening a book.

(continued)

ELL–BEWCONNECTION

ELL students quickly learn through physical movement and modeling. Use the BEW research hand jive to teach this genre.

Teach: The focus here must be to communicate to your students the actual purpose of a research project. Ask them if they have ever really wanted to learn the answer to certain questions. Many will respond with questions that have aroused their curiosity. Most elementary and middle school students typically research a topic because they want to extend personal knowledge in an area. Some, however, will choose a topic to show off expertise in an area of personal interest.

2. Audience

Say: "You need to know the audience you are writing for. You will be writing this research paper for a particular audience, such as another student or a younger student in the school, or to put in a classroom book. You need to find out how much this audience knows about your topic."

Do: Have your students complete a Who Is My Audience? worksheet (see Student Worksheet 8.1 at the end of the chapter). This will help them better identify their audience. When they have finished, tell students to save this worksheet in their Rough Draft Writing Folder.

3. Purpose of the study

Ask: "Why are you doing this research paper?"

Say: "No, the correct answer isn't because it's part of your school assignment. The purpose of the study is to find an answer to a question you are curious about."

4. Research question

Ask: "What is the question that you would like to find an answer to? It should be something that you would really like to know and is worth spending a lot of time to find out."

Background for Elementary Grades: In the early primary grades, young writers should work with a single, basic research question. Because most young students understand a question in spoken language, you can provide them with an oral question that they transcribe into written form. This becomes their research question. Very young writers, such as kindergarten children, may need a class-written question or need to participate in an actual class investigation to get them started. This procedure is optional for second and third graders, but by the time children reach third grade, they will be able to determine a research question independently. Refer to your specific state standards when teaching the how-to's of composing a research question.

Background for Upper Elementary Grades and Middle School: When students reach upper elementary and middle school age, more than one related research question should be used in order to complete an age-appropriate research project. Again, check your state standards to fulfill the specific requirements. As an additional organization aid and focus tool, ask students to complete Student Worksheet 8.2, Ready, Set, Go! Let's Research (at the end of this chapter).

5. Research sources

Say: "This word answers the question, 'Where do I find the information that I need?' "

Background: If you're from our generation, research sources have greatly expanded since we were in school. The Internet provides an enormous resource for student research and places it literally at their fingertips. Ask your students, "Where can you find some of the answers to your research questions?" and they will tell you, "The Internet, books, magazines, and the library." A trip to the school library may be in order for young authors to learn such things as finding a book on a specific topic or how to do an Internet search on a topic.

6. Research data

Say: "*Research data* is the term that means the actual information that answers your question. This is all the information that you'll find from books in the library or on the Internet."

7. Research references (bibliographies)

Say: "This term refers to the sources where you found the answer to your question."

Teach: Select the type of bibliography format that your school district adheres to. We recommend the MLA manual.

Step 2: Conventions and Grammar

Different genres require different building blocks. A special building block needed for research writing is the *point of view* in which the selection is written. Research is generally written in first-person or third-person point of view. Research uses past-tense verbs because it has already happened or been completed.

 Professor Write's Interactive Teaching Strategy

Conventions and Grammar

1. Point of view

Say: "When you write your research paper, the *point of view* that you write it from is important. There are two perspectives that research papers are written from: first person and third person.

(continued)

Chapter 8 Research Papers

163

If you write from the first-person point of view, you will be writing *I* did it or found it. If you're writing from the third person you will be writing *he* or *she* did it or found it."

Background: Young authors may not be ready to learn these two perspectives. In that case, teach them to write from the first-person point of view because it is easier to understand.

2. Verb tense

Say: "When writing a research paper, the verb tense is important to consider. You must use the past-tense form of the verb to write your research paper. This is because the information for research projects already exists."

Step 3: General Vocabulary

When writing a research paper, there are certain vocabulary words that tend to be overused. When this happens, it makes your students' research papers redundant. The most frequently overused words in research papers are transition words and research adverbs, and they are presented in Table 8.4. Expanding your students' research vocabulary base is easy when you create a Web of Words. Tack your Web of Words in front of your class and write a transition word in the square, such as *also*. Have a thesaurus for each child in your class. Ask your students to use their thesaurus to find synonyms for the word *also*. Use the class responses to create a Web of Words with new words to use as research transitions words.

After your students have completed the class Web of Words, you may want to create class charts from these frequently used transition terms and give one to each student.

Table 8.4   Research Transition Words

also	otherwise
and	as a result
in addition	what's more
too	after all
besides	although
therefore	alternatively

Five Steps in Phase II: Prewriting

Step 1: Multisensory Experiences

The hands-on experiences you use during this Prewriting Phase depend upon the topics of your students' exploration. If your students are researching particular states in the United States, have maps and puzzles available for students to look at. If part of the research involves state flowers, provide authentic experiences on how your state flower shows up in official places. If you are researching a science subject, such as mammals, then consider scheduling a museum visit so that students can see some authentic examples. This will help them address the importance of their research question. We've found that there are some common field trips that work well, depending upon the curriculum subject matter. Examples are presented in the Writing Tips.

WRITING TIPS

Writing Tips: Multisensory Experiences

- Use your social studies curriculum, and choose an interesting unit that lends itself to research. Add a research paper unit to enrich your social studies unit to write across the curriculum.

- In grades K through 2, use your science curriculum and enhance it with a research paper. Consider topics such as *Parts of a Bug, Volcanoes,* or *Planets.*

- Third Grade, *Our Earth:* Bring in a globe, pictures of deserts and mountains and oceans, or pictures of a related topic such as pollution.

- Fourth Grade, *State History* or *People in History:* Have pictures of state flags; allow students to dress up like their historical figure. Is there a veteran who could come in and provide some oral history?

- Fifth Grade, *A State in the United States:* Start a postcard collection to put into a literacy box for your school, with postcards from different states for students to look at. Find out which students have grandparents that live in a different state and ask them to send something that represents that state.

- Sixth Grade, *A Country in the World:* Take a cyber trip to different countries. Ask students to bring in objects that have the words "Made in . . ." on the back. Make a poster that says *hello* or *welcome* in different languages that match the countries you are researching.

Step 2: Wheel of Thought

Just as with other genres, students (especially young authors) experience difficulty in finding and narrowing a research topic. Research papers are no exception to this rule. Creating a class Wheel of Thought will help students write their own research topic that is workable even for young authors.

First, coordinate this research project with your existing curriculum. Science, social studies, or history curricula provide great opportunities for student-written research projects. We will use science as the subject for our teacher example in this chapter. Our students in third grade must complete a research project on our earth. This topic is much too large for third-grade students to develop without defining a focus.

FIGURE 8.1

Third-Grade Classroom,
Broad Topic

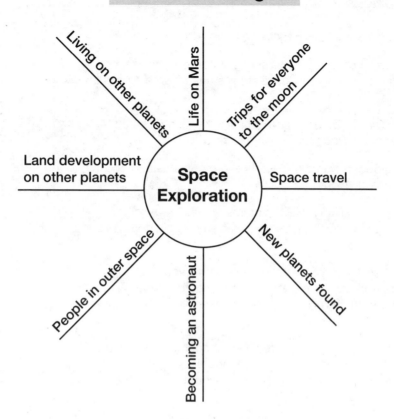

Wheel of Thought

Living on other planets

Life on Mars

Trips for everyone to the moon

Land development on other planets

Space Exploration

Space travel

People in outer space

Becoming an astronaut

New planets found

Start by telling your students, "You're going to write a research paper on a topic that is interesting." Now, write *Space Exploration* in the center of the Wheel of Thought. Your students will begin to come up with ideas from their own experiences as well as those discussed in your science curriculum. As your students tell you their ideas, record them on each ray of the class Wheel of Thought. Figure 8.1 is a teacher example of a Wheel of Thought that was developed with one of our third-grade classes.

Notice, once again, that the student topics listed on the class-created Wheel of Thought are still too large. To remedy this problem, have the students complete individual Wheels of Thought. Tell your students, "Select the theme of your research and write it in the center of your Wheel of Thought." Because students learn best through modeling, it's now your turn. As an example, we've selected the theme of *Mars Exploration* for our research project and will consequently write *Should*

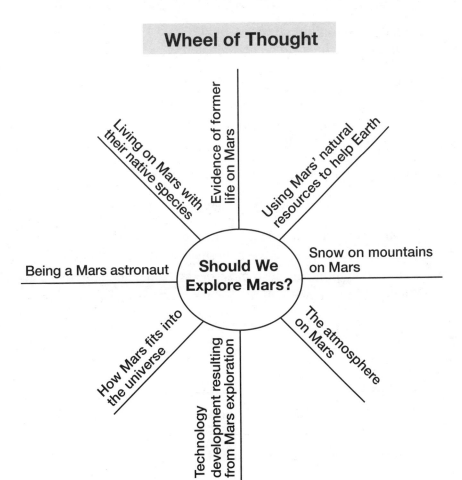

FIGURE 8.2
Focused Example

Wheel of Thought

- Evidence of former life on Mars
- Living on Mars with their native species
- Using Mars' natural resources to help Earth
- Being a Mars astronaut
- **Should We Explore Mars?**
- Snow on mountains on Mars
- How Mars fits into the universe
- Technology development resulting from Mars exploration
- The atmosphere on Mars

we explore Mars? in the center or our Wheel of Thought (Figure 8.2). The objective here is to narrow the topic. Give examples of how different types of exploration occur on Mars. On each ray of the Wheel of Thought, write some specific topic ideas like: existence of life on Mars, was there water on Mars, and more scientific knowledge on microorganisms.

After the teacher demonstration, it's now time for your students to do two things. First, they will write their selected space exploration theme in the center of their personal Wheel of Thought and then they will write specific topic ideas on the rays.

Your students will have many concepts written on their Wheels of Thought. The phrase written in the center of the Wheel of Thought becomes the topic. Tell your students to highlight the three concepts listed on the rays of their Wheel of Thought that they would be most interested in finding out about. These three areas will now become the areas to be investigated.

Step 3: Genre Format and Voice

It's time to start teaching your students the key building blocks of a research paper. These building blocks define the unique format and voice of the research genre.

The key building blocks we will address in this section are as follows:

1. Teaching students how to find and collect research data

2. Teaching students how to complete the Blueprint for organizing a research paper

Collecting the Research   Now it's time to start our research. Arrange a media center visit and have the media specialist assist your class in the research process. Perhaps a short discussion on how your school media center is set up would be helpful. Because most media centers contain the same basic elements, you should familiarize your students with all the sections. We've prepared Table 8.5 to assist you.

Table 8.5   Media Center Sections

Media section	DVDs, tapes, and CDs are kept here
Reference section	Dictionaries, encyclopedias, almanacs, atlases, thesauruses
Computer card catalog	Computer index to everything
Fiction	Novels and stories
Nonfiction	Factual books
Computers	Computer lab section
Newspapers and magazines	Periodicals

When your students know where specific sources can be found, teach them to use a computer card catalog (if one is available). Tell them that a computer card catalog lets them find their research sources by looking up information in one of three ways: by the author, by the title of the book, or by the key word or subject. Show your students the *call number* for a book. When they find the call number on the computer screen, they can easily find the book on the bookshelf by following the number progression until they come to it.

In addition, your students should have an understanding of how to look up information in encyclopedias, almanacs, atlases, and the Internet. The older the author, the more sophisticated their source searches should be.

While your students are visiting your school media center and beginning their investigations, make sure they've brought along their Rough Draft Writing Folders. Attach a resealable bag that contains a stack of 3 × 5 note cards to their Rough Draft Writing Folder. Using note cards, students can begin to collect source information on their *source cards* and data on their *research topic note cards*. This procedure will act as an organizational aid in both areas. When the media center visit is over, students should know more about the different sources available and how to find them.

Professor Write's Interactive Teaching Strategy

Teaching Genre Format and Voice: Doing the Research

1. Teaching note card recording: Source note card

Say: "Look up each source. Remember, a source is where you find your information. If the source has the information you want to help you answer your question, then take a 3 × 5 card and list all the information that identifies the source so you can put it in your bibliography later. These cards are called your *source cards*. Each source card will get its own letter of the alphabet, starting with A, in the upper right hand corner. This type of labeling will help you know if you have all your source cards at the end."

Background: Students must be made aware of the correct method for citing references when collecting resource information. The primary resource used for formatting reference citations is the MLA manual. Reference citation rules can be tricky for different types of media. Teach these methods at age-appropriate levels. Even kindergartners can answer the questions, "So how do you know that?" or "Where did you find that out?" Citing references at this age may only require a single word or, for beginning kindergartners, it could even be a picture. However, in middle

(continued)

school, students should be aware of more advanced citing techniques, such as referencing material in the body of a paragraph and how to present quotations correctly. If you teach them to put their source cards in the correct format, it will be easier for them to do their bibliography later. Display a visual reference of the correct format and walk your students through recording the first and second source correctly on their source note cards.

2. Teaching note card recording: Research topic (information) note card

Say: "Read about your topic from each source. Take notes from the sources that have good information about your question. Don't copy the exact words unless you intend to use a direct quote, because otherwise you have plagiarized. This means stealing someone's work. Use a different card for each piece of information. Code it at the top to match your source card such as A-1 and A-2, where A stands for the source card and 1 stands for the first piece of information selected from that source. Go through each source and make cards that pertain to your topic. These become your *research topic note cards*. You will write your notes down on your note cards to record in your Blueprint later."

Teach: "Now organize your research topic note cards by the main ideas that will provide the answer to your research question. Give each main idea a short name and write it at the top of each card that talks about that main idea. You'll have cards from different sources in each pile; however, each pile refers to only one main idea, and that main idea is written on the top of each card. These will be the cards that give you the ideas of what to write in your detail paragraphs on your Blueprint." Some of your students might benefit by putting a shape or color on the top left corner of each card to signify the cards that are on the same main idea (Figure 8.3).

"Decide the order of the main ideas for the detail paragraphs. Which information should come first, second, third, and so on, in order to answer your research question the best?"

FIGURE 8.3

Sample Information Card

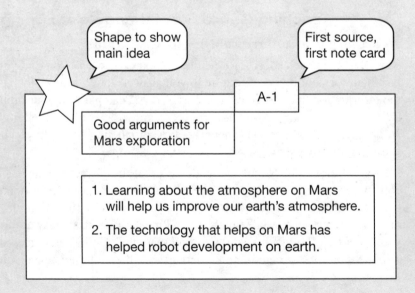

Blueprint Note Taking   Research papers of elementary and middle school students should follow a specific format. It's now time to teach these formatting steps to your students using the Blueprint as an organization tool. Because you have already taught the basic Blueprint shapes and purposes in previous genres, your students should recall them easily. The key teaching concept here is to incorporate all the requirements of a well-done research paper into BEW format. Let's start with the research paper introduction.

Professor Write's Interactive Teaching Strategy

Teaching Genre Format and Voice: Teaching the Format

1. The purpose of the introduction paragraph

Ask: "What shape is this? [point to the oval shape on a class Blueprint]."

The students will answer, "It's the oval."

"What type of paragraph does the oval represent?"

The students answer, "The introduction or beginning. We put our notes for the introduction in the oval."

"What is the job of the introduction or beginning of a research paper? The introduction of a research paper must introduce the topic. It should start with general statements, move to more specific ideas, and end with your research question. It should spark an interest in your topic for your audience. It introduces your topic, and states your research question. To use our writing Blueprint correctly, we must also look at the size that our introduction will be in comparison with the rest of the paper. How big is an introduction or beginning?"

Students respond, "Medium size [and show you the size with their hands]."

Background: The depth of your student research projects will depend upon their grade levels and your state benchmarks for individual grades. For instance, a research paper for kindergarten students may be as simple as a picture and three statements that answer a question. As students advance, more in-depth research is required.

Teach: The introduction must give general knowledge about the problem or question that students will answer. It should tell why the answer to this question is important. Is it something that affects everyone? How relevant is the answer to the author's audience? The introduction must also contain a concise statement of the student's research question.

(continued)

2. The topic sentence

Ask: "What type of sentence should the introduction or beginning paragraph start with?"

"A topic sentence," will be their response.

"What's a topic sentence?"

"That's what it's all about."

Teach: Topic sentences are very important because they act as a hook to draw the reader into the paper. A great topic sentence in a research paper draws the audience into the research and makes them want to read more. Teach the strategies outlined in the BEW writing process for creating a great topic sentence, such as ask a question or tell an interesting fact (see Chapter 3).

3. Research question

Say: "You must write a research question that you would like to find an answer to." To begin this process, state the class theme for the research project.

Teach: Always select a broad class theme from which your students will choose a research topic to write about. Tie this theme to your curriculum standards. Social studies and science also provide good subject matter for research themes. Be certain that the topics that your students choose within the class theme are narrow enough to be managed by your student researchers.

Say: "The most important sentence that you can write is your research question. Your entire project revolves around this question. Decide how you will write your research topic in a question format. It should be a sentence that restates your research topic as a question."

Ask: "What type of sentence will you write for your research sentence?"

Student Response: "A sentence that restates my research topic as a question."

4. The purpose of the detail or middle paragraph(s)

Ask: "What shape is this? [point to one of the squares on the Blueprint]."

The students will answer, "It's a square."

Then ask, "What type of paragraph do the squares in our Blueprint represent?"

They will tell you, "The detail or middle paragraphs."

"Yes, we'll put our notes for our research details in the Blueprint squares. How big are the detail or middle paragraphs? Large [and ask students to show you with their hands]."

Say: "The detail paragraphs section of your writing will be the largest section, because it contains all the research information that answers your questions. Your research paper will have at least three detail paragraphs that refer to the research question. There will be a detail paragraph for each of the researched main ideas from your research topic note cards. Gather all your note cards

172

together. Sort them by main idea—the way you labeled each card in the top left corner. Each main idea topic of your note cards has a specific place to be written on the Blueprint." While pointing to the three Blueprint squares say, "All your notes go here—a square for each different main idea topic."

Background: A research paper written by younger authors may not have three paragraphs. Younger students may include this information in a single well-written paragraph. This paragraph should include at least three sentences that point out three facts that answer their question. The general rule of having three supporting research facts to answer the student-proposed questions should remain consistent across all grade levels. Remind your students to develop smooth transitions between these detail paragraphs.

Say: "Remember, as you write your notes in the Blueprint squares, make sure that your information follows a logical order and stays on the topic."

5. The purpose of the summary

Ask: "What shape is this? [point to the rectangle on the Blueprint]."

The students will answer, "It's a rectangle."

Then ask, "What type of paragraph does the rectangle in our Blueprint represent?"

They will tell you, "The rectangle represents the summary paragraph."

"Yes, we'll put our notes for our research summary or ending paragraph in the Blueprint rectangle. How big is the summary paragraph? Small [ask students to show you with their hands]."

Say: "The summary or ending paragraph must restate your research question. Yes, say the question again! You want to emphasize this question. Then highlight your three research points briefly. End your paper with a good statement that leaves a lasting impression in the minds of your audience."

ELL–BEWCONNECTION

Learning to summarize is an important skill for ELL students to learn. Teach this concept by using examples from their papers.

Step 4: Blueprint Note Taking

Now that students understand the relationship between their research topic note cards and the Blueprint, it's time to organize their paper by taking notes on the Blueprint. Start by giving your example for the topic. Complete your notes on a class Blueprint for your introduction, detail paragraphs, and your conclusion. Remind students that they are using the ideas they found in their sources, not the exact words, which is plagiarism. Give examples of how to put something into your own words. Also model how to use an exact quotation with quotation marks and how to cite the source and page number.

Now it's time for your students to do the same. Make sure that your students have all of their note cards and any worksheets handy in their Rough Draft Writing Folders. Your students may need more time for this step because they must critically analyze their research and synthesize it into each of the three squares in their Blueprint (Student Worksheet 8.3).

Step 5: Talking Paragraphs

So far, your students have successfully found a workable and narrow research topic, conducted their own research, formulated a research question, and planned and organized the answer to their research question in BEW format. Now the time has come for your students to talk out the notes from their Blueprints into complete sentences and paragraphs. But you go first! You must model this technique for your students. Place a copy of your Blueprint on an overhead or digital projector as you point to each different Blueprint shape and speak your notes aloud, turning them into full spoken sentences and paragraphs.

Then it's your students' turn. Ask your class if there are any student volunteers who would be willing to come to the front of the class to demonstrate their talking research paragraphs. Encourage your class to listen carefully to make sure they hear whether all the elements needed for a winning research paper have been integrated in their peer's talking paragraphs. Review these concepts:

- Is the topic narrow enough?

- Did the author write a first-class research question?

- Can you hear the different spoken paragraphs as they begin?

Occasionally, at the beginning of this exercise, your students may be reluctant to do talking paragraphs in front of the class. We've found that some enticement may be needed, like giving a highlighter to the person who tries first. You'll notice that your students will begin to volunteer readily for this exercise, not necessarily for the enticement, but because they find it helpful to their writing project. Next, tell your students to find a partner. Have each student complete a talking paragraph with their partner. Our students constantly tell us, "Talking paragraphs help me get things straight in my mind." Sometimes, especially with research reports, our students ask us to listen to their talking paragraphs before they begin to write. This BEW technique—talking paragraphs—is an extremely powerful student organizational tool.

Two Steps in Phase III: Writing

The writing phase of the BEW process is probably the easiest phase for your students to accomplish. This is especially true for research papers. The process writing format in BEW makes writing the draft a snap for your students. Be certain to have all your Webs of Words that were developed to enhance research vocabulary posted in your classroom.

Step 1: Writing the Draft

Students have learned about their topic, researched their key question, and used their note card topics and notes to record on their Blueprint. Then they talked out those notes in their talking paragraphs. We predict some of your students will have already revised their notes at this point. Now, ask your students to use their notes from their Blueprint to begin writing their rough drafts. They should also use all the materials developed during the prewriting phase that have been saved in their Rough Draft Writing Folders to assist them in writing their first draft. Take the class through the writing of each paragraph by modeling your own introduction using your Blueprint notes. Then model your detail paragraphs and, finally, your summary. Give your students enough time to write each paragraph after you have modeled yours.

Use a class period to help your students write their bibliographies. If you have put a bibliography poster in your room, students should have written their source cards to match the formats listed in it. At this point, they need only alphabetize their source cards and double-check them before recording them in written form at the end of their paper.

Step 2: Title Writing

Next, review BEW title-writing strategies from Chapter 3. Remind your students that titles should reflect their personal research project. Titles shouldn't be generic or uninteresting, but should entice the audience to want to read the research paper. Give some examples from your repertoire. Bring in research papers written by other authors and discuss the titles—good and bad!

Five Steps in Phase IV: Authentic Editing

Steps 1 through 3: Editing

It's now time to begin developing an authentic editing rubric for your students' research papers. Just as in the other genres, this process is led by the teacher, and student responses should be in accordance with the research genre format. Ask your students to develop a rubric that will be used for students' self-editing, peer editing, and teacher conferencing. The three categories that students must use to develop their rubric remain the same for all genres:

1. Genre Format and Voice
2. Vocabulary and Word Usage
3. Spelling and Grammar

Children of all grade levels can collectively write a research paper rubric. Table 8.6 is a sample from one of our second-grade classes. Remember, this is only a sample and should not be used in

Table 8.6   Second-Grade Authentic Editing Rubric

Research Genre Format and Voice

Did I have an introduction paragraph?	Yes	No
Did I ask my research question in the first paragraph?	Yes	No
Do I have a detail paragraph?	Yes	No
Did I give three good answers to my question?	Yes	No

Vocabulary and Word Usage

Did I use my research words?	Yes	No

Grammar and Conventions

Did I start my sentences with capital letters?	Yes	No
Did I end my sentences with end marks?	Yes	No
Did I use -*ed* verbs?	Yes	No
Do I have different-length sentences?	Yes	No
Did I check all of my spelling?	Yes	No

any of your classes. To be effective, *your rubric must be developed for a specific writing selection by your class.*

These second-grade students did a fine job creating their research paper rubric. This is probably because this group of students really enjoyed their research project topics!

Of course, more advanced students will create a more detailed rubric. Let's look at a research paper rubric created by our fifth-grade students (see Table 8.7).

This group of fifth-grade students enjoyed their research topics too. They really felt that they had become experts on their research questions and weren't shy about letting everyone know.

By the time students reach middle school, the curriculum standards for writing research papers become very detailed. Students are expected to spend time out of class researching and obtaining information from many different sources. These projects become a major part of a student's workload

Table 8.7   Fifth-Grade Authentic Editing Rubric

Research Genre Format and Voice	Least to Best
1. Do I have an introduction paragraph?	0 1 2 3 4
2. Did my introduction paragraph start off generally and narrow to the research question?	0 1 2 3 4
3. Did I state my research question in a question format?	0 1 2 3 4
4. Is it a topic that can be researched?	0 1 2 3 4
5. Did I find three points that answer my question?	0 1 2 3 4
6. Did I find good research for documentation?	0 1 2 3 4
7. Did I write up my research in separate paragraphs with topic sentences?	0 1 2 3 4
8. Do I have a summary paragraph?	0 1 2 3 4
9. Did I restate my research question in the summary paragraph?	0 1 2 3 4
10. Did I summarize my research in the summary?	0 1 2 3 4
11. Did I include a bibliography?	0 1 2 3 4

Vocabulary and Word Usage	Least to Best
1. Do I have my research stated in a question?	0 1 2 3 4
2. Did I use research terms?	0 1 2 3 4

Grammar and Conventions	Least to Best
1. Did I write the paper with past-tense verbs?	0 1 2 3 4
2. Did I check my spelling?	0 1 2 3 4
3. Do I have subject–verb agreement?	0 1 2 3 4

during a semester. This is evident when you look at the rubric created by our middle school students in BEW style (see Table 8.8). These middle school students have definitely internalized the building blocks for research papers.

Table 8.8 Middle School Authentic Editing Rubric

Research Genre Format and Voice	Least to Best
1. Did my introduction include a good description of the problem?	0 1 2 3 4
2. Is my research question clearly stated in the introduction paragraph?	0 1 2 3 4
3. Did I write a good transition sentence between each paragraph?	0 1 2 3 4
4. Did I find at least three supporting answers to my research question?	0 1 2 3 4
5. Did I write each of these answers in a well-organized paragraph?	0 1 2 3 4
6. Does each paragraph have a topic sentence?	0 1 2 3 4
7. Is my paper well organized and does it follow a logical order?	0 1 2 3 4
8. Do I have a summary?	0 1 2 3 4
9. Did I restate my research question in my summary?	0 1 2 3 4
10. Did I summarize my research in the ending paragraph?	0 1 2 3 4

Vocabulary and Word Usage	Least to Best
11. Did I use the past-tense form of the verb?	0 1 2 3 4
12. Did I use the correct research terms?	0 1 2 3 4
13. Did I include a bibliography?	0 1 2 3 4

Grammar and Conventions	Least to Best
14. Did I check my spelling?	0 1 2 3 4
15. Did I have descriptive words?	0 1 2 3 4
16. Did I present my research in a logical way?	0 1 2 3 4
17. Did I use a variety of sentence types?	0 1 2 3 4

After the authentic editing rubric has been created, make copies of the rubric for each of the editing steps. First, each of your students should be given a copy of the rubric to edit their own work. Additional copies are required for peer editing and teacher conferencing. When your students have completed the self-editing step of BEW with their authentic rubric, they should continue on with the remaining BEW editing steps. After each step, students correct and rewrite their research paper drafts until they are ready to complete the final writing selection.

Step 4: Final Copy Writing

After all the hard work has been done, it's now time for your students to write their final research papers. Tell your students, "While looking at your rough draft writing, and using all your editing comments, begin to write [type] your final research papers." Because they know how they will publish their research papers, they will undoubtedly be excited and do their best work.

Step 5: Teacher Assessment

Perhaps you haven't seen a young author's research writing selection. Just in case you're wondering what a finished selection for an early elementary student's research paper looks like, we've included a proficient example and a nonproficient example. The first student selection is the proficient example. Their topics were based on the general theme of *volcanoes*. This theme created a great deal of interest in the class. The teacher felt that much of the interest was generated by a science DVD on volcanoes that the students watched at the beginning of the research project (see below).

First-Grade Research Paper Writing Sample: Proficient

How Does It Work?

Volcanoes can be scary. They can hurt many people when they explode. There are many volcanoes in the world. Why does a volcano erupt?

Volcanoes erupt because of nature. It is a thing that happens in nature a lot. It is part of the things that happen on the earth.

There is a special reason as why volcanoes erupt. It is because inside the earth gets very hot. This hot rock is called magma. It melts and goes to the top of the earth.

When the melted rock gets to the air it explodes. This is because gas gets bigger and makes steam. Then there is a big explosion.

There isn't anything that scientists can do to stop volcanoes from exploding. Volcanoes erupt because it's part of nature. It happens when inside rock melts and raises to the top. I hope none explode soon.

Scary Volcanoes

I saw a volcano explode on a DVD at school. It was scary. We don't have any volcanoes in our state. I wonder what makes a volcano explode in the air? I hope that I don't ever see a real one explode. When they explode it can hurt many people.

This first-grade student knew the question that she wanted to ask: How do volcanoes explode? She stated it in a question format and proceeded to find the answer. Later, this student constructed a model of a volcano to share with her class. Now that sure shows interest in a topic!

The student who wrote the second (shown at the left) selection also wanted to learn more about volcanoes. As you can see, science was a high-priority subject for this class. Unfortunately, the second student wasn't quite as skillful as his peer.

The very first mistake this student made was not stating a research question. He just wrote facts about a volcano and how it erupted. Also, sentence structure was a real problem with this selection. The limited sentence structure interfered with the comprehensiveness of the piece. How are your young authors' research papers written? Are they proficient like the student who wrote the first selection?

As students progress through various grades, research papers become more and more complicated; however, research building blocks remain the same. The depth of research, length of the selection, and sophistication of student research projects increase year by year. By the time students are in upper elementary and middle school, it isn't unusual to have students submit final selections that are between fifteen and twenty pages in length. Many students create charts, graphs, maps, and illustrations on their computers that effectively assist in answering their research questions.

The most critical building block for all research papers is developing a research question that can be investigated. Because it isn't possible to include lengthy research papers from upper elementary and middle school projects in this book, we present proficient and nonproficient introductory paragraphs, including the research question, for upper elementary and middle school students. Generally, if the introductory paragraph is well written and includes a well-defined research question, the remainder of the paper also tends to be well written.

One of our fourth-grade students just had to know how bees made honey. Apparently, he had a beehive in his attic and became fascinated with it. The beginning of his unedited paper is shown in at the left.

Fourth-Grade Research Paper Writing Sample: Proficient Introduction

Buzz, Buzz!

Buzz, buzz, buzz everywhere around me. Then, ouch, I got stung, by a bumble bee. I thought those are terrible bugs. They are good for nothing. Then I thought of the honey that I liked. I wanted to know how awful bugs like bees made honey? Just how do bees make honey?"

As you can see, all the elements of a well-written introductory paragraph are included in this proficient student example. You can be assured that the remainder of his paper was equally proficient.

Let's look at a nonproficient fourth-grade research paper investigation (shown at the right). This student was interested in environmental issues and selected the research topic, *Why Is the Sky Blue?*

From the very beginning, this student's research project runs into trouble. The topic that he selected isn't very good for his grade level nor is it really one that can be easily investigated. The remainder of his research project was nonproficient as a result of poor topic selection.

Middle school students can dig deep for their research. Again, the importance of writing an explicit, definable research question that can be investigated is critical. One of our middle school students selected a current topic that is on everybody's mind: high gas prices and the development of electric cars. His proficient introduction and research question is shown below.

Obviously this student has a real interest in cars. It's a great question that's relevant today. He develops his paper very well by carefully following the building blocks for writing a research paper. Included in the rest of the paper are diagrams for building these cars and their production, research on the amount of money a family of four would spend on gas per year, an analysis of gas costs versus electrical costs, and a cost analysis for electric cars versus traditional fuel burning. This project is very lengthy and very well done, and he followed the research paper building blocks.

Why Is the Sky Blue?

The sky is blue. There are clouds in the sky. Why does the sky have a blue color?

Middle School Research Paper Writing Sample: Proficient Introduction

Alternatives to Gas

The world revolves around fuel. Everybody needs fuel of some sort or another. We use gas to cook, and gas to drive our cars. Today, gas prices are going up and up. It doesn't look like they will ever stop. We need to find other fuel sources to drive our cars. Scientists have found many different ways to make fuel. Instead of finding different fuel types, why don't we just change the type of cars that we drive? How about driving an electric car to school? Electric cars have been around for a while now. How are electric cars made and how much money would a family save on gas by owning one?"

Section II

Drive or Walk

With the raise in gas lately I am walking everywhere. I don't get a ride to school anymore. Where will it stop? Is it going to cost more to pay for gas than to buy a car?

Gas prices have never been this high before in history. I think that gas prices might get up to 10.00 a gallon. It's going to cost more to put gas in a car than it will to buy the car. We should make smaller cars like they have in Europe. We don't need these very big luxury cars to get places. We need to conserve our fuel.

Just as our fourth-grade author who did not write a proficient example, our second middle school student made the same error. Right from the start he selected a topic that was too large and that could not be effectively researched (shown above).

Sometimes even middle school students can go astray when writing research papers. This student had some trouble at the beginning of his paper.

We hope that comparing the differences between a successful student writing sample and one that isn't helps you assess your own students' writing. How are your students doing writing their research papers?

Three Steps in Phase V: Publishing Phase

Research papers can make wonderful additions to the Kids Korner of your school library, especially if embellished with artwork to match the topic. A research paper is the perfect assignment for writing across the curriculum, connecting science or social studies concepts with literacy activities. When your students find they can choose the topic for their research, watch them get motivated!

In Summary: Research Writing

Yes, even young authors enjoy research. The key to teaching students to write successful research is getting them to find a topic that holds their interest. Is there a question that your students have a burning desire to find the answer to or an issue that they feel passionate about? When your students

Table 8.9   Three-Week Teaching Schedule for Research

	Monday	Tuesday	Wednesday	Thursday	Friday
Week 1	Vocabulary				
	Prewriting Strategies on Research Question				

	Monday	Tuesday	Wednesday	Thursday	Friday
Week 2	Vocabulary Review				
	Research: Sources and Notes	Research: Sources and Notes	Research: Sources and Notes	Record Notes on Blueprint in Proper Order	Writing the Draft

	Monday	Tuesday	Wednesday	Thursday	Friday
Week 3	Writing the Draft	Writing the Draft	Editing 1. Self-editing 2. Peer Editing	Editing 1. Teacher Conferencing 2. Final Copy Writing 3. Teacher Assessment	Publishing

are captivated by their topics in conjunction with BEW teaching strategies, they have a recipe for success. Follow the three-week schedule for teaching research projects we've included (Table 8.9). Remember to remain flexible, however. If your students need more time to research their topics, provide the necessary changes.

FEATURE: Research Paper Writing Prompts

Research projects are a great way to have your students write across the curriculum. Science and social studies are two subjects that lend themselves to providing interesting research papers. Formulate writing prompts around interesting lessons taught in these two subject areas, based on your state and local curriculum, and your students will experience great success in writing this genre.

Genre: Research Paper

Student Name _____   **Research Theme** _____

Who Is My Audience?
1. Exactly who will be my audience for this research paper? ☐ my peers   ☐ my teachers   ☐ my family   ☐ another group
2. My audience interest level on this topic is ☐ high interest level   ☐ moderate interest level   ☐ low interest level
3. My vocabulary should be ☐ very detailed   ☐ somewhat detailed   ☐ not detailed
4. Is there something about my audience that I should consider when writing my selection? ☐ yes   ☐ no

Genre: Research Paper

Student Name _____

Ready, Set, Go! Let's Research

1. Think of your research topic. What is it?

_____

_____

_____

2. Now write your research topic area of interest into a question. This becomes your *research question*.

_____

_____

_____

3. What three points or areas of investigation answer your research question best?

   1._____

   2._____

   3._____

Genre: Research Paper

Student Name _____

Topic _____ **Date** _____

State your research question.

_____ _____

_____ _____

Investigation One

_____
_____
_____
_____
_____
_____

Investigation Two

_____
_____
_____
_____
_____
_____
_____

Investigation Three

_____
_____
_____
_____
_____
_____
_____

Restate your research question and summarize your research points.

_____ _____ _____

CHAPTER 9

Poetry is like an artist's drawing. The words of a poem paint a picture filled with imagery that communicates the poet's innermost feelings. It's writing that uses the poet's imagination to create an intimate emotional link between the writer and the reader.

Poetry Writing

What Is Poetry?

Poetry is written art! Successful poets give insight to their most intimate feelings. Poetry challenges the author's ability to write concisely, use rhyme, rhythm, alliteration, and poetic diction. The old adage, *Everyone's a poet*, is absolutely true. Everyone has a poem inside of them just waiting to emerge.

Key: Poetry can take many different forms, such as ballad, limerick, haiku, cinquain, and blank and free verse, to name only a few.

When you're out on the playground with your students you can *hear poetry in the making*. Could it be that young children arrive with an inborn instinct for creating and understanding poetry? When you're outside with your children as they jump rope, notice how their voices echo a rhythmic beat. You know, that sing-song sound of moving rope followed by little feet touching the ground perfectly timed with their patter songs. In poetry we call it *rhythm*. When children play, they make up their own songs and sayings—and poetry emerges. Children have the ability to let their imaginations run unfettered. They think nothing of taking a standard song or rhythm and making it their own by adding their own words. And it is here that poetry is born. Somehow, however, this natural affinity gets lost at the classroom door and writing poetry as an assignment becomes a chore.

Poetry Building Blocks

Our students enter our classrooms daily with the most critical building block of poetry: their own imagination. It is our job to help them capture the essence of that childhood imagery on paper. Table 9.1 highlights the additional building blocks for writing great poetry.

Common Student Mistakes: What Poetry Is *Not*

Misunderstanding of Rhyme

Not: Your poem doesn't make sense with the rhyming words you've selected.

Oh! You mean it doesn't have to rhyme?

Almost all children come to school with the belief that poetry *must* rhyme. This isn't surprising because most childhood poetry from Mother Goose to Dr. Seuss *does* rhyme. Many students think that's all poetry is. Students who are unfamiliar with blank verse will listen to a poem that's being read to them and say, "Oh that's not any good. It doesn't even rhyme." Students need to be taught that poetry comes in more shapes, sizes, and forms than any other kind of literature. Expanding students' view of poetry beyond the couplets of simple nursery rhymes is necessary to help them write better poetry and become better poets.

Table 9.1   Poetry Building Blocks

Genre Purpose	To communicate the poet's innermost thoughts and feelings; writing that uses the poet's imagination to create an intimate emotional link between the writer and the reader
Building Block	1. *Rhyme:* repetition of similar sounds at given intervals 2. *Meter:* a combination of stressed and unstressed syllables in a line of poetry 3. *Poetic Diction:* the poet's use of vocabulary and writing style to communicate meaning 4. *Form:* the arrangement of words on the written page such as line, verse, and stanza
Genre Writing Techniques (elements of poetry)	1. *Similes:* making a comparison using the words *like* or *as* 2. *Metaphors:* comparison of two objects that are completely different 3. *Alliteration:* repeating consonants in words that are adjacent in a line 4. *Personification:* giving animals or inanimate objects human characteristics 5. *Rhyme Scheme:* understanding the pattern of rhyme in a type of poem and using that pattern when writing in that style
Genre Format and Voice	1. Concise wording to communicate meaning 2. Understanding the various formats or forms of each type of poetry 3. Painting a mood or feeling with words

A Can't-Do Mind-set

Yes, you can write poetry!

I didn't think I could write it but I did.

You'll find many students who feel they just can't write poetry. They're really not even willing to try. Have you encountered these students in your teaching career? Students who have this type of attitude tend to be unaware of the variety of types of poems covered by the poetry genre. Well, unlock the poet inside of them by reading a wide variety of different kinds of poetry in class. They'll soon get beyond rhyming as the key characteristic of poetry!

So, Why Teach Poetry?

Poetry is definitely a unique genre to teach. If you're asking yourself, "Why should I teach poetry anyway?" the correct answer isn't because it's part of our state benchmarks. It turns out that unlike other genres, learning to write poetry has some definite advantages for our students that will enhance their general reading and writing abilities. Poetry helps our students

- Learn to choose specific, carefully thought-out vocabulary words
- Use voice in their writing across all genres
- Get in touch with their senses
- Write concisely
- Express their emotions through writing
- Learn about parts of speech in an interactive way using, for example, metaphors and similes

In addition, poetry is a great way to teach writing to our at-risk student population because poems are shorter than stories. Special needs, at-risk, and our ELL students often have a short attention span for reading. Poems are short and will hold their interest. The fact that poems can be short also helps with writing. Because of this, many of our special needs students can channel their creativity and find comfort in writing in this genre as opposed to others.

Teach the Genre Using BEW Phases

Three Steps in Phase I: Authentic Vocabulary

Step 1: Written Expression Vocabulary

Phase I in BEW describes methods for teaching authentic vocabulary. Don't forget to teach the BEW Big Ten words we described in the vocabulary phase (Chapter 1). Because there are many different types of poetry, this genre's vocabulary teaching unit can be very expansive and will vary depending upon the type of poetry that you are teaching. Only teach the specific vocabulary words that are relevant to the type of poetry that students are currently writing. Build on these vocabulary words throughout the year. The following includes examples of some basic poetry vocabulary words that every student should be familiar with.

Professor Write's Interactive Teaching Strategy

Teaching Poetry Vocabulary Words

1. Genre

Say: "Today we will talk about poetry. Poetry is really like art. It paints a picture for you with words instead of colors. This genre appeals directly to your emotions and challenges you to share your feelings with your audience."

Teach: Start your poetry unit instruction by reading various poems to your students. These poems should serve as a model for the type of poetry that your students will soon create. Some of your students may not have heard the type of poetry that you're teaching. Familiarize them with great poems.

Audience: When you write poetry, you hope that whoever reads the poem understands the picture that you paint with your words. This genre is really an interpretation of your own personal view of an event or sensation. That's what makes this genre special.

Teach: Poetry is your imagination run wild. It's your chance to turn everyday ordinary events into the extraordinary. You must let your imagination soar. Of course, children usually don't have much difficulty in this area.

2. Poetic diction

Teach: When you write a poem, you don't usually use as many words as you do when you write an essay, and you write these words in a certain style. So every word that you put in your poem has to be selected carefully, because it helps draw the picture you have in your mind.

Background: An important part of this lesson is helping your students visualize a picture of what they want to say in their poem, then describe in words what they see in their mind. This is *imagery*. Can they describe what it looks like, smells like, feels like? Can they do this in a way to match the rhyme and rhythm that needs to be in their poem? Finding just the right word is poetic diction.

Step 2: Conventions and Grammar Vocabulary

Each and every genre requires different building blocks. When you plan your poetry genre unit, recognize that there are many types of poems, each with their own requirements. This is what makes a poetry unit such a fun and enjoyable genre to teach. There are many different types of poetry, and the form involved in writing each type of poetry is unique. Will it have three lines like a haiku, or five like a cinquain or limerick? Will it have multiple stanzas and a refrain, like a ballad? A diamante poem, for instance, is written in such a way that it looks like a diamond when complete. Students must understand these elements to recognize poetry when they see it in written form.

Elements of Poetry

Teach: When we write poetry, we put our words together in very special ways to help paint a vivid word picture. We want our audience to see our topic the same way we do, so we have to say it in a special way. Your students will experiment with different words in their poems until they can find just the right word they need. There are many special ways to describe people and objects in poems. These are called *elements of poetry*.

Background: Teach the different elements of poetry to your students, modeling them and practicing them with your topic and type of poetry.

Similes: A simile is when one thing is compared with another thing using the words *like* or *as*. This can help the audience picture just what the author is picturing. For example, *The branches of the tree are like a gigantic umbrella,* or *The lake was as smooth as glass.*

Metaphors: Another powerful way to compare your topic with something else is to say it *without* using *like* or *as*. For example, *Your words were the sword that wounded my heart.* This is called a *metaphor.*

Alliteration: Sometimes you will want to write your poem in a way that some of the words stand out as more important than the others. You can do that with alliteration—when several of the key words in a line repeat the same sound. For example, "*I saw a simple seesaw.*"

Personification: You use personification when you write words that say that an animal or object does something as if it were a person. For example, *The wind whistled a sad song.*

Rhyme Scheme: While teaching elements of poetry, it's good to remind students about rhyme scheme, if that is part of their poetry type. Rhyme happens at the end of a line. If students study a model of their type of poem, they can label the rhyme scheme using an alphabetic abbreviation. A letter is used to represent a line. A repeated letter represents lines that rhyme. In a couplet, the rhyme scheme is *aa,* because both lines rhyme. For example, a couplet from Edgar Allan Poe's poem "The Raven" says, "Once upon a midnight dreary, as I pondered weak and weary." After they have practiced the rhyme scheme, then they can work with their ideas and construct a poem with a similar rhyme scheme.

Step 3: General Vocabulary

The precision of the words used in poetry is an important element in this genre. All children can learn to use poetic diction when it is taught at their level. Using the Web of Words concept to expand your students' writing vocabulary is the answer. Create many Webs of Words with vocabulary built on your class writing topic. Student vocabulary and poetic word selection will be enhanced by this exercise. A vocabulary-rich environment will give your students word selection choices when they need to find just the *right* word to write. The Web of Words can be used to build skills related to this building block of poetry. It helps students find and select the precise word phrases that are required for poetry (see Table 9.2).

Table 9.2   Poetry Word Choice and Vocabulary Builder

Building Block Element for Poetry Usage	Definition
Alliteration	This technique occurs when one of the leading sounds of a word is repeated, such as **R**obert **r**abbit **r**oamed **a**round
Assonance	This technique occurs when the vowel sound in the middle of a word is repeated in the middle of a second word, such as *tune* and *spoon*
Diction	Vocabulary usage and word order are key here. Diction changes the order of a sentence and makes it more complex. For example, look at the sentence: *He fell down while skating.* Let's use more expressive vocabulary and change the word order of this sentence to create a more interesting format. *While rambunctiously skating on the ice rink, he lost his balance, sliding fast and furiously to a dead stop at the wall.* Note the order change and new vocabulary used in sentence two. That's diction!
Imagery	This technique asks the readers to form a concrete mental image of the event, person, place, or time that the author has described. Imagery is a visual image that the author paints, much like an artist. Look at this fourth-grade student example of poetry: *Oh, the forest* *Quiet wonder,* *Woods and rivers, streams and flowers,* *Seas of leaves, petals and weeds.* Now that's imagery.
Irony	This technique says the opposite of what is in the speaker's mind. The audience usually knows what is meant. For example, an ironic statement might be, *"It's OK; I like to wear my dinner,"* by somebody who has just had their dinner dumped into their lap by a clumsy waiter.

Five Steps in Phase II: Prewriting

You may be asking yourself: How do I motivate my students to write poetry? The answer is simple! Prewriting strategies are the key to having your students produce exciting poetry.

Step 1: Multisensory Experiences

Because there is a definite relationship between the poet's senses and the written poem, set the stage for these experiences. Create literacy boxes and bags that relate to your class poetry topics. Let your students share these experiences together. Turn the ordinary into the extraordinary through your senses.

Anyone ready for a field trip? Real-life field trips, especially to museums and parks, where art and nature can be experienced, are great ways to give students opportunities for adventure that can be written in poetic form. Awaken your students' senses by giving them a Sensory Log (see Student Worksheet 9.1 at the end of this chapter) to take with them on the trip. As they go from experience to experience, have them record their feelings and thoughts in the log while each experience is fresh in their mind.

Step 2: Wheel of Thought

If you're just beginning your poetry teaching adventure, try focusing on an element of nature as a beginning topic with your students. Nature provides a great basis for using creative language and imagery in poetic form. Not only that, everyone can relate to one element or another of nature. Begin your poetry Wheel of Thought by writing *Things of Nature* in the center circle. Ask your students to reflect on special times they've had with nature and then quickly record their ideas on the rays of the Wheel of Thought.

After you have helped them to develop their personal topic based on nature, let them write that topic in the center of their personal Wheel of Thought. They need to write their specific feelings or thoughts about that event or activity in the rays on the wheel. Ask them questions to stimulate their visual images and what they heard or felt.

Step 3: Genre Format and Voice

There are many types of poetry that are written by elementary and middle school students. Your school curriculum and state standards will act as a guide for teaching the types of poetry expected for your grade level. Genre format and voice instruction will depend on the type of poetry being taught. Each of the building blocks should be demonstrated to your students by reading them poems in each poetry type. Your students will then start to mimic these forms when creating their own poetry.

The specific genre format and voice taught will reflect the structure of the type of poem you're teaching. Adapt the BEW Professor Write teaching strategies according to the specific type of poem that you are teaching. For example, the format and structure given for a limerick will be different

ELL–BEWCONNECTION

Appealing to the senses is a great way for ELL students to connect to the world around them. Create poems that are related to the senses.

from that of a ballad. See Table 9.3, which describes some of the different types of poetry taught in grades K through 8.

Table 9.3 Types of Poetry Taught in Grades K through 8

Types of Poetry	Unique Elements
Acrostic	With this type of poetry, the first letter of each line spells a word vertically. This is a unique feature that students love to work with.
Ballad	The topic for this type of poetry is usually folklore or legends. Ballads also tend to be romantic. A ballad often has a stanza that is repeated, called a *refrain*. That is why ballads are frequently set to music. Ballads have a rhythmic meter that is most often iambic. Typically, the second and fourth lines rhyme.
Cinquain	This is an unrhymed poem. It's a great poem to teach parts of speech. Young poets can really have fun with this one. It has five lines, gradually increasing the number of words in each line from one to four with the last line back to one and with specific types of words in each line.
Clerihew	This type of poetry is about a person or character. It is a silly verse that usually has two couplets with an *aabb* rhyme scheme. The format is easy. 1. A person or character is named 2. A characteristic of the person is stated (end rhyme scheme with line 1) 3. A second characteristic is stated 4. A third characteristic is stated (end rhyme scheme with line 3) This is also a favorite of young poets.
Diamante	This is a very structured type of poetry with words that form a diamond shape when written on paper. This is also an excellent type of poetry to teach parts of speech to upper elementary and middle school students. It is a good format for contrasting two opposing words.
Didactic	This type of poem teaches a lesson.
Epic	This is a type of narrative poetry that tells a story about a hero.

(continued)

Section II

Fable	Everybody has heard of Aesop's Fables. These are great examples of fables to read to your kids. These poems are written to teach a lesson. The main characters of a fable are usually animals.
Free Verse	Beginning middle school poets quickly catch on to the methods for writing free-verse poetry. This type of poetry doesn't use rhyme or a patterned rhythm. The lines are written to match natural pauses in reading. It is rich in word choice, mood, and feeling.
Haiku	These are favorite poems for many grades. Their subjects are usually those of nature and the poem is written in the past tense. They follow a traditional Japanese pattern of unrhymed lines. The first line has five syllables, the second line has seven syllables, and the third and last lines have five syllables. There are seventeen syllables in all.
Limerick	A limerick is a funny poem that is typically nonsense. It has a specific rhyme scheme. The rhyme is *aabba*. It also has a distinctive meter.
Monorhyme	This type of poem is one that all children recognize and enjoy writing. It has an end rhyme scheme that is the same for all lines.
Ode	An ode is a lyric poem, usually of some length, that is written to praise a person or object. It has no fixed rhyme scheme, and it uses rich and intense expressions.
Quatrain	This type of poem has four lines (or four-line stanzas) with a special rhyme scheme (*abab*).
Song	This type of poetry is sung! It has lyrics or lines that are sung and a refrain that's repeated just like a song (see *ballad*).
Sonnet	This type of poetry is usually identified with Shakespeare. It has fourteen lines with an iambic pentameter meter and a distinctive rhyming scheme.
Tongue Twister	This type of poem is one young authors love to listen to. It has lines that are difficult to say aloud, because of its use of alliteration. Oh yes, and it doesn't have to rhyme.

Professor Write's Interactive Teaching Strategy

Genre Format and Voice: Poetry Format

Materials: Show a poem of the type you want your students to write. Use an overhead projector to display that type of poem so that your students can see the written format.

Say: "Poetry has many different formats. Today we're going to learn about basic poetry format or, simply, how it's written. Just as narratives are written in sentences and paragraphs, poetry is written in lines."

Teach: Students will need to understand that many types of poetry are written as lines across the page. Lines of poetry don't have to be a complete sentence; they can be phrases or parts of a sentence. Each new line in a poem starts with a capital letter.

Your students already have an understanding of a paragraph in writing. Showing the connection between paragraphs in prose and stanzas in poetry will increase their awareness of this type of format.

Background: As you teach various types of poetry to your class, use the Professor Write strategies (teach, model, practice) to instruct the necessary vocabulary words for that type of poetry. For example, vocabulary related to lyric poetry will be different than structured cinquain poems. The vocabulary words that you teach will vary based on the type of poetry that you are teaching.

Say: "Lyric or verse poetry is often based on something called a *couplet*. This is a pair of lines that rhyme."

Demonstrate: Read some examples of couplets that you've written, students have written, or others have published. Students will hear the concept of the end rhyme scheme when a couplet is read to them (see Student Worksheet 9.2 at the end of this chapter).

There are many, many different types of poetry within this genre. You will probably choose a type related to those you are reading in your literacy series or in your curriculum. Therefore, you will need to learn the specific conventions and grammar of that type of poetry. One thing is for sure, if you follow the teaching style outlined by Professor Write (teach, model, practice), your students will have a thorough understanding of each and every genre element that you teach!

Key: For samples of different types of poetry to share with your students, go to www.shadowpoetry.com/resources/wip/types.html.

Step 4: Blueprint Note Taking

No matter what type of poetry you're teaching, have your students write down their notes in a poetry Blueprint. Specialty Blueprints, as well as a generic one, are included as Student Worksheets 9.3 through 9.6 at the end of this chapter.

Step 5: Talking Paragraphs

Yes, we recommend using talking paragraphs even with poetry writing. After students have written their ideas into notes on the Blueprint, they can practice putting them into lines and speaking them aloud to a peer. The peer can listen and give ideas regarding whether the word picture is a good one or whether it matches the rhyme scheme or rhythm that is needed with the style of poetry they are writing. The peer can clap the measure, for example, to check whether the number of beats is correct for a haiku or the number and type of words is correct for a cinquain. At this time, your students will *hear* their poems and revise them if needed. They only need to change their notes on the Blueprint, rather than rewrite a whole draft, which is the next phase.

Two Steps in Phase III: Writing

Step 1: Draft Writing

Using all their assembled notes, logs, and ideas, students should now compose their poems on paper in their Rough Draft Writing Folders. As with other genres, support each student in writing during this phase. Model writing a poem from Blueprint notes, whether it is one of your own or your student's. Writing will be a breeze.

Step 2: Title Writing

Titles of poems reflect the topic or the message the poet is communicating to the reader. A poem's title should mirror the uniqueness of the poem itself. The key in writing effective titles for poems is creativity. Students should write the titles for their selections last, because this will help them write titles influenced by the actual words of the poem. The BEW title-writing strategies (Chapter 3) work just as well for poems as they do for other writing selections.

Five Steps in Phase IV: Authentic Editing

Steps 1 through 3: Editing

ELL–BEWCONNECTION

ELL students require immediate feedback for correcting writing. Use the three steps of the BEW editing phase to provide them with this feedback.

Just as with the other three genres we include in this book, students should create an authentic editing rubric with you for the poems that they've composed. This rubric must include student entries in three important areas of assessment:

1. Vocabulary and Word Usage
2. Genre Format and Voice
3. Grammar and Conventions

198

The specific class-generated rubric will be constructed relative to the type of poem that is being written. For example, if your class is writing a cinquain, the genre format and voice category of the rubric must include items like: "Did I use five lines?" and "Do I have the right number of words in each line (1, 2, 3, 4, 1)? Does each line express the correct part of speech?" Students will mimic back to you all the genre format and voice elements and building blocks that you've taught them, and that they, hopefully, have included in their poems. This authentic editing rubric will change with each and every type of poetry that your class creates, according to its characteristics. This class-generated rubric will be used for self-editing, peer editing, and teacher–student conferencing. Each authentic editing rubric will reflect the type of poetry taught and will include the specific format and language that you have worked on with your students. This is critical for teacher assessment.

Step 4: Final Copy Writing

After the three steps of editing are complete, students will move on to writing their final copies. Many middle school and upper elementary students like to type and print their poetry on specialty papers. For example, one of our middle school students wrote a poem about mountain climbing and found paper with mountains highlighted in the background. This was the perfect artistic touch for portraying a mountaintop adventure. Let your students show their creativity in developing an artistic format for their final creations.

Step 5: Teacher Assessment

Assessment of this genre is somewhat different than the assessment of other genres. A great deal of the assessment will depend on whether the student followed the rules for the specific poetry type as reflected in the rubric. For example, did the poem have the correct number of lines and follow the correct form for that type of poem? Did the student follow the correct building blocks? However, because poetry is so artistic in nature, there are other elements that enter into the assessment. We recommend that you pay particular attention to the oral presentation of student poetry to assess the emotional impact that the poem has on both you and the students in the class. Any evaluation of poetry needs to rely at least partially on the instinctive appeal the poem has to the audience.

Student Examples

If you're new to the venue of teaching poetry in the K-through-eighth-grade student arena, you must be wondering: What type of poetry can a student write? Well, the sky is the limit. Student poetry depends on your students' ability to relate to their senses in a spectacular way. We offer a set of student-written poems for you to enjoy, all of which we consider proficient writing. Nature is a topic

ELL–BEWCONNECTION

ELL students quickly learn through modeling. Allow students to hear and see the poetry of others!

for poetry that usually results in excellent student examples. Read the fourth-grade student's poem (below left), "Oh, The Forest," as he conveys the *wonders of the forest* that he sees. He uses imagery beautifully to communicate his vision of the forest.

Again, nature is the setting for another poem written about the forest by a fifth-grade student (below right). This short, well-written poem communicates the presence of wildlife and fish in the forest. He sets a somewhat whimsical tone by his word choice and text placement of fish-and-hook lines. What a great job!

Fourth-Grade Poetry Sample

Oh, The Forest

Oh, the forest
Quiet wonder,
Woods and rivers, streams and flowers,
Seas of leaves, petals and weeds,
Going on and on.
Deer and wolf, fox and hawk
All call the forest home.
Gentle forest, how you awe me,
Wind playing tunes upon the trees.
The acorn falls, the birds call,
All is peaceful,
All is beautiful here.

Fifth-Grade Poetry Sample

The Forest

As the elk go ambling by
The eagles patrol the sky.
And the wolves down on the ground,
Are waiting, not making a sound.
And the fish in the brook,
Avoiding the fisher's hook,
Upon the sky look,
As the trees are swaying The Forest

200

Let's explore nature and its related experiences one more time with this fourth-grade student as he writes about seasons (below left). We can see that this student is definitely in touch with his senses.

Let's look at a different style of poetry written by a fourth-grade student (below right). He writes about Petey Bill for his selection. This poem just puts a smile on your face. Petey Bill is an example of pure imagination gone wild. Are your students writing poems like Petey Bill?

Fourth-Grade Poetry Sample

Seasons

When flowers begin to blossom,
When birds begin to sing,
When the moon gets all sullen
Because the sun takes up too much day,
Then I know that it is spring.

When the sun is burning,
When flowers are all abloom,
When the bullfrogs are a-calling,
Then I know it is summer.

When trees lose their green glory,
When acorns all fall down,
When the horses all do frolic,
Then I know it's truly fall.

When the birds are gone,
When snow falls gently down,
When bears are in their slumber,
Then I know that winter is here.

Fourth-Grade Poetry Sample

The Legend of Petey Bill

Petey Bill, he saved the day;
He really chased the clouds away.
When a dragon came to Petey's town,
He chased it up, he chased it down.
Then, finally, with a level head,
He sent the dragon home to bed!

Petey Bill, he met a witch,
But not a hair did Petey twitch!
His quite large mouth he opened wide
Showing the witch all the teeth inside;
Then, finally, with a level head,
He filled the witch with lots of dread!

Petey Bill, he met a ghost,
He stopped and looked and ate his toast.
When he was finished, with a level head,
He looked up and "BOO!" he said.
The ghost ran away and is running still,
And all this thanks to Petey Bill!

Three Steps in Phase V: Publishing Phase

Do you have a Parent–Teacher Conference Day coming up? Parents love to walk down the halls and see student poetry hanging on the walls. Another idea is to have student poems written and read out loud at an American Legion for Veterans Day, or at a senior center for a Grandparents Day Gathering.

ELL–BEWCONNECTION

ELL students may excel in poetry writing because poems can be short in length, but meaningful!

In Summary: Poetry Writing

Everyone can be a poet! All your students can find a type of poem that has a style that matches their own creative expressions. Be sure they have many opportunities to hear a variety of styles of poems. Capture that talent with young authors. Develop it as they move from elementary to middle school. If you're uncertain about the daily teaching schedule that we recommend for teaching poetry, look at our teaching chart. Allow students to add artwork, fancy lettering, or other creative touches as they publish their poems. Your poetry units will help you to see new aspects of your students that you never saw before.

Table 9.8   Two-Week Teaching Schedule for Poetry Writing

	Monday	Tuesday	Wednesday	Thursday	Friday
Week 1	Vocabulary	Vocabulary Review	Vocabulary Review	Vocabulary Review	Vocabulary Review
	Prewriting Strategies Multisensory Experiences				Prewriting Strategies Blueprint Note Taking
	Monday	**Tuesday**	**Wednesday**	**Thursday**	**Friday**
Week 2	Vocabulary Review	Vocabulary Review	Vocabulary Review	Vocabulary Review	Vocabulary Review
	Writing the Draft	Writing the Draft	Editing 1. Self-editing 2. Peer Editing	Editing 1. Teacher Conferencing 2. Final Copy Writing 3. Teacher Assessment	Publishing

WRITING TIPS

Writing Tips: Poetry

- Be sure to read aloud multiple examples of the type of poetry that you want your students to write.

- Display examples of the poetry style on posters for students to use as a pattern.

- Allow students to share their poems with other students when their final selections are finished. A *poetry slam* is a great way to share student selections.

FEATURE: Poetry Writing Prompts

If you're wondering what topic you should pick for your students to begin writing, *Back to Nature* is the best bet! Here are some additional ideas.

1. Wait for the first big thunderstorm of the season. The time is right for a poem. Ask your students to describe the sights, sounds, and emotions that the thunderstorm aroused in them. Students should describe this storm using the poetry format that you're teaching.

2. A change of seasons makes a fantastic topic for poetry. On the day of the first snow, have your students look outside the classroom window. Write a poem about the first snowfall of the year.

3. How about fall? Wait for a windy fall day and ask your students to look outside your classroom window. Ask them what signs of fall they see. Have them write a fall poem based on the type of poetry that you're currently teaching.

4. Try a *window observation strategy* for a topic. Ask your students to look outside the classroom window and focus on one object intently. Just as an artist would draw a picture of that object, tell them to paint a picture with their words that describes the object within the poetry format that you're teaching.

5. *Pocket poetry* topics are great fun! Have your students reach into their pockets and pull out one object. Tell them to write a silly poem describing where that object came from using the format that you're currently teaching in class.

6. Plan an outside walk around the neighborhood. Tell the students to put on their "sensory hats" and be aware of their environment. Let them bring their Sensory Log with them. Ask

them to focus on something special in the neighborhood, record notes, and then write a poem about their experience.

7. Take a field trip to the zoo. Have your students focus on one animal they saw at the zoo and write a poem describing this animal. Don't forget to have them bring their Sensory Log with them.

8. Ask students to write a poem about something they want more than anything in the world. It can be an object or an excursion. Have them write a poem about this using the type of format that you're teaching.

9. Tell students to write a poem about what they would do if they won a million dollars. Details are the key here. They can write the poem in a realistic way or perhaps even something silly.

10. Students can write a poem about something that they crave on a cold winter's day when they're walking to school. Describe it in concise, vivid language, according to the type of poem that your class is writing.

11. Give your students a daily word. Ask them to write a poem incorporating all the words that rhyme with that word. Specify a type of poem or special end rhyme scheme.

12. Do *grab bag poetry* for a change. Fill a brown paper bag with common objects. Ask your students to pick one object out of the bag. Tell them to turn the ordinary into the extraordinary. Have them write about the object that they've selected from the brown bag.

13. Have students write synonym–antonym poetry lines for a challenge. Students should write down a word and then a synonym for that word. Then, tell them to write a word of opposite meaning. Write a poem of opposites.

14. Have students write about themselves. Have them write a poem about how they are feeling that very moment!

15. Have your students pick a classmate and write a poem as if they were that other person. Share the poems with the class.

16. Have your students write a poem from the perspective of their favorite pet. Make sure they follow the format that you're teaching in class.

17. Pick a song, any song that your students know. Have your students change the words, keeping to the rhythm and beat of the melody. Young poets just love this one.

Genre: Poetry Writing

Student Name _____ **Topic** _____

Place where you are recording information:

_____

_____

Are there any special sounds that stand out in your mind?

_____

_____

How about any interesting sights?

_____

_____

Is there a special aroma?

_____

_____

How does this place make you feel?

_____

_____

What will you remember most about this place? Why?

_____

_____

Will you visit it again?

_____

_____

Genre: Poetry Writing

Student Name _____ **Poem Topic** _____

Key Word	Key Word	Key Word	Key Word	Key Word
Rhyming Words	Rhyming Words	Rhyming Words	Rhyming Words	Rhyming Words

Genre: Poetry Writing

Student Name _____ **Poem Topic** _____

Line	Word Count	Word Type	Your Words
1	One word	Noun: title or name of subject	
2	Two words	Adjectives: describing the title	
3	Three words	Verbs: describing action related to title	
4	Four words	Describe a feeling about the title	
5	One word	Refer back to the title of the poem	

Section II

HAIKU BLUEPRINT

Genre: Poetry Writing

Student Name _____ **Poem Topic** _____

Mood for your poem: _____

Line	Number of Syllables or Beats	Your Words
1	Five	
2	Seven	
3	Five	

Genre: Poetry Writing

Student Name _____ **Poem Topic** _____

Line	Number of Words	Your Words	Your Words
1	One	Noun (contrasting to line 7)	
2	Two	Adjectives (describing line 1)	
3	Three	Action verbs (relating to line 1)	
4	Four	Nouns (first two relating to line 1, last two relating to line 7)	
5	Three	Action verbs (describing line 7)	
6	Two	Adjectives (describing line 7)	
7	One	Noun (contrasting to line 1)	

Hint: Pick the two nouns you want to contrast and fill in lines 1 and 7 first.

Section II

DIAMANTE BLUEPRINT

Genre: Poetry Writing

Student Name _____ **Poem Topic** _____

Understanding and composing a written response to reading assists students in developing analytical higher order thinking and writing skills. The IRA frequently states this goal as a writing objective. Performing this task is not usually considered a genre on its own; however, because of the importance of this type of writing, effective teaching strategies need to be discussed. Here, students are asked to compare and contrast different texts, finding similarities and differences.

Response to Reading

What Is Response to Reading?

As you read the daily newspaper I'm sure that you have a reaction to certain articles that you read. Some may make you laugh whereas others may enrage you. A well-written article or story definitely elicits an emotional response! You might not realize it, but everyone who reads, watches television, or sees a great film has a reaction to it. Think about it! When you read a great nonfiction book or see a fantastic movie, if you're not happy with the ending you feel like shouting, "That's not right!"

It makes you want to rewrite the ending! Response to reading on a theme or question allows the writer an outlet to state this kind of opinion. The writer substantiates this viewpoint with evidence gleaned from the reading selections. With the BEW process *response to reading* is defined as a writing selection that requires the author to form an opinion on a proposed topic or prompt and then write a response based on that opinion, incorporating concepts from the reading selections to support the opinion.

To lay the appropriate building foundation to be successful in this writing endeavor, the author must know and understand the purpose of this writing process:

1. The first purpose is to form an opinion on the writing prompt question.

2. The second purpose is to back up that opinion in a logical way with information from the reading.

Key: Students may be asked to respond to reading selections based on a central theme or question. In different states this type of writing may be called *response to literature* or *cross-text writing* or a *review of literature in higher education*; however, the same type of format and teaching strategies are applicable. Student responses may be requested on reading selections from different genres. For example, one reading selection could be a narrative story and the other a poem. On the other hand, both selections could be from the same genre.

Response to Reading Building Blocks

What are the building blocks for composing a *response to reading* writing assignment? There are three key building blocks for students to learn.

The first building block used as the foundation for successful completion of this type of student writing begins with critical reading skills. The student must have the ability to read and comprehend the theme of the selections that are to be used for supporting a stated position.

The second building block is the ability to formulate an opinion or position statement in response to the question or writing prompt. These prompts are usually thematic or current event oriented.

The third and last building block is weaving the theme through the writing selection while supporting the author's position. In other words, the author must be able to show a connection between the two reading selections that supports his or her stated opinion. The theme must be woven through the selection like thread through a tapestry (see Table 10.1).

Table 10.1   Response to Reading Building Blocks

Writing Purpose	To increase students' analytical and higher order thinking skills
Building Block Features	1. Using reading skills to comprehend the selections 2. Understanding the question or writing prompt 3. Forming an opinion on the question or writing prompt 4. Supporting the opinion with details from both reading selections
Format and Voice	1. *Introduction:* Respond to the writing prompt question by affirmation or disagreement and then restate it clearly as a position statement 2. *Detailed Paragraphs:* Usually two detailed paragraphs at a minimum are required. Detail paragraph 1 supports the position statement by giving examples from reading 1. Detail paragraph 2 supports the position statement by giving examples from reading 2. 3. *Summary:* Restating the question and the author's position using the titles of the readings; restating the connection between the readings and giving some new level of thinking or learning based on the readings.

Common Student Mistakes: What Response to Reading Is *Not*

Writing a Summary

> *Not:* Don't just write story summaries!

> *Oh, no, it's not a summary!*

A common student mistake is that students simply retell the story much like a summary without answering the proposed question. They may have every detail written down, the story in perfect chronological order, and it could even be extremely well written; however, there is no connection to the question that has been asked. It's like asking somebody what they think about the Blue Jays and having the person respond with a complete history of the team. Although that information could prove interesting, it isn't what was asked!

Providing Story Details

Not: Don't just give an opinion!

Oh, no! You mean I was supposed to tell details from the story?

Many times students just answer the writing prompt with no reference to the readings. They just give their opinion based on their own feelings or experiences. This is not the desired response. Students must use examples and details from both stories that are well developed and clearly written in this type of writing response.

Giving Equal Time to Reading Selections

Not: Don't use just one story!

Oh, no! I was supposed to use details from both stories equally?

When students are given two reading selections that relate to a prompt, many students have a tendency to expand on the reading selection that is their favorite. Both reading selections must be given equal treatment in the writing selection. In addition, the argument should be constructed in a logical, easy-to-follow format, with details and examples from each reading selection. Students should make a new Rough Draft Writing Folder for every response to reading assignment.

Teach Response to Reading Using BEW Phases

Three Steps in Phase I: Authentic Vocabulary Phase

Step 1: Written Expression Vocabulary

In Phase I of BEW, we describe how to teach authentic vocabulary words. Begin by reviewing the Big Ten vocabulary in the generic BEW process as explained in Chapter 1. In addition, teach the words that label this writing selection. Teach the concept of responding in writing to a theme that they have read in specific stories.

Professor Write's Interactive Teaching Strategy

Teaching Response to Reading

1. Response to reading

Say: "Today we will talk about response to reading. This is a writing assignment that answers a question where you agree or disagree with a basic idea and support it with evidence from the reading selections. I want to know what you think!"

Teach: Before you practice this concept with actual reading assignments, conduct a quick teaching lesson using movies that your students know. This activity will teach these basic principles quickly and easily. For example, create a writing prompt such as, "Everyone has a hero to look up to. Do you agree or disagree?" Justify your answer by using examples from the movies *Superman Returns* and *Spiderman*.

Do: Draw two columns on the board and list the ways that the main characters are heroes in the movie and list the characters that look up to them. Relate this data back to the writing prompt, "Everyone has a hero to look up to."

Teach: The objective is to teach your students to respond to a key concept (or theme) that they can identify or talk about from the selected readings. They are looking for how the two movies (or stories, poems, and so forth) are alike or connected to the theme. This is such an important skill. Conduct a class discussion on the points your students share with you. Now that your students understand the concept relating to an experience that is part of their world (a movie), they can relate the same concepts to the selected readings.

2. Opinion

Say: "All of you have an opinion about topics or events. A response to reading essay requires that you write how you feel about the topic asked."

Do: Conduct a class discussion about your students' opinions on various age-appropriate topics. Draw a connection between the opinions that they have just expressed and the opinions they will be asked for in the response to reading.

> **TIP:** Some states use this type of writing in their high-stakes testing. If your state requires students to identify differences in reading selections as well, repeat this same teaching principle with a class discussion that focuses on contrasting concepts.

Step 2: Conventions and Grammar

The basic principles for grammar and conventions hold true in writing this type of selection. Make sure you check your state standards to include all those that are grade appropriate. General grammar rules hold true.

ELL students may not have a sufficient understanding of the required vocabulary to complete this assignment. Teach specific vocabulary words associated with this type of writing.

TIP: A good, dependable thesaurus written at your students' appropriate grade level will enhance this process.

Step 3: General Vocabulary

General vocabulary building strategies used in response to reading must include a knowledge base of words that are frequently used during this process. There are specific trigger words used in reading selections and writing strategies that actually alert the reader to a comparison that is just ahead. These words are significant words that must become a part of your students' vocabulary.

How do you teach these words? Through our Web of Words teaching strategy. Create a Web of Words on art roll paper and display it in front of your classroom. Ask students to think of synonyms for each word and write them on the graphic organizer.

Start with the word *compare*. Ask your students to think of synonyms for the word *compare* and write them down in your Web of Words. Then create a chart using the words suggested by your class and pass them out to each of your students (see Table 10.2). Have the students place the chart in their Rough Draft Writing Folders. These synonyms can also be used as transition words and phrases in this type of writing and will enrich the writing quality. All children can learn to use specific transition words and phrases when they are taught at an appropriate grade level. Specific transition words or phrases give the reader a clue that similarities or differences are being discussed. The degree of language sophistication will depend on your grade level. (If your curriculum standards include the term *contrast,* follow the same procedure with another Web of Words using synonyms for *contrast.* Create a chart and give it to your students to place in their Rough Draft Writing Folders.)

Table 10.2   Comparing Trigger Words and Phrases

in the same way
at the same time
similar
like
likewise
resembling
akin

Five Steps in Phase II: Prewriting

Step 1: Multisensory Experiences

One way to have students understand similarities in text and respond to them is to have students read the story or text and then, if a movie version of the same story is available, watch it. Students can then experience two different versions of the same story and write about it.

If possible, have students take field trips that are story related. Remember, cyber trips are a great way to give students these experiences as well.

Step 2: Wheel of Thought

During this step, two Wheels of Thought will work wonders to increase students' understanding of the story line to answer the proposed question. First, write the question on the board. Then ask those students who agree and those who disagree with the writing prompt to form two groups. Have students in each group complete a Wheel of Thought—one on story A and one on story B—according to their group's opinion. Ask each group to elect a student spokesperson. Have each student spokesperson present their group's Wheel of Thought to the class. Later, when students begin to take their individual notes, place these Wheels of Thought in clear view for the class.

Step 3: Genre Format and Voice

It's time to start teaching your students the building blocks for a response to reading. After your students learn each of these elements, they will use them to construct their assignments and write them in the proper format. The format that we use in the BEW process involves our Blueprint.

Professor Write's Interactive Teaching Strategy

Teaching Genre Format and Voice

1. The purpose of the introduction paragraph

Ask: While pointing to the oval shape on a class response to reading Blueprint, ask your students, "What shape is this?"

The students will answer, "It's an oval."

"What type of paragraph does the oval represent?"

The students should answer, "The introduction or beginning."

"What is the job of the introduction or beginning in a response to reading?"

"It introduces your topic and tells your opinion."

"To follow our writing Blueprint correctly, we must also look at the size or how long our introduction or beginning will be in comparison with the rest of the story. How big is an introduction or beginning? Medium size [and ask students to show you with their hands]."

Teach: The introduction paragraph of a response to reading must identify the topic and state the author's position. It must start with general thoughts on the topic and end with identifying the specific opinion of the author and naming the titles of the literacy selections that have been read.

(continued)

2. The topic sentence

Ask: "What type of sentence should the introduction or beginning start with?"

"A topic sentence" will be their response.

Teach: Topic sentences are very important because they act as a *hook* to draw the reader into the argument. A great topic sentence is essential in a response to reading.

3. State your opinion

Say: "Decide what your opinion or answer to the topic question will be."

Teach: In a response to reading, authors must state their opinion on the topic or question. This means they need to state their opinion on what they believe or don't believe regarding the topic. Then the authors must back up their opinion with details and examples from two (or more) reading selections.

4. The purpose of the detail or middle paragraphs

Ask: While pointing to the first square on a Blueprint, ask your students, "What shape is this?"

The students will answer, "It's a square."

Then ask, "What type of paragraph does the square in our Blueprint represent?"

They will tell you, "The detail or middle paragraphs."

"Yes, we'll put our notes for supporting our arguments from the first reading selection in this Blueprint square. How big are the detail or middle paragraphs? Large [and ask students to show you with their hands]. The detail paragraphs section of your response to reading will be the largest section of your paper because this section contains your reasoning and three strong argument points." (Repeat this process for the second square on the Blueprint that corresponds to the second reading selection.)

5. The purpose of the summary or ending paragraph

Ask: While pointing to the rectangle on the Blueprint, ask your students, "What shape is this?"

The students will answer: "It's a rectangle."

Then ask, "What type of paragraph does the rectangle in our Blueprint represent?"

They will tell you, "The summary or ending."

"Yes, we'll put our notes for the ending in the Blueprint rectangle. How big is the summary or ending paragraph? Small [and ask students to show you with their hands]. The summary or ending section of your writing will be the smallest section because it contains a final review of your arguments."

Teach: The summary in a response to reading is where authors must restate their opinion and the names of the readings that support it. Authors may want to add anything that they've personally learned from these stories that applies to them. Every story has a lesson to be learned. Students should question: What did I learn from this experience? Did I learn something about myself or the theme?

6. Transitions

Say: "Transitions make your words flow smoothly from one paragraph to another. Your paragraphs must flow into each other like a flowing river. This is called a *transition*. Make sure your story flows." (See Student Worksheet 10.1 at the end of this chapter for a response to reading Blueprint.)

Step 4: Blueprint Note Taking

Your students are ready to take out their Rough Draft Writing Folders and begin filling out their Blueprint. Begin by modeling the process of note taking for your students on the Blueprint using your personal example. As you make notes on your Blueprint, tell the students what you are writing. Remember to include all the building blocks necessary for a well-written response to reading.

It is important to leave your recently modeled teacher Blueprint visible for your students to see as they write notes in their own Blueprints. Your students will use your Blueprint for a guide as they take notes in their own Blueprint.

ELL–BEWCONNECTION

ELL students require modeling of new concepts for mastery. Model your story from your notes.

Step 5: Talking Paragraphs

Start by modeling the talking paragraph concept to your students. Point to your notes in your Blueprint and speak your potential paragraphs using your notes as a guide for developing full sentences. After your students have finished taking notes on their Blueprints, it's their turn. Ask for student volunteers to model talking out their notes from their Blueprints. At this point, students can easily revise or add editing changes to their Blueprint notes because they haven't yet committed to writing the actual paragraphs. Yes, they will self-correct when reading their paragraphs out loud!

Two Steps in Phase III: Writing

Step 1: Draft Writing

As a result of all the prewriting activities, students will now have their response to reading mapped out. It's time for them to write their rough drafts using their notes from their Blueprints. This is the time to structure the writing process, modeling what you would think and do based on your own

Blueprint. What would you write for your topic sentence? Paragraph by paragraph, lead your students through the writing phase.

Step 2: Title Writing

Title writing for response to reading can be very interesting. For example, one of our students wrote a very clever title after reading the two selections that reflected the central theme about heroes who were successful in life—and he believed in heroes! His title was, "Follow Your Dreams." As with the other writing types, don't write titles until *after* the rough draft has been completed, and make sure you use the BEW title-writing strategies covered in Chapter 3.

Five Steps in Phase IV: Authentic Editing

Steps 1 through 3: Editing

Just as with the other writing types, the authentic editing phase should be used with a response-to-reading selection. This means that students start by giving their teachers feedback regarding what should be included in the *editing rubric* used in all three steps of editing: self-editing, peer editing, and teacher conferencing. Engage your students in a discussion of what the key elements are for a well-written paper. Prompt them, but don't give away the answers. In the BEW process, there are three important areas for writing rubric assessment. By organizing your class rubric in these three categories, students will begin to understand and remember the different sections.

1. Genre Format and Voice
2. Vocabulary and Word Usage
3. Spelling and Grammar

The contents of the Genre Format and Voice section of the rubric will depend on the concepts covered in your teaching.

Step 4: Final Copy Writing

After completing the first three authentic editing steps, your students are ready to take their edited rough drafts and use them to write their final copy. They should also anticipate publication as they write.

Step 5: Teacher Assessment

When it comes to response to reading, be sure to review your state standards. Because this type of student writing can be developed in more than one way, depending on your state standards, it's important to understand exactly what your state requires. Departing from those requirements when

> **TIP:** Some state high-stakes tests actually require your students to edit peer selections and respond accordingly. If your students cannot internalize the editing concepts necessary for a genre, and can only edit by a rubric that you provide, how will they be successful? Creating a class rubric, authentically, is the key!

you teach will lead to confusion and poor performance when your students are tested. Know your state benchmarks and conform to them when you teach the BEW way!

When teaching very young children, such as kindergartners and first graders, you may have to provide more assistance, because these children are still struggling with learning concepts in print. Asking them to read two relatively difficult selections and then write an essay based on those readings can be an onerous task. Instead, read the selections to your students and then have them write a single paragraph as a response to your readings. This activity will teach these organizational concepts to very young children. For example, we read two stories to our first-grade students: Aesop's Fable *The Tortoise and the Hare* and *The Little Engine That Could.* After the students heard both stories, we asked them, "Should you always keep trying and never give up? Yes or no? What did the tortoise and the little red engine do?" One of our first-grade student's unedited paragraphs is shown at the right. You can be assured that this student understands the central theme in the stories: Don't give up. She chose to agree with it and then wrote a response to reading selection in an age-appropriate manner.

Another sample from our third-grade class is shown on page 222. The class read the story of John Henry and "All Star" (a poem about a boy who wanted to play in the NFL). All the students were asked to write on this prompt: We all have goals in life. Do you agree or disagree? Explain your answer with details from the story of John Henry and the poem "All Star."

Upper elementary and middle school students should follow the identical writing patterns as those of younger students. They should follow the genre format and voice section of this chapter to develop their response to reading selection. Because of the lengthy reading selections, upper elementary and middle school writing examples in this area tend to be quite long and, consequently, we did not include sample writing selections.

First-Grade Response to Reading: Proficient

No, we can't give up. The turtle in the story never stopped. He was slow. He was never afraid of the rabbit winning the race. The rabbit thought for sure he was going to win and stopped a whole bunch of times. But the turtle just keep going. The little red engine did the same thing. He never stopped even when he came to a big hill he said, I think I can. The little red engine did it. The little red engine and the turtle never stopped and they did it. Don't stop and you will do it and be happy.

Phase V: Publishing

Use the Publishing Phase as a learning experience in your school! The response to reading selections are a great way for students to learn writing skills from other students. For example, let your students share their writing selections with other classes that may have read the same selections. Students learn from their peers. What an opportunity this type of writing provides for student learning!

Everyone has goals in life. If you didn't you'd just be a couch potato. John Henry and the boy in All Star had great goals for each of their very own lives. Each of them had different endings.

John Henry had an interesting life and ending to it too. One day John Henry was asked to enter a contest. He was challenged to drill through the mountain and come out the other end before a man with a drill. John Henry was a miner and a really, really good one. He accepted the challenge and it became his very own goal. He worked really, really hard to win the contest and achieve his goal. He drilled and drilled and drilled more and more. John got lost. Nobody could find him. They found him and he had died drilling through the mountain. John was born with a hammer in his hand and died with a hammer in his hand. He died trying to make his goal.

All Star had a big, big, big dream. He wanted to play on television on the NFL. To make his goal he went to football practice every day. He worked so hard that he was really tired. All Star would always get up even when he was knocked down in a game. He never quite trying to make his goal.

Both John Henry and All Star worked hard to make their goal. John worked so hard that he died trying with a hammer in his hand. All Star would never give up. Each time he was knocked down it didn't matter he just ran and worked harder. Everybody needs to work as hard at their goals as John Henry and All Star.

In Summary: Response to Reading

Response to reading is a type of writing that should be included in each child's curriculum. The ability to read, synthesize, and respond to various types of written material is a higher order thinking skill that all students should master. We realize that many students such as our at-risk population, special needs students, and ELL students can experience extreme difficulty with this type of writing. Many of these students will have a difficult time just reading and comprehending the provided selections. To assist all students with this task, try books on tapes or even DVDs of the reading selections (when they are available). When students have a variety of prewriting strategies that strengthen their understanding of the text at hand, greater success in writing is achieved.

If you're unsure of how to prepare for this type of classroom writing selection, look at our two-week teaching schedule. This schedule is one that should be followed after the reading selections have been completed.

Table 10.3   Two-Week Teaching Schedule for Response to Reading

	Monday	Tuesday	Wednesday	Thursday	Friday
Week 1	Vocabulary	Vocabulary Review	Vocabulary Review	Vocabulary Review	Vocabulary Review
	Prewriting Activities 1. Sensory Activities 2. Wheel of Thought	Prewriting Activities 1. Genre Format and Voice	Prewriting Activities 1. Genre Format and Voice	Prewriting Activities 1. Genre Format and Voice	Prewriting Activities 1. Blueprint Note Taking 2. Talking Paragraphs
	Monday	**Tuesday**	**Wednesday**	**Thursday**	**Friday**
Week 2	Vocabulary Review	Vocabulary Review	Vocabulary Review	Vocabulary Review	Vocabulary Review
	Writing Activities 1. Writing the Draft	Writing Activities 1. Writing the Draft 2. Title Writing	Editing 1. Self-editing 2. Peer Editing	Editing 1. Teacher Conferencing 2. Final Copy Writing 3. Teacher Assessment	Publishing

FEATURE: Response to Reading Writing Prompts

Are you having a difficult time thinking of writing prompts for your students? Well, if you can't think of a writing prompt for your response to reading curriculum, try one of the ones that we've listed here. Students will respond best if the prompt is one that they can connect with in their own lives.

1. We all have heroes in our lives. Do you agree or disagree? Support your answer with details from both reading selections.

2. There are times in our lives when we must show courage. Do you agree or disagree? Support your answer with details from both reading selections.

3. We all have goals in our lives that we try to achieve. Would you agree or disagree? Support your answer with details from both reading selections.

4. Everyone has a special dream. Do you agree or disagree? Support your answer with details from both reading selections.

5. Education is important. Would you agree or disagree? Support your answer with details from both reading selections.

6. Problem-solving skills are important skills to have in your life. Would you agree or disagree? Support your answer with details from both reading selections.

7. To be successful, you have to keep trying and never give up. Do you agree or disagree? Use the reading selections to support your opinion.

8. Even in hard times, some people can see the good. This helps them change things for the better. Do you agree or disagree? Use the reading selections to support your opinion.

9. Everyone is afraid at some time in their life. Good things can come from overcoming that fear. Do you agree or disagree? Support your opinion with details from the reading selections.

10. Setting a goal can help many people achieve things they never knew they could do. Do you agree or disagree? Support your opinion with details from the reading selections.

11. Taking a stand is not always popular, but it helps people consider all sides of an issue. Do you agree or disagree? Use your reading selections to support your opinion.

12. People can learn life lessons when taking care of animals or pets. Do you agree or disagree? Use your reading selections to support your opinion.

13. It is what's inside of you that counts, not your outer appearance. Do you agree or disagree? Support your opinion with details from the reading selections.

For younger children you can use Aesop's Fables, fairy tales, and simple children's books to help you choose topics. For example, if you picked a theme about bullying and the importance of standing up for yourself, you could use *Jack and the Beanstalk* (the giant who steals and threatens and comes after Jack) and the story of *The Three Little Pigs* (the wolf who comes after each pig), and how the book characters prevail. Be creative. Talk to your school librarian. There are so many stories you can incorporate into oral and written response to reading activities.

Student Worksheet 10.1 Response to Reading Blueprint

Introduction:
State your opinion.

______________________ ______________________
______________________ ______________________

Ideas from first reading

____
____
____
____
____
____

Ideas from second reading

____
____
____
____
____
____

Summary: Restate your opinion and tell what you learned.

______________________ ______________________ ______________________

Section III

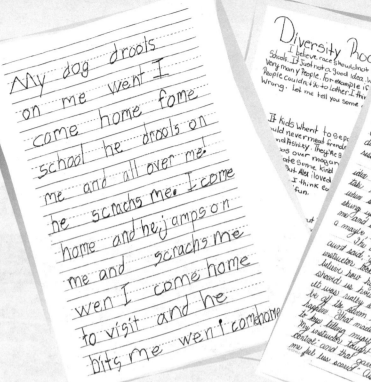

Interactive Creative Activities for Teaching Writing

Chapter 11   Kindergarten through Grade 2

Chapter 12   Grades 3 through 5

Chapter 13   Grades 6 through 8

Chapter 14   Planning for the Future

Kindergarten through Grade 2

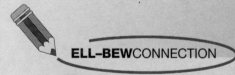

ELL–BEWCONNECTION

ELL students quickly learn
through physical modeling
and movement. Use the
BEW hand jives and jingles
to teach different genres.

It's no secret that young children enjoy playing games! Young authors will learn new writing vocabulary words through our hand jives and jingles. They'll be inspired to write stories and learn other genres because of their new-found writing skills acquired as a result of participating in our creative learning experiences. Try our games and activities to teach your young authors: interactive strategies for learning writing vocabulary; skill-building activities for learning genre building blocks; and remedies for common grammar errors.

These skill-building activities can be taught as part of your writing curriculum or used as student reinforcement. Have a great time with them or create your very own.

Interactive Strategies for Teaching Writing and Genre Vocabulary

Genre Format

Grades: K through 2	Interactive Strategy	Your Own Ideas!
Ask, *"What is . . ."*	**TIP:** Teach and use the proper writing words found here consistently.	
Genre	Lead choral response: • *What type of writing are we doing?* • *Who's my special audience?*	
Personal narrative	Lead choral response and hand jive: Put hand over heart and extend other hand out to the side: • *This is my story.*	
Informational (sequential)	Lead choral response and hand jive. Simulate writing a list with your hands: • *Putting things in order*	
Research	Lead choral response and hand jive: Put both hands in front of you and mimic opening a book: • *Look things up in a book.*	
Fantasy	Lead hand jive. Use a "make-believe" look, with eyes up and hands outward at shoulder level, palms facing up in a wondering position. • *It's make-believe.*	
Poetry	Lead hand jive. Put hands over heart with palms open. Lead a song, clapping the rhythm: • *I think that I shall never see, a poem as lovely as a tree.* *(or favorite class poem)*	
Persuasive	Lead pantomime and choral response. Put three fingers up to your head to demonstrate changing someone's mind with three good reasons, and say: • *Changing somebody's mind with three good reasons*	
Magazine article	Hold left hand palm up (like a page of a magazine) and scroll down it with your right index finger, as if reading an article. • *Writing for a magazine*	

Interactive Strategies for Teaching Writing and Genre Vocabulary

Genre Elements

Grades: K through 2	Interactive Strategy	Your Own Ideas!
Ask, "What is . . ."		
Topic **Topic sentence**	Lead choral response to the tune of "The Hokey Pokey": • *That's what it's all about.* • *That's what it's all about* [say the topic].	
Sentence **Complete sentence**	Lead choral response (and add the appropriate punctuation mark): • *Who/what + a doing = a sentence.*	
Simple paragraphs **(Writing complete** **sentences on topic)**	Model examples of two to three sentences that follow one topic. As students progress, lead choral response to teach sentences needed in a paragraph, three sentences on one topic, extending three fingers, then one: • *3 on 1* Hold up one finger, and probe, "What is the number one sentence?" • *Topic sentence* Hold up two fingers and identify what it will be: • *A detail that goes with the topic* Hold up three fingers and identify what it will be: • *A detail* **Example:** 1 = Topic idea: dog 2 = Detail: wags tail 3 = Detail: has spots These notes can be turned into a three-sentence paragraph.	
Introduction paragraph	Ask, "What's the first paragraph called?" • *The introduction* "What's the purpose of the introduction?" • *It introduces the topic* or *It's the beginning of the story* "How big is the introduction?" Students show with their hands: • *Middle size*	

Grades: K through 2	Interactive Strategy	Your Own Ideas!
Detail paragraph	Ask, "What's the second paragraph called?" • *The detail paragraph* "What is the purpose of this paragraph?" • *It tells the details about the topic* or *It tells the middle of the story* "How big is the detail paragraph?" Students show with their hands: • *The longest*	
Summary paragraph	Ask, "What is the last paragraph called?" • *The summary or The conclusion* "What is the purpose of the summary paragraph?" • *To tell about the topic in a short way* or *To tell the ending of the story* "How long is the summary paragraph?" Students show with their hands: • *It's the shortest.*	
Rough draft	Lead choral response: • *Sloppy copy*	
Word wrap	Lead word-wrap dance with arm swinging left to right while saying: • *We write side to side, side to side, side to side.*	
Indenting paragraphs	Lead students in hand action: • *Put two fingers on the left side of the first line and put a dot. This leaves a space for indenting.*	
Edit	Lead choral response while making erasing motion: • *Fixing our mistakes*	
Peer edit	Lead choral response while making erasing motion: • *Helping our peers fix their mistakes*	
Conference	Demonstrate hands "talking" to each other (open and close fingers): • *Talking about it together*	
Illustration	Lead choral response: • *A picture*	*(continued)*

Grades: K through 2	Interactive Strategy	Your Own Ideas!
Speaker	Ask who's the speaker, while pointing to own mouth [teacher]: • *The person talking*	
Listener	Ask who are the listeners, while pointing to own ears: • *The people listening, not talking*	
Portfolio	Hold up the real portfolio. Lead choral response: • *A collection of my work*	

Skill-Building Activities for Learning Personal Narrative Building Blocks

Genre Writing Techniques Personal Narrative: Character Development (Who Are My Characters and What Do They Say?)

Grades K through 2, Character Development

Activity 1: Oral Language Game: *Who Am I?*

ELL–BEWCONNECTION

ELL students learn quickly in small groups. Have them participate in skill-building small-group activities.

Think of a popular character that your students would know. Write the name down on a piece of paper and put it on your desk. Now have students try to figure out who the character is via many, many questions you ask them, such as: Who wears a cape? Who flies through the sky? Who is faster than a speeding bullet? The first student to answer, "Superman" wins! When a particular student guesses the correct answer, it's their turn. Ask them to write a name of a character down on a piece of paper, put it on your desk and the game begins again!

Possible Characters

Abe Lincoln, Spiderman, SpongeBob Squarepants, characters from recently read class stories, famous people, you, the school principal, another teacher, the school media specialist, a policeman, a fireman, a nurse, a doctor, a dentist, a lawyer

Resources

Board game: *Anybody's Guess: The Riotous Game of Revealing Clues* (Golden Inc.)
Board game: *Twenty Questions* (University Games)

Grades K through 2, Character Dialogue or Voice

Activity 2: Oral Language Game: *Switch Voices*

Write the words "From Another Person's Point of View" on the board. Select a fable or story that your students know really well, like *The Three Little Pigs*. Select students to role-play each character in the story. Have them tell the story in front of the class and have them speak the part of each of the characters just as if they were the characters in the story. When they have finished the story, have each of the students who role-played a story character retell the story from their character's point of view.

Resources

Readers theater resources for teachers and students. Check out this student interactive website: www.cdli.ca/CITE/langrt.htm.

Grades K through 2, Character Dialogue or Voice

Activity 3: Puppet Shows: *Puppet Talk!*

All students love to speak through puppets. Have students bring in an old sock and provide plenty of felt scraps that they can use to construct their own puppets. Have your students work in groups of three. Tell them their puppets are three new students in your school. Have them act out their first day at the new school by talking to each other through the puppets.

Resources

A box of ideas for kids: *Dramatic Play Writing Boxes* (Lakeshore Publishing)

Grades K through 2, Character Dialogue or Voice

Activity 4: Oral Language Game: *What Would It Say?*

Pick an object in your classroom, any object, perhaps a book or a toy. Show it to the class and ask them to pretend that the object can talk. Ask them, "What would the _____ say to you and why?" Have students respond to the class orally with its story. This will help your students hear and explore the power of adding dialogue to their stories.

Grades K through 2, Character Dialogue or Voice

Activity 5: Oral Language Game: *Guess Who's Talking?*

Have your students put their heads down. Walk around the classroom and tap one child on the shoulder. Have that child quietly ask the question, "Who am I?" Ask the rest of the students to put their heads up and guess which classmate asked the question just from hearing their voice. Relate this activity to voice in writing. We each have a different-sounding voice.

Variation: Instead of having the selected student say, "Who am I?" ask the student to say something about themselves or give a favorite expression. Have your class guess who spoke the words. Or have the selected student use a favorite expression of somebody else in the class. Have your class guess who is actually doing the talking and whose favorite expression they used.

Grades K through 2, Character Development

Activity 6: Oral Language Game: *Felt Board Stories*

Many teachers of young children know the fun of using felt board characters in teaching narrative stories. Be sure you have several sets of felt characters so students can play with them on the felt board and tell you the story of what is happening.

Variation: Students can bring in action figures and use them as characters in a story. When using these action figures, students can speak with various accents or special voices. Another idea is to allow students to use finger puppets for this type of activity.

Genre Format and Voice for Personal Narrative:
Format: A Story with a Beginning, Middle, and End

Grades K through 2, Format:
A Story with a Beginning, Middle, and End

Activity 1: Oral Language Activity: *Storytelling Story Starters*

Prepare a number of different sentence strips on pieces of paper using storytelling prompts such as (1) Tell us about your favorite pet. (2) Tell us about your favorite birthday. (3) Tell us about your most memorable trip. (4) Tell us about your favorite toy. (5) Tell us about your favorite vacation. (6) Tell us about your new bike. (7) Tell us about your favorite food. (8) Tell us about your favorite holiday. (9) Tell us about something that you're really good at doing. (10) Tell us about your favorite subject in school. (11) Tell us about your favorite sport. (12) Tell us about the time that you felt really, really good. Put all these story starters in a brown paper bag and shake them up. Have your students sit in a circle and let them take turns pulling a sentence strip from the bag and telling their story to the class. *Hint:* Tell students they have three minutes to tell their story, and set a kitchen timer. When the timer goes off, it's the next person's turn.

Grades K through 2, Format:
A Story with a Beginning, Middle, and End

Activity 2: Cut-and-Paste Activity: *How Does It Happen?*

Read a short fairy tale to your class, such as *Cinderella*. Then write the story in three paragraphs (a beginning, middle, and ending paragraph) on a sheet of 8 x 11 paper, but mix up the order (for example, put the ending first). Then pass out the paper to your class. Have them cut out each paragraph and paste the paragraphs on another sheet of paper in the correct order.

Suggestion: Depending on the age of your students, you might want to draw a black line around each paragraph to help them know where to cut. Older students could be reminded that a paragraph starts with an indented sentence.

Grades K through 2, Format:
A Story with a Beginning, Middle, and End

Activity 3: Tell Me a Story: *Story Time*

Invite a professional storyteller to tell stories interactively to your class. Your students will learn about the parts of a story (beginning, middle, and end) through the experience of participating, listening, and enjoying the lively performance of the storyteller. If a professional storyteller isn't in your budget, purchase a storytelling CD. These CDs have story background sound effects that will mesmerize your students.

Resources

National Storytellers Organization: www.storynet.org

Dr. Debra Christian's exciting stories on CDs: hometown.aol.com/DebraC4

Changar, H. 1995. *Story Telling Activities Kit*. New York: The Center for Applied Research in Education.

Grades K through 2, Format:
A Story with a Beginning, Middle, and End

Activity 4: Sound Effects Story: *Simulating a Sound*

Select a favorite fable or story that vividly incorporates sounds. Get a box of rhythm instruments from your music teacher. Talk about the sounds in the story and have the students decide which instrument defines each sound best. As you read the story aloud, have the students play the sounds when you read that specific part of the story. For example, if you read a section where there is a

Section III

loud bang in the story, have a student hit a drum. Read the story a couple of times and allow different students to play the instruments that simulate the sounds in the story.

Resources

Look up some of our favorite websites for storytelling with animated sounds. Use these with your young authors:

Storytime with animated sound effects to be used interactively with your class: www.grinabit.com/Books.html

Kids' stories: www.candlelightstories.com/soundstoryblog/SoundStoryBlog.htm

Grades K through 2, Format:
A Story with a Beginning, Middle, and End

Activity 5: Drawing and Speaking Activity: *Picture Flip Card*

Give students three 5 × 7 note cards that have a hole punched in the upper left corner and are tied together. On the first card, write "Story Beginning." On the second, write "Story Middle (Details)." Write "Story End" on the third. Tell students to draw a picture representing the three parts of their own story. You may want to give them a selected topic, such as My School Day, My Birthday Party, or Learning to Ride My Bike. This is a simple activity that is especially good for kindergarten or beginning writers.

Grades K through 2, Voice

Activity 6: Splashy Words

Kids love to write fun-sounding words. Write different words on the board or cards using onomatopoeia (words that imitate their sound), such as *bang, yuck, splish, splash.* Ask students to pronounce the words one at a time according to how they sound.

Variation: Do a takeoff on this game by writing words in a way that matches what they mean, like writing the word *tiny* in very small letters. Use cadence and timing in your spoken voice to say the word. The word *Tall* would be drawn out when spoken.

Resources

Read this book to your young authors to teach the concept of onomatopoeia: Robinson, M. 1993. *Cock-a-Doodle-Doo!* New York: Doubleday Books for Young Readers.

Grades K through 2, Voice

Activity 7: Role-play: *Changing Roles*

Prepare some cards with the names of different professionals, such as *teacher, policeman, fireman, principal, doctor, parent, school nurse,* or *librarian.* Give students a situation in which the professional will have to respond by talking. For example, "You were caught playing with matches." Have different students pick a card and talk to that situation as if they were that character. This will help them hear the voice of different people.

Variation: For younger authors, it is appropriate to select different story characters for students to role-play, such as their own pet, animals at the zoo, or maybe even a cartoon character like Spiderman.

Resources

Board game: *Win, Lose or Draw: The Picture Charade Game* (Walt Disney)

Skill-Building Activities for Learning Persuasive Writing Building Blocks

Genre Writing Techniques for Persuasive Writing: Point of View (What's My Point of View?)

Grades K through 2, Point of View

Activity 1: Game: *Point-of-View Game*

Write pronouns (*I, we, he, she, it*) on small cards for your students. Tell them it's time to play the Point-of-View Game. Bring two students to the front of the room. Give them a sentence with one of their names in it as the subject. For example, "Mary went to the mall yesterday." Have one student draw a card with one of the pronouns written on it. Then have the other student use that pronoun in your sentence to replace the word Mary. For example, "She went to the mall yesterday" or "I went to the mall yesterday." Relate these concepts to writing with pronouns. Explain how the pronouns we use in writing a persuasive paper tell a story with a special point of view. Because their stories will be told by them, they will use *I* in their stories.

Grades K through 2, Point of View

Activity 2: Role-play: *Arguments*

Prepare some note cards with the names of two types of people who might be arguing such as Father and Son, Brother and Sister, or even Best Friends. Also include a situation or problem that those two people will argue about. Have two students act out those roles. For example, the situation for Father and Son might be that the son wants to go to a baseball game but the dad says he's too busy to take him. The situation for the best friends might be that they are at a restaurant and can't agree on the pizza toppings for their pizza. Remind students after they have each tried to argue their point of view in a winning way that this is the objective of a persuasive paper.

Grades K through 2, Point of View

Activity 3: Role-play: *Doctor, Doctor*

Ask your students, "Who is an expert on knowing how to stay healthy?" Your students will respond by saying, "A doctor." Let students work in pairs. One student should persuade the principal to install a candy machine and a soft drink machine in the school. The other student should play the expert—the doctor. Let the student and doctor debate this issue, and remind the students that they need to stay in character. Have some fun with this. Let the doctor wear a play stethoscope or white coat, for example.

Variation: Play Teacher, Teacher by having a debate between a student and a teacher over longer recess. Play Principal, Principal by having a debate between a student and the principal over wanting to go to a water park for a field trip.

Genre Format and Voice for Persuasive Writing: Taking a Stand and Three Good Arguments

Grades K through 2, Taking a Stand

Activity 1: Oral Language Activity: *Cast a Vote*

Prepare two to three questions on sentence strips to read aloud to your class using debatable issues that are age appropriate for your class. They should be phrased in a way that your students can answer, "Yes, I agree" or "No, I don't agree." For example, "We should have assigned seats at lunchtime," or "The school should serve pizza each week," or "We should go to school in the summer." Read the sentence strip aloud and ask students who say "yes" to move to one side of the room, and ask those who say "no" to move to the other side of the room. Read your question again, and ask each group for a choral response, saying, "Yes, we agree" or "No, we don't agree." Then point out that this is an argument; there are two sides that believe they are right. This is called *taking a stand.*

Grades K through 2, Taking a Stand

Activity 2: Class Survey: *What Do You Think?*

Prepare three to five questions that are relevant to your class that could be considered "hot topics." An example is: "Should students be allowed to watch TV during lunchtime?" Organize an appropriate time for your students to survey other students about this question. Have your students tally the yes and no votes that others give them, and then total the final answer. Collect all the surveys and provide a grand total of those who agree and those who disagree. Tie this into a graphing activity. Remind students that either of the answers is fine; no one is a winner or loser. You are just learning the importance of taking a stand.

Grades K through 2, Three Good Arguments

Activity 3: Oral Language Activity: *Three Reasons Why*

Give your students a debatable hot topic, such as, "Should we be allowed to bring our favorite stuffed animal to school?" Tell students to take a stand and answer "Yes, I agree" or "No, I don't agree." Give them five minutes to think of three good reasons for their stand. Walk around the room and call on a volunteer to share his or her reasons. Say to that student, "What do you think and why?" and hold up three fingers. The student should raise a finger for each of the three reasons, counting up to your three-finger prompt. Continue around the room.

Variation: Give each student a persuasive Blueprint and have the students number the square paragraphs with 1, 2, and 3. Then ask them to write their three good reasons in the squares.

Grades K through 2, Three Good Arguments

Activity 4: Oral Language Activity: *Good Reason or Not*

Select a topic of interest to your class. Prepare a number of reasons for which students might agree or disagree with that topic. Write each reason on a sentence strip. Make some of these choices reasonable and some of them absurd. Share the question that you want students to consider. Then hold up one of the reasons and ask your class to read it aloud together. Then ask, "Good reason or not?" Ask the class to respond in unison. This is good practice for developing good persuasive arguments.

Grades K through 2, Three Good Arguments

Activity 5: Hands-on Activity: *Best for Last*

Select a topic of interest to your class for which they can make up three good reasons for either agreeing or disagreeing with the topic. Have them write their arguments in the three squares on a persuasive Blueprint. Then ask them to cut out each square and clip them together using a paper-clip. Have students trade their reasons with a partner, who gets to decide the best order of the arguments, saving the best one for last. Let the students discuss each other's perspective.

Grades K through 2, Three Good Arguments

Activity 6: Oral Language Activity: *I Should Have That!*

Tell your students they have thirty seconds to find an object in their pocket or desk. Have them hold that object and find a partner. Give each partner two minutes to give three good reasons why they should have the other partner's object. Both students should get the opportunity to persuade their partner that they should get the object. Then, ask for a team to present both sides of their argument (three good reasons) in front of the class. Record each of their three reasons on the board. Ask the class which student gave the most convincing argument and why.

Skill-Building Activities for Learning Research Building Blocks

Genre Writing Techniques for Research Papers: Writing the Research Question and Finding the Information

Grades K through 2, Writing the Research Question

Activity 1: Oral Language Game: *Questions Quest*

Select a research theme from your curriculum. Write a number of possible topics based on that theme. Then, together as a class, write these questions on sentence strips. This will teach your young researchers how to write a good research question. Make sure that you leave these research questions posted in your classroom. A great way to do this is to create an interactive class bulletin board that focuses on the research topic. Each day you may want to add an answer to one of the research questions on the bulletin board. Keep this activity going until you have three answers for each research question posted.

Resources

Need some help creating interactive bulletin boards? The following book gives pattern ideas for elementary bulletin boards: Burke, K., and J. Kranhold. 1979. *The Big Fearon Bulletin Board Book.* Carthage, IL: Fearon Teacher Aids. (Yes, 1979. Copies are available from amazon.com. There is also a 1999 version available.)

Grades K through 2, Writing the Research Question

Activity 2: Oral Language Game: *Question or Not?*

Because young researchers have difficulty understanding the difference between a question and a statement, try this game. Pick research topics on which your class will soon be formulating questions. On large sentence strips, write a number of research statements and research questions. One by one, hold these sentence strips up in front of your class and have your students read them in unison. Then ask your class to tell you if what is written is a *question* or *not*. Students should respond with the word *question* if the sentence strip has a question written on it; they should respond with *not* if the strip has a research statement written on it. Go through these quickly with your class. Finally, ask students to write a question about a research topic that they may want to know the answer to. This activity will give your students practice in writing research questions.

Grades K through 2, Writing the Research Question

Activity 3: Hands-on Activity: *Green Thumb*

In order for very young researchers to understand this genre, why not start out with a class research project that is teacher directed? Very young children understand nature and plants, so start with this activity. Propose two class research questions that ask, "How long will it take a seed to grow into a plant?" and "What should we do to help it grow?" Plant a fast-growing seed in a pot in the classroom and place it on a sunlit windowsill. Make sure students water and fertilize the plant on a regular basis. Each day, record the plant's growth pattern on a chart that is visible to your students. Within a short time, the seed will grow and you will have an ongoing research project that your students can experience right in their classroom. Be sure to record the three things that made the plant grow on the growth chart. Create a bulletin board based on this project. Lead daily discussions about the plant's growth pattern.

Grades K through 2, Writing the Research Question

Activity 4: Cyber Trip: *Planets*

If your class is investigating a research project about planets, the following website is a must-visit site. Your students will be involved one hundred percent in their research projects by taking a cyber trip to The Science Factory Children's Museum and Planetarium Exhibits at www.sciencefactory.org/newsletters/2005/may_05.shtml.

Grades K through 2, Finding the Information

Activity 5: Cyber Trip: *Online Investigation*

Science inquiries are a great way for young researchers to begin understanding and writing their projects. Young students enjoy science and the elements of nature. Reinforce the concept of searching for source information online. If you're looking for a great website that includes many topics suitable for young researchers, check out a site that provides interactive research information on 329 different topics applicable for K through 2 research projects, Websites for Our Class, at www.csubak.edu.

Grades K through 2, Finding the Information

Activity 5: Cyber Search: *Can You Do the Dewey?*

With some guidance from you, even very young researchers can learn to use the media center and find sources. To complete this activity you will need an Internet hookup in your media center, with individual student computers or a digital media presentation method for class viewing. Your students can learn the Dewey decimal system by using the interactive website Can You Do the Dewey? at http://thrall.org/dewey. This website has three links: (1) a check link, to test your knowledge regarding the Dewey classification system; (2) a meet Dewey link, which provides information about the man who invented this system; and (3) a Dewey decimal system link, to learn how to use this system interactively. After each cyber lesson, let your students find research services using the Dewey decimal system themselves in the school media center.

Genre Format and Voice for Research Papers:
Three Good Supporting Research Points

Grades K through 2, Three Good Supporting Research Points

Activity 1: Oral and Written Language Development: *Finding Facts*

Your young authors can learn to support a research topic with three facts, which is the early elementary version of a research paper. Give your students a topic such as "Where do bears live?" Students can brainstorm and use the library to learn three facts about this topic. Young authors may then record their three facts by drawing three pictures, one for each fact. They can also be directed to the following website to find information as well as examples: ArtHouse: Make it Your Own! at www.storyboardtoys. com/gallery/Cecily.htm. This website shares elementary students' completed research projects with coordinating artwork. If your students are interested in publishing their finished papers on this website, merely follow the kid-friendly submission instructions.

Grades K through 2, Three Good Supporting Research Points

Activity 2: Oral Language Activity: *Three-Answer Activity*

Select a topic that your students are familiar with. Compose a question on this topic for your class and write it on the board. Ask your class for answers to this question. Write three answers to this question by labeling the answers numerically: 1, 2, and 3. Repeat this class exercise several times with simple questions and student responses. Relate this activity to writing a research paper by emphasizing that students must also have three answers to their questions.

Skill-Building Activities for Learning Poetry Building Blocks

Genre Writing Techniques for Poetry: Using Rhyme and Rhythm

Grades K through 2, Using Rhyme and Rhythm

Activity 1: Listening to Poetry: *Let's Hear a Poem This Week!*

Try this website to share poems with your students. This interactive poetry blog site allows your students to hear different poetry weekly. Take a cyber trip to www.everypoet.com. Lead a class discussion about the type of poetry that your class has just heard. Can they write the same type of poem? Students must have exposure to different types of poetry to be able to compose it.

Grade K through 2, Using Rhyme and Rhythm

Activity 2: Fill-in-the-Blank Poems: *Silly Poems*

Most young poets like silly poems, and they're a great way to teach rhyme and rhythm. Select a nursery rhyme that your students are sure to know, like "Mary Had a Little Lamb." Write this nursery rhyme on the board and leave out the last word of each verse. Let the students fill in their own word to each verse. They will learn rhyme and rhythm from this exercise. If you're unsure of which nursery rhymes to use, try an interactive poetry website. Giggle Poet includes fill-in-the-blank poems, silly poems, songs, limericks, and poetry theater activities and is located at www.gigglepoetry.com.

Grades K through 2, Using Rhyme and Rhythm

Activity 3: Web of Words, Word Families: *Building Rhymes*

Our Web of Words is a great way to help young authors hear rhyming words. Write a word such as *hat* in the center square of the Web of Words. Ask students to think of all the rhyming words that they can that rhyme with *hat*. Write all the rhyming words that your students can think of in additional squares on the web. If some of your students need assistance with this activity, let them use Young's (2006) *Scholastic Dictionary of Rhyming Words* (kids love this book). Then create silly rhyming sentences with your class from the Web of Words. Have your students illustrate their silly sentences and put them on the bulletin board in your classroom.

Genre Format and Voice for Poetry:
Word Choice and Connecting with Your Senses

Grades K through 2, Word Choice

Activity 1: Oral and Written Language Activity: *Sound Words*

Children love to write with onomatopoeia. Use this writing device and your students will enjoy searching and selecting words for their poems. Play word games with onomatopoeia. Write a list of words on the blackboard that use this device, such as *brr*, *tick-tock,* and others. Now rewrite these words and have the students pronounce them as they are written: BRRR, T-I-C-K–T-O-C-K. Young authors, especially, will pick up on this writing device when composing their poems. They are exceptionally creative!

Grades K through 2, Word Choice

Activity 2: Oral and Written Language Activity: *Same Sounds*

Young authors love to have fun with words. Teach your young authors how to use alliteration as a word choice selection in their poems. Practice this activity until your students become comfortable with it. Select an initial consonant, such as the letter S. Write this letter on the board. Then write a word beginning with the same letter next to it, such as *Sam*. Write as many words as possible that start like Sam, until you have written a string of these words. It would look like this: *Sam, silly, swam, sensibly,* and so on. You students will soon get the idea of beginning words with the same sound—alliteration! This writing technique creates interesting verses when used in poetry.

Grades K through 2, Word Choice

Activity 3: Oral and Written Language Activity: *Teaching Similes*

Even young authors can spice up their writing with similes. Create a chart on your blackboard with comparisons using *like* or *as*. Make sure these comparisons relate to your students' senses or activities that they are very familiar with, at least at first. Create a chart like this one:

- I was as hungry as _____.

- He was as slow as _____.

- She was as fast as _____.

Have your students fill in the blanks with their own ideas. You may want to ask students to illustrate these examples. Create a *Simile Sentence Book* and give one to each of your students. They will always remember how to write similes after this activity!

Grades K through 2, Connecting with Your Senses

Activity 4: Hands-on Activity: *Sensational Sensory Stations*

Students will connect with their senses through this activity. Collect a number of small shoe boxes. Cut a hole in the side of these boxes so that a child's hand can fit through the opening. Place a number of different-textured items in the box. Create a station in your classroom for these boxes and call it: Sensational Sensory Stations. Let students place their hands in the different boxes and describe what it is that they feel. Have them attempt to identify what they believe is in each box from just touching the object. Let them share this experience with the class. Your students will automatically formulate descriptive words that relate to their senses through this experience.

Grades K through 2, Connecting with Your Senses

Activity 5: Written Language Activity: *The Here and Now*

To connect with the world around them, students must write in the here and now! Have a small rhythm instrument, such as a triangle or a drum, in your class. Tell your class that when they hear this instrument it means *poetry call*. They must stop where they are and listen for the writing prompt. This element of surprise adds an interesting factor to the writing process for students. When there is an interesting event, perhaps after a fire drill or when there is a thunderstorm occurring, have a poetry call and tell your students it's time to write. Ask students to write notes for their poem in their Sensory Logs or poetry Blueprints about the event that is happening now (related to your writing prompt). Question them regarding what it is they hear, see, or feel about this event. They should record this information and share it with the class or a peer. This activity will begin to teach students to look, feel, and experience the world around them in the here and now, and to enjoy the spontaneity of a quick verse.

Resources

Need some help in brainstorming activities for your students to write in the here and now? Visit this wonderful website for ideas: www.readwritethink.org.

Remedies for Common Grammar Errors

Grades K through 2, Common Student Writing Errors

Common Error 1: Not Using Proper Punctuation Marks

Young students will leave out capital letters at the beginning of sentences and punctuation marks at the end of sentences very frequently.

Remedy 1: Teacher-Led Editing

As students are writing their rough drafts, have them number their sentences. Tell students to exchange papers and give each student a highlighter. Lead a peer editing session just for capital letters at the beginning of sentences and punctuation marks at the closing of sentences. Tell your students to put their finger on the first letter of each sentence, beginning with number one. Ask them, "Does it start with a capital letter? If it does, tell your neighbor, Good job. If it doesn't, put a dot on that letter with your highlighter." Have your students continue with the same process for end marks throughout the entire writing selection. Then have students exchange papers and correct their own punctuation mistakes. This activity will reinforce the concepts of capitalization at the beginning of sentences and end marks at the end of sentences.

Remedy 2: Interactive Books

Young students like pop-up books. Here's one that focuses on students selecting the correct punctuation marks for young authors. Try reading it to your class and have them select the correct pop-up correction! Petty, K. and J. Maizels. 2006. *Perfect Punctuation Pop-Up*. New York: Dutton Children's Books.

Grades K through 2, Common Student Writing Errors

Common Error 2: Sentence Fragments

Young authors are notorious for writing fragments instead of complete sentences. Reinforce and teach the concepts of sentences requiring a who/what and a doing to your class by doing the following fun skill-building activities.

Remedy 1: Oral Language Game—Sentence or Not?

Create two game cards for each student, one 3×5 card with *Not* written on it and the other with *Sentence*. Give a set of these cards to each student. Begin the game by writing a sentence or a fragment on the board. Turn to your class and ask them, "Sentence or not?" Your students should then hold up the card giving the correct response. If the statement is a fragment, ask a student to turn it into a complete sentence. Repeat this activity as frequently as you can. Your students will really enjoy this game!

Remedy 2: Who/What + A Doing = A Sentence

Place this sentence strip on your board. Formulate sentences with your class by using their names and activities in which they frequently participate. As you write the sentences on the board, have your students read the sentences in unison. Ask them to identify the two parts of each sentence. Remind them that their sentences must have the same two parts as the sentences on the board or it is *not* a sentence.

Grades 3 through 5

Are you looking for creative skill-building activities that are fun to reinforce your students' learning concepts in the areas of writing vocabulary and genre? Then read on! This chapter highlights: interactive strategies for learning writing vocabulary; skill-building activities for learning genre building blocks; and remedies for common grammar errors.

These skill-building activities can be used in isolation or can be used in conjunction with your writing lessons. Each of the three main sections that follow includes creative, interactive teaching concepts. Make sure to come up with some of your own ideas! One thing is for sure, your students will benefit from these experiences and have fun at the same time. Enjoy!

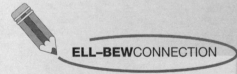

ELL–BEWCONNECTION

ELL students will remember different genres through their association with these catchy hand jives.

Interactive Strategies for Teaching Writing and Genre Vocabulary

Genre Format

Grades: 3 through 5	Interactive Strategy	Your Own Ideas!
Ask, *"What is . . ."*	**TIP:** Teach and use the proper writing words found here consistently.	
Genre	Lead choral response: • *What type of writing are we doing?* • *Who's my special audience?*	
Personal narrative	Lead choral response and hand jive: Put hand over heart and extend other hand out to the side: • *This is my story.*	
Informational (sequential)	Lead choral response and hand jive. Simulate writing a list with your hands: • *Putting things in order*	
Research	Lead choral response and hand jive. Put both hands in front of you and mimic opening a book: • *Look things up in a book.*	
Fantasy	Lead hand jive. Use a "make-believe" look, with eyes up and hands outward at shoulder level, palms facing up in a wondering position: • *It's make-believe.*	
Poetry	Lead hand jive. Put hands over heart with palms open. Lead a song, clapping the rhythm: • *I think that I shall never see, a poem as lovely as a tree. (or favorite class poem)*	
Persuasive	Lead pantomime and choral response. Put three fingers up to your head to demonstrate changing someone's mind with three good reasons, and say: • *Changing somebody's mind with three good reasons*	
Magazine article	Hold left hand palm up (like a page of a magazine) and scroll down it with your right index finger, as if reading an article: • *Writing for a magazine*	*(continued)*

Grades: 3 through 5	Interactive Strategy	Your Own Ideas!
Myth/legend (add in fourth grade)	Flex your muscles with both arms and say: • *Writing about heroes and gods from long ago*	
Adventure (add in fourth grade)	Using an excited voice, twirl an imaginary lasso, saying: • *Yi-ha, action!*	
Mystery (add in fifth grade)	Look through a magnifying glass for a clue, saying: • *Whodunit?*	
Tall tale (add in fifth grade)	Pretend to stretch a long rubber band and say: • *Stretching the truth*	
Position paper (add in fifth grade)	Remind students this is a persuasive paper, then stand and spread your legs apart with hands on your hips and say: • *This is where I stand.*	
Historical fiction (add in fifth grade)	Remind students this is a narrative, then stroke your chin (as if pulling on your beard) and say: • *Long, long ago . . .*	

Interactive Strategies for Teaching Writing and Genre Vocabulary
Genre Elements

Grades: 3 through 5	Interactive Strategy	Your Own Ideas!
Ask, "What is . . ."		
Topic **Topic sentence**	Lead choral response to the tune of "The Hokey Pokey": • *That's what it's all about.* • *That's what it's all about [say the topic].*	
Sentence **Complete sentence**	Lead choral response (and add the appropriate punctuation mark): • *Who/what + a doing = a sentence.*	

Grades: 3 through 5	Interactive Strategy	Your Own Ideas!
Simple paragraphs (Writing complete sentences on topic)	Lead choral response to teach sentences needed in a paragraph, three sentences on one topic, extending three fingers, then one: • *3 on 1* Hold up one finger, and probe, "What is the number one sentence?" • *Topic sentence* Hold up two fingers and identify what it will be: • *A detail that goes with the topic* Hold up three fingers and identify what it will be: • *A detail* **Example:** 1 = Topic idea: dog 2 = Detail: wags tail 3 = Detail: has spots These notes can be turned into a three-sentence paragraph.	
Introduction paragraph	Ask, "What's the first paragraph called?" • *The introduction* "What's the purpose of the introduction?" • *It introduces the topic* or *It's the beginning of the story* "How big is the introduction?" Students show with their hands: • *Middle size*	
Detail paragraph	Ask, "What's the second paragraph called?" • *The detail paragraph* "What is the purpose of this paragraph?" • *It tells the details about the topic* or *It tells the middle of the story* "How big is the detail paragraph?" Students show with their hands: • *The longest*	
Summary paragraph	Ask, "What is the last paragraph called?" • *The summary* or *The conclusion* "What is the purpose of the summary paragraph?" • *To tell about the topic in a short way* or *To tell the ending of the story* "How long is the summary paragraph?" Students show with their hands: • *It's the shortest.*	*(continued)*

Section III

Grades: 3 through 5	Interactive Strategy	Your Own Ideas!
Rough draft	Lead choral response: • *Sloppy copy*	
Word wrap	Lead word-wrap dance with arm swinging left to right while saying: • *We write side to side, side to side, side to side.*	
Indenting paragraphs	Lead students in hand action: • *Put two fingers on the left side of the first line and put a dot. This leaves a space for indenting.*	
Edit	Lead choral response while making erasing motion: • *Fixing our mistakes*	
Peer edit	Lead choral response while making erasing motion: • *Helping our peers fix their mistakes*	
Conference	Demonstrate hands "talking" to each other (open and close fingers): • *Talking about it together*	
Illustration	Lead choral response: • *A picture*	
Speaker	Ask who's the speaker, while pointing to own mouth [teacher]: • *The person talking*	
Listener	Ask who are the listeners, while pointing to own ears: • *The people listening, not talking*	
Portfolio	Hold up the real portfolio. Lead choral response: • *A collection of my work*	

ELL–BEWCONNECTION

ELL students lack age-appropriate vocabulary. Teach writing vocabulary the BEW way.

Skill-Building Activities for Learning Personal Narrative Building Blocks

Genre Writing Techniques for Personal Narrative: Character Development (Who Are My Characters and What Do They Say?)

Grades 3 through 5, Character Development

Activity 1: Oral Language Game: *What Am I?*

Tell your class you are going to play a game describing characteristics of things they know. Find pictures of items that your students would typically play with on the playground or at recess. Put one picture or item in a shoe box and place it in front of your class. Tell your students that they need to guess what item is in the box based on the clues that you give them. Instruct them to listen closely. Give your students characteristics of the item. For example, if you have selected a ball, tell your students, "It bounces," and "It can travel through the air." Ask your students to guess the object by your clues. The first student to answer wins the round! Continue for several rounds. This activity provides class examples of object traits and characteristics. This will help students hear rich descriptions of characteristics that can help as they develop their characters.

Possible Items

Baseball, Frisbee, jump rope, football, Nerf ball, marbles, jacks; pictures of a slide, swing set, basketball hoop, monkey bars

Resources

Board game: *Twenty Questions* (University Games)

Grades 3 through 5, Character Development

Activity 2: Oral Language Game: *Beat the Clock!*

On one set of 3×5 cards, prepare descriptions of characters that are popular with your students, perhaps from reading stories or watching television programs. On the second set of 3×5 cards, write the name of the character so that each description has a character name match. (We suggest a group of approximately twenty cards for this activity.) Break your students up into groups of four. Set a timer for three minutes and have the first team of four students try to match all the character descriptions with the character names. When the timer goes off, it's the next team's turn to do the same. The team of students that matches the most cards wins. Everybody learns to describe characters in detail.

> **ELL–BEW**CONNECTION
>
> Use these fun activities to help your ELL students learn the building blocks of different genres.

Section III

Grades 3 through 5, Character Development

Activity 3: Oral Language Game: *What's in the Egg?*

Purchase a class set of plastic dinosaur eggs. Give each student an egg to take home at the end of the day. Tell your students that their homework is to put one object in the egg. When the students return to school the next morning, they are to give the class clues by describing the object in the egg. The key is not to tell what the object is, but to describe its characteristics so that other students can guess the object. The first student to guess the mystery object wins, and then it's their turn to do the same. Continue with the game as long as you like! This game teaches students to use verbal descriptions to describe the characteristics of objects. They will soon learn that describing characters in their stories will result in a genuine uniqueness—just like it does for objects.

Genre Format and Voice for a Personal Narrative: Format: A Story with a Beginning, Middle, and End

Grades 3 through 5, Format: A Story with a Beginning, Middle, and End

Activity 1: Written Language Activity: *What Happens Next?*

Select an age-appropriate short story to read to your class. Read the story and stop just before the story ends. Tell your students to finish the story with a *good* ending. Set a timer and give your students ten minutes to write down the story ending. When the timer goes off, ask students to share their story ending verbally with the class. After the class has shared their story endings, read the actual story ending. Did any of your students write the actual story ending? This activity will facilitate student understanding of story parts. Students will soon understand that stories must have an ending.

Grades 3 through 5, Format: A Story with a Beginning, Middle, and End

Activity 2: Oral and Written Language Activity: *Stories in the Round*

Break your students up into groups of three. Select a topic for this story time. Pass out three index cards to each group of students. Write *Beginning* at the top of the first card, *Middle* at the top of the second, and *End* at the top of the third. Each student needs to hold one of each of the three story parts. Tell the students holding a *Beginning* card that they have three minutes to tell the beginning of the story, then set a classroom timer for three minutes. When the timer goes off, everyone needs to stop. Then have the students with a *Middle* card continue the middle of the story, starting from where the first students left off. Set the timer for five minutes and say "Go." Stop them when the timer rings. Now the students with an *End* card must tell the story ending. Set the timer for two minutes and follow the same procedure. When the story has been completed, have each student write the entire story beginning, middle, and end on their paper. Have one person from each group share the story with the class. This activity promotes understanding the parts of a story.

Grades 3 through 5, Format: A Story with a Beginning, Middle, and End

Activity 3: Oral and Written Language Activity: *Magazine Magic*

Select a student topic such as animals. Bring a number of magazines and brown paper lunch bags to class. Give each student a brown paper bag, magazine, 3×5 cards, scissors, and a glue stick. Tell your students to find as many animals as they can from the magazine. They need to cut out each one individually and paste it on a 3×5 card and put it in the brown paper bag. Set a timer and have students do this in the time that you have allotted. Then have students pull out the animal cards one at a time and tell an animal story using all the characters (animals) they have cut out. Then ask them to write their story and glue it on the face of the brown paper bag. Repeat this activity throughout the year using various class topics. Timed activities such as this one will give your students practice in writing stories quickly, just like the standards required in your high-stakes state tests.

Grades 3 through 5, Format: A Story with a Beginning, Middle, and End

Activity 4: Reading and Thinking Activity: *Plays*

Students enjoy reading and acting out plays in school. Try letting your students perform for their peers or younger classes. This provides review of the parts of a good story: a beginning, middle, and end. Need some ideas? The following website includes fun plays that teach story parts with an accompanying audio CD. Your students will love the plays from *Speak Out! Readers Theater* (Pacific Learning Company) available online at www.pacificlearning.com.

Grades 3 through 5, Voice

Activity 5: Oral and Written Language Exercise: *Whose Line Is It?*

Prepare a number of large call-out bubbles from construction paper. Ask your students what their favorite sentence is and have them write it down on a call-out bubble. Collect the bubbles and hold one up in front of the class and ask the students in your class if they can identify whose line it is. Then post the bubble on a bulletin board. Save the rest of the bubbles and follow this same procedure with one or two call-out bubbles every day.

Variation: Cut out a few more call-out bubbles and ask a couple of your students to record your favorite lines. Post these too! Your students will learn that their verbal expressions can be recorded in written form as one of their identifiable characteristics: voice!

Grades 3 through 5, Voice

Activity 6: Oral Language Activity: *Guess Who?*

Pick one of your class's favorite authors. Read a short-story selection by that author to your class. Ask them to identify the author by just listening to your reading. Lead a class discussion about how they have come to know who wrote the story. Talk about word choice, word fluency, and writing style. This activity will help your students have an understanding of writing style or author's voice. Good authors for this activity are Peggy Parish (Amelia Bedelia books), Barbara Park and Denise Brunkus (Junie B. Jones series), Shel Silverstein's poetry, or Marjorie Sharmat and Marc Simont (Nate the Great books).

Variation: Instead of a children's author, use a historical document and read it in character, using the statesman's voice as you read from the Declaration of Independence, the Constitution, and so forth.

Skill-Building Activities for Learning Persuasive Writing Building Blocks

Genre Writing Technique for Persuasive Writing: What's My Point of View? Appeal to the Senses!

Grades 3 through 5, Point of View

Activity 1: Oral Language Game: *Let's Go Fishing!*

Get a small fish bowl and fish net. Write a number of first-person pronouns (*I* and *we*) and third-person pronouns (*he*, *she*, and *it*) on small pieces of paper. Put these pieces of paper in the fish bowl. Tell your students it's time to go fishing. Select a student to fish a piece of paper out of the fish bowl. Have the student read the pronoun on that paper aloud to the class. Ask the class if that specific pronoun is first person or third person. Then ask for volunteers to say a sentence with that pronoun. Teach your students how the pronouns that we use in persuasive writing selections are first or third person. This game will help them get the idea.

Grades 3 through 5, Point of View

Activity 2: Oral Language Game: *Role Switch*

Put all your students' names in a bag. Shake them up and pick one name. Ask that student to switch roles with you for an argument. Construct some preselected arguments, such as our class shouldn't have any homework; each student should get an A in this class; or each class should have fifteen minutes of free time every day. Have the selected student role-play the argument from your perspective. This will allow your students to understand arguing from a different point of view.

Grades 3 through 5, Appealing to the Senses

Activity 3: Appealing to the Senses: *How Would You Feel?*

Think about and write different scenarios in which individuals would respond emotionally to an issue. Write them down and put them in a bag. Have students draw a card from the bag. Ask each student to answer the question, "How would you feel if [fill in the blank with the scenario that they selected from the card]?" This will help students understand how to appeal to the emotions of their audience in a persuasive argument. For example, scenarios could include a new house being built in the field where they have their tree house or play softball, or desserts are being removed from school lunches for health reasons.

Genre Format and Voice for Persuasive Writing: Taking a Stand and Three Good Arguments

Grades 3 through 5, Taking a Stand

Activity 1: Class Activity: *Survey Surprises!*

Students love school surveys. Use this to your advantage when teaching persuasive arguments. Pick a hot issue in your school, maybe one to do with recycling in your school and community or even an investigation of school homework policies. Work with your class and develop a persuasive question that can be used as a survey question. For example, "Should we recycle in our school?" or "Should we have a no-homework policy for weekends in our school?" Create a student worksheet and tell students that they have two days to survey twenty-five students in their school regarding this question. When the students bring in their results, have them tally the numbers of students who were for or against the proposed question. Have students present their results to the class and give brief reasons for supporting each side of the question. This activity helps assist students in understanding how to take a stand and how to recognize the opposing side of an argument.

Grades 3 through 5, Taking a Stand

Activity 2: Oral Language Activity: *Court Case*

Create a mock courtroom in your class. Appoint a judge, jury, and audience. Present a topic to the class, such as "Should there be a fine or penalty for littering on the school grounds?" Appoint two attorneys: one to argue the case for the topic and the other to argue the case against the topic. Run this like a debate or just request closing arguments. Let the jury and the audience vote on which attorney presented the better argument. There is a website that relates to this called Lesson to G. It's located at civicallyspeaking.org/fairness.html. This site has links to elementary, middle, and high school ideas.

Grades 3 through 5, Taking a Stand

Activity 3: Oral Language and Listening Activity: *Special Speeches*

Most speeches provide an example of an individual taking a stand on an issue in public. Students will learn how to take a stand by listening to popular speeches. Are you unsure of where to find some of these speeches? Download them from the following website: www.history.com/media.do. This is a fabulous website for historical videos and speeches; check it out!

Grades 3 through 5, Three Good Arguments

Activity 4: Oral Language Activity: *Three Reasons Why*

Give your students a debatable hot topic, such as "Should we be allowed to bring a favorite toy to school each day?" Tell students to take a stand: "Yes, I agree" or "No, I don't agree." Give them five minutes to think of three good reasons for their stand. Walk around the room and call on volunteers to share their reasons. Ask, "What do you think and why?" and hold up three fingers. The student should hold up one finger for each of their three reasons to match your three-finger prompt. Continue around the room.

Variation: Give each student a persuasive Blueprint and have them number the squares with 1, 2, and 3. Then ask them to write their three good reasons in the squares.

Grades 3 through 5, Three Good Arguments

Activity 5: Oral Language Activity: *Good Reason or Not*

Select a topic of interest to your class. Now prepare a number of reasons that students might agree (or disagree) with that topic and write each of them on a sentence strip. Make some of these choices reasonable and some of them absurd. Share the question that you want students to consider. Then hold up one of the reasons and ask your class to read it aloud together. Then say, "Good reason or not?" and ask for them to respond in unison. This is good practice for developing persuasive arguments in grades 3 through 5.

Skill-Building Activities for Learning Research Building Blocks

Genre Writing Techniques for Research Papers: Writing the Research Question and Finding the Information

Grades 3 through 5, Writing the Research Question

Activity 1: Oral Language Game: *Jeopardy—What Am I?*

Bring a small rhythm instrument such as a drum to class. Also, collect a variety of small items in a bag (a can opener, a small pot, silverware, paper clips, or anything else that students would know) to be used for this game. Select one of these items, cover it with a small towel, and put it on a table in front of your class. Tell your students to listen carefully as you give them clues regarding the object's identity. Start with the purpose of the object such as a small pot by saying, "I'm used to cook food. What am I?" The students should answer you as if they're playing the game *Jeopardy,* by saying, "What is a pot?" By chance, if students forget to state their answer in question form, hit the drum and say, "Forfeit." If they actually guess the object from the first clue, move on to the next object. In the event that they don't guess the object from the first clue, give them two additional clues describing characteristics of the object. Using a can opener as an example, you might say it can use electricity to operate or it can be used manually and then ask your students to guess what the object is. The purpose of the game is to guess what the object is with only three clues. If students aren't able to discover the identity of the object using three clues, remove the towel from the object and move on to the next item. This activity will familiarize students with how to formulate a good question—the key to writing a great research paper.

Resources

Board game: *Twenty Questions* (University Games)

Grades 3 through 5, Writing the Research Question

Activity 2: Hands-on and Writing Activity: *Ingenious Invention!*

Tell your students that they are about to become an *ingenious inventor* just like Thomas Edison.

They must invent a *thingamajig* that every student in the country wants. Children love to use their imaginations during this exercise. First, tell them they must think of an invention. If you need some student examples, check out the websites listed in the Resources to inspire your students. Next, have them write down three facts about their invention: what it is used for, what it looks like, and why everybody needs one. Finally, have students present their invention ideas and their three facts to your class. Many students may even choose to draw a picture of their thingamajig or construct a sample object out of paper or cardboard! Your class must ask the inventor questions about the invention, such as "Where did you get the idea for this invention?" or "What else could this invention be used for?" Lead a class discussion around the fact that many inventions begin or have begun in this fashion. The purpose of this exercise is to help your students develop questions related to a specific topic. Yes, students will draw the connection between their own inventions, and the role of research and development in the writing of a research question.

Resources

If your students can't think of an invention idea, have them check some of our favorite websites:

Invention Convention: Examples of Student Inventions: www.eduplace.com/science/invention/resources/real_inventions.html

The Bakken Science Program Students: www.thebakken.org/students/ebsp/prespring02/index.htm

Grades 3 through 5, Writing the Research Question

Activity 3: Oral Language and Writing Game: *Twenty Questions!*

Children certainly do know how to ask questions! Why not turn this aptitude into a research learning experience? First, your students will need twenty 3 × 5 cards, one large sheet of construction paper, a ruler, and markers. Ask each student to pick a great research topic. After that has been decided, pass out all the listed materials. Tell your students to write twenty questions about their research topic on one side of their twenty 3 × 5 cards. Your students may already know the answer to some of their twenty questions. Questions to which your students don't know the answers must be researched. Give this as a homework assignment for the next two days. Tell your students to find the answers to their unanswered questions and write the answers down on the reverse side of the cards. When students have completed their twenty-card question-and-answer assignment, they're ready to develop their own game. Let your students be creative by drawing a game board that represents an idea having to do with their research topic. Tell your students to draw a game board just like one that they would buy, with a start and finish line, and a place to put their question cards in the center. Use pennies to move around the board. They must now decide the game rules, such as how many spaces each player should move if they answer the question correctly and so forth. When finished, your students will have creatively written a research question and begun a research writing project. Let them enjoy their newly created game with others!

Resources

If your students can't think of their own game, have them look at some fun interactive games created by NASA's observation website, Fun & Games, located at http://nasa.gov/audience/for students/index.html.

Grades 3 through 5, Finding the Information

Activity 4: Hands-on Group Activity: *Scavenger Scurry!*

Elementary students don't always understand how or where to find information on a topic. They don't know what it means to research a topic, so try this activity. Select a class research topic such as a science project on the formation of different types of rocks. Collect various types of specialty rocks and write information on 3 × 5 cards about each rock type. Use very descriptive language to describe the rocks that you will hide. Your students will have fun with this activity. Tell them, "It's time for a scavenger hunt," and ask them to find the rocks that you've hidden on the playground. Form groups of five students from your class. Give each group of five students a set of descriptive cards describing the special rocks that you've hidden (five or six types would be great). Give your students fifteen minutes to find the rocks outside. When the time is up, have your students return to class. Ask each group of students to read the description of the rock that you've written on the 3 × 5 card and the one that they've found. Have the class decide, "Does the description match the rock?" If so, that team gets a point. Go through this same process with each group until they all have had the opportunity to discuss their findings. Relate this searching-for-rocks scavenger hunt to searching for research information. Students will relate looking for descriptive information that matches their topic to this game activity.

Variation: Scavenger hunts can be used for any genre or any cross-curriculum learning activity.

Grades 3 through 5, Finding the Information

Activity 5: Cyber Trip: *Can You Do the Dewey?*

Today, even our young students are great with computers. Some are just plain fantastic investigators when it comes to using the Internet. This learning experience will channel the computer talent of your students while teaching them research skills. Make learning the Dewey decimal system exciting as well as practical for finding materials in the media center. For this activity you need an Internet hookup in your media center with individual student computers or a digital media presentation method for class viewing. Teach the Dewey decimal system by using the interactive website Can You Do the Dewey? located at http://thrall.org/dewey. This website has three links: a check link, to test your knowledge regarding the Dewey classification system; a meet Dewey link, where information about the man that invented this system is shared; and a Dewey decimal system link, to learn how to use this system interactively. After each cyber lesson, let your students determine whether they can "Do the Dewey" for themselves in the school media center.

Grades 3 through 5, Finding the Information

Activity 6: Cyber Trip: *Fact Monster*

Most elementary students need multiple sources to gather research facts. If your class is writing a research project requiring information from almanacs, try this website: Fact Monster: Online Almanac, Dictionary, and Encyclopedia located at www.factmonster.com. Your class will have a great time experiencing and learning about almanacs from this interactive website.

Genre Format and Voice for Research Papers: Developing Three Good Supporting Research Points

Grades 3 through 5, Three Good Research Points

Activity 1: Oral Language Activity: *Pick Three*

Select a class research topic with a narrow focus just like you would for your very own research topic. Make five class sets of 3×5 cards with your research topic written on one card in bold letters. Then write six supporting research answers to your question on the other cards in each set. Make sure only three of the six cards have accurate supporting information about your research topic. Break up your class into five learning groups. Instruct your students that each group must select the best three supporting details that answer the research question. Set a class timer for ten minutes and when the timer goes off, ask each group to share their findings with the class. Ask your students to give reasons for choosing their supporting details. Lead a class discussion on the importance of finding at least three facts that can support your research question and why some are better than others. This exercise will assist your students with finding great supporting details for developing their research papers.

Grades 3 through 5, Three Good Research Points

Activity 2: Oral and Written Language Development: *Listen and Learn*

Your students will learn how to construct a great research paper by reading or hearing one in class. Make sure that you read well-done research papers to your class. If you're wondering where you can get this type of information, try one of our favorite student-friendly websites, ArtHouse: Make it Your Own! located at www.storyboardtoys.com/gallery/Cecily.htm. This website shares elementary students' completed research projects with coordinating artwork. If your students are interested in publishing their finished papers on this website, simply follow the student-friendly submission instructions that are available.

Skill-Building Activities for Learning Poetry Building Blocks

Genre Writing Techniques for Poetry: Using Rhyme and Rhythm

Grades 3 through 5, Using Rhyme and Rhythm

Activity 1: Oral and Written Language Activity: *Web of Words*

Create many Webs of Words with rhyming words. Write a word in the center of the web and then create an entire web of rhyming words with your students. Your students may need some assistance to come up with difficult-to-rhyme words, so have a class set of Scholastic's *Rhyming Dictionary* (Young, 2006) available for all to use. Then, using the class-created Web of Words, have students write rhyming sentences in couplets. This will prepare them for using rhyme in various types of poetry.

Variation: Create many different Webs of Words with rhyming words that can be used in a silly poem. A topic that our students enjoyed writing on was "If Principals Could Fly." Students would then add lines creating a poem with an end rhyming scheme in couplets. For example,

> If principals could fly, Mrs. Blumberg would fly high in the sky,
> She would see everyone from high in the sky.
> Have fun creating silly rhyming couplets.

Resources

Board game: *What's the Rhyme?* (Sorting Houses: Lakeshore)

Grades 3 through 5, Using Rhyme and Rhythm

Activity 2: Oral and Written Language: *Make It Your Own!*

Pick a common poem or jingle that all your students know. Create a worksheet leaving the last word off each line. Make copies of this worksheet, give one to each student, and tell them to finish the poem with their own words. Have fun with it! Are you unsure of a poem or jingle to use with your class? Find one on this great website, Fill-in-the-blank poems located at http://3www.poetry teachers.com/poetryfun/poetfun.html. If your students are having trouble with rhyme in poetry, give them some help. Download any of this free PoemMaker software for use with Windows. This software will help your students generate poems from selected words: www.ihsan.biz/#poemmaker. Another good website is www.janecutler.com/games/poemmaker.html.

Grades 3 through 5, Using Rhyme and Rhythm

Activity 3: Listening Activity: *Can You Hear It Now?*

Just as with any other genre, your students will learn to write poetry if you create a poetry-rich classroom environment. Read a wide variety of poems to your students where rhyme and rhythm are present. Read poems to your students daily and ask them to listen for the rhyming words and poetry meter. Try these websites: www.poetryarchive.org/childrensarchive/home.do or www.poetry4kids.com or www.gigglepoetry.com.

Resources

Are you unsure of where to find poetry that your students will enjoy? Look at one of our favorite poetry anthologies: Moger, S. 2006. *A Poem for Every Day!* New York: Scholastic. Are you interested in playing some children's poetry for your students to listen to in class? Try this website: http//poetryvlog.com.

Genre Format and Voice for Poetry:
Word Choice and Connecting with Your Senses

Grades 3 through 5, Word Choice and Connecting with Your Senses

Activity 1: Cyber Trip: *Off We Go!*

The best way to get your students to write poetry is for them to have a good understanding of its various forms and types. Why not take a cyber trip to the Poets Pantry Virtual Field Trip website? This website will introduce the various formats and styles of poetry, and your class will meet some real poets. Make sure you save this location among your Favorites: www.tramline.com/lit/poet/index.htm. After the cyber trip, lead a class discussion on the variety of poetry your students have just been exposed to. Ask them what their favorite type was and why. Focus on the Building Blocks of Poetry covered on the cyber trip.

Grades 3 through 5, Word Choice and Connecting with Your Senses

Activity 2: Writing Activity: *Journal Journey*

Create a sensory journal for your students and have them assemble it. A simple cover that includes their name and *Journal Time* works well. Fill the inside of the journal with special sensory journal recording sheets, which are designed to help your students relate to the world around them. They should record information on their topics such as: What sounds do you hear? What does it look like? How does it smell? Is there a special characteristic of the thing or place that stands out in your mind? An important part of writing interesting poetry is the poet's ability to *stop, look,* and *listen* to the environment. Remind your students to carry their poetry journals with them every place they go. They never know when a poem will emerge!

Grades 3 through 5, Word Choice and Connecting with Your Senses

Activity 3: Poetry Writing Activity: *Focus, Focus!*

Chances are that your students won't select poetry-writing topics on their own until they become more familiar with the genre. This means it's up to you to help them find interesting topics to write about. Try this. Keep a small rhythm instrument like a triangle hanging in your room (or a bell or chime). When your students have completed their lessons or you feel it's time for a change of pace, hit the triangle three times. Tell your class this is a signal that it's poetry-writing time. It's time to drop everything and write poetry. Give them a focused topic to write on, such as window poetry. Here they must focus on one object or event happening right outside their window. Have them describe it in a poetry form that you've taught in class. They should write the poem and be prepared to share it with your class. Limit this activity to ten or fifteen minutes. It's just a poetry break.

Grades 3 through 5, Unique Poetry Styles

Activity 4: The Power of Poetry

There is a great website that can help you, as the teacher, learn the different poetry styles. This includes cinquain, acrostic, and shape poems. Go to www.readwritethink.org/lessons/lesson_view.asp?id=798.

Remedies for Common Grammar Errors

Grades 3 through 5, Common Student Writing Errors

Common Error 1: Writing Only Short, Simple Sentences

Students at this age level aren't very confident in their writing skills. Consequently, they often write short, choppy sentences. Does this type of student writing sound familiar to you?

Remedy 1: Stretch It

Stand in front of the class with a rubber band in your hands. Tell your students that the rubber band that you're holding represents the length of their sentences. Ask your students to read a few of their sentences out loud. If the sentence is short, just hold the rubber band in place. Ask another student to expand on the sentence that was just read to the class. If the sentence is longer, stretch out your rubber band a little longer. Tell your students you want their sentence length to stretch or even break your rubber band. As their sentences grow, you stretch the rubber band longer and longer.

Remedy 2: Sentence-Combining Exercise: *Sentence Growing*

Create your own game! Write a number of simple sentences on 5 × 7 cards. Then write a number of conjunctions on 3 × 5 cards. Divide your class into groups of three students and call them *teams*. Set a timer for three minutes. Tell students to combine as many sentences as they can until the timer rings. When the timer goes off, say, "Stop!" The team with the largest number of correctly combined sentences wins a no-homework pass.

Remedy 3: A Board Game: *Scrabble Sentence Cube Game* (S & R Games)

Students will enjoy this board game and will learn to build complex sentences at the same time.

Common Error 2: Spelling Mistakes

Do your students misspell words frequently? Do they lose context meaning in their writing because of terrible misspellings? You're not alone. Students at this grade level may still be using inventive spelling when writing.

Remedy 1: Create Topical Dictionaries: *Spelling Help!*

Students just don't like looking up words in dictionaries. They will, however, enjoy making their own topical dictionaries and will use them! Before your class begins a topic, select a number of new vocabulary words that they may have a difficult time spelling. Put these words in alphabetical order and write the definitions with your class. Put them in a folder with the name of the topic on the front. Let students keep these student-created dictionaries in their Rough Draft Writing Folders.

Remedy 2: Love Those Gadgets

For your students with special needs, allow them to use an electronic spelling device such as the Franklin spelling products. This will allow them to get the correct spellings of those difficult words.

Grades 6 through 8

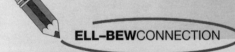

ELL–BEWCONNECTION

ELL students quickly learn
through physical modeling
and movement. Use the
BEW hand jives and jingles
to teach different genres.

By the time students are in middle school they have already acquired considerable instruction and skills in the area of written expression. Frequently, however, middle school students lack motivation to write. Do you know any students who fall in this category?

The major complaint middle school students have about writing (and they are not shy about sharing it) is, "I hate writing!" If these words are not being said by students in your middle school writing classes, you are indeed fortunate. However, if you are like the rest of us, try some of our interactive creative strategies for teaching and reinforcing writing concepts. These new ideas will motivate your students. As a matter of fact, many of them will actually begin to enjoy writing.

This chapter contains three main sections: interactive strategies for learning writing vocabulary; skill-building activities for learning genre building blocks; and remedies for common grammar errors.

We've included our interactive creative strategies for teaching writing to use with middle school students. The key to success with these students is to perform these interactive strategies in an age-appropriate fashion. You will use the same jingles and hand jives, but in a nondramatic way. Your students will appreciate the similarity to what they have learned in previous grades. Yes, middle school students as well as adults will respond positively to these techniques when used in a more adultlike manner.

ELL–BEWCONNECTION

ELL students lack the necessary writing vocabulary meanings to understand each genre. Teach them the BEW way!

Interactive Strategies for Teaching Writing and Genre Vocabulary

Genre Format

Grades: 6 through 8	Interactive Strategy	Your Own Ideas!
Ask, *"What is . . ."*	**TIP:** Teach and use the proper writing words found here consistently.	
Genre	Make students aware of the following: • *What type of writing are we doing?* • *Who's my special audience?*	
Personal narrative	Review the meaning of this genre with your class: • *This is my story.*	
Informational (sequential)	Review the meaning of this genre with your class: • *Putting things in order*	
Research	Review the meaning of this genre with your class: • *Look things up in a book.*	
Fantasy	Review the meaning of this genre with your class: • *It's make-believe.*	
Poetry	Review the meaning of this genre with your class: • *I think that I shall never see, a poem as lovely as a tree* (or favorite class poem).	*(continued)*

Grades: 6 through 8	Interactive Strategy	Your Own Ideas!
Persuasive	Review the meaning of this genre with your class. Put three fingers up to your head to demonstrate changing someone's mind with three good reasons, and say: • *Changing somebody's mind with three good reasons*	
Magazine article	Hold left hand palm up (like a page of a magazine) and scroll down it with your right index finger, as if reading an article: • *Writing for a magazine*	
Myth/legend	Flex your muscles with both arms and say: • *Writing about heroes and gods from long ago*	
Adventure	Using an excited voice, twirl an imaginary lasso, saying: • *Yi-ha, action!*	
Mystery	Look through a magnifying glass for a clue, saying: • *Whodunit?*	
Tall tale	Pretend to stretch a long rubber band and say: • *Stretching the truth*	
Position paper	Remind students this is a persuasive paper, then stand with your legs apart with hands on your hips and say: • *This is where I stand.*	
Historical fiction	Remind students this is a narrative, then stroke your chin (as if pulling on your beard) and say: • *Long, long ago . . .*	

ELL–BEWCONNECTION

ELL students will internalize and apply writing vocabulary words when they are taught first.

Interactive Strategies for Teaching Writing and Genre Vocabulary

Genre Elements

Grades: 6 through 8	Interactive Strategy	Your Own Ideas!
Ask, *"What is . . . "*		
Topic **Topic sentence**	Remind students to say: • *That's what it's all about.* • *That's what it's all about* [say the topic].	
Simple paragraphs (Writing complete sentences on topic)	For students who need this reminder, teach three sentences on one topic, extending three fingers, then one: • *3 on 1* Hold up one finger, and probe, "What is the number one sentence?" • *Topic sentence* Hold up two fingers and identify what it will be: • *A detail that goes with the topic* Hold up three fingers and identify what it will be: • *A detail* **Example:** 1 = Topic idea: dog 2 = Detail: wags tail 3 = Detail: has spots	
Introduction paragraph	Ask, "What's the first paragraph called?" • *The introduction* "What's the purpose of the introduction?" • *It introduces the topic* or *It's the beginning of the story* "How big is it?" • *Middle size*	*(continued)*

Grades: 6 through 8	Interactive Strategy	Your Own Ideas!
Detail paragraph	Ask, "What's the second paragraph called?" • *The detail paragraph* "What is the purpose of this paragraph?" • *It tells the details about the topic* or *It tells the middle of the story* "How big is the detail paragraph?" • *The longest*	
Summary paragraph	Ask, "What is the last paragraph called?" • *The summary* or *The conclusion* "What is the purpose of the summary paragraph?" • *To tell about the topic in a short way* or *To tell the ending of the story* "How long is the summary paragraph?" • *It's the shortest*	
Rough draft	*Sloppy copy*	
Indenting paragraphs	*Like a computer, tab in to start a new paragraph*	
Edit	Remind students to say the following to themselves: • *Fixing our mistakes*	
Peer edit	Remind students to say the following to themselves: • *Helping our peers fix their mistakes*	
Conference	• *Talking about it together*	
Illustration	A picture	
Portfolio	Hold up the real portfolio, and remind students that it is • *A collection of my work*	

Skill-Building Activities for Learning
Personal Narrative Building Blocks

Genre Writing Techniques for Personal Narrative: Character Development: Who Are My Characters and What Do They Say?

Grades 6 through 8, Character Dialogue

Activity 1: Written Language Activity: *Drop Everything and Write*

Your students will learn about writing effective character dialogue if they must use it to communicate with you and their peers. During this activity, tell your students that for the next ten minutes of class they cannot talk at all. The only way they can communicate with you and others is through writing. All questions and communications will be conducted only by writing dialogue to each other. Set a timer and begin. At the end of the ten minutes, lead a class discussion on the effectiveness of your students' written communication. Ask them if they were able to get their points across. Did they find they had to express their questions or answers more fully when they couldn't talk? Connect this exercise to the writing process by stating that the written communications in their stories are only as effective as the words that they choose. Select them carefully when developing characters in their stories.

Variation: Have a Drop Everything and Write in the Lunchroom Day. Announce to the school in the morning what the lunch menu that day will be. Teachers can write the choices on the board. Fifteen minutes before the lunch bell rings, give students a small piece of paper or a note card. Have students write down their lunch order, spelled correctly, to give to the lunch servers. If they want a salad, they need to write down the ingredients they want in their salad, including the dressing. If they want a carton of milk, they have to write it down. Make sure each student has his or her lunch order ready before going to the cafeteria. We really tried this and it was a success (the lunch staff agreed to it!). Be sure to debrief afterward and find out who didn't get a drink because they forgot to write it down. Connect this concept to the importance of word choice in narrative writing. Each detail counts.

Grades 6 through 8, Character Dialogue

Activity 2: Written Language Activity: *Dialogue Communication Boards*

Students do like to communicate with you. Mount a small dialogue bulletin board outside your office or classroom. Communicate with your students using written notes. They will look forward to receiving your notes!

Variation: Media Center Dialogue Boards. Hang a small bulletin board near the Kids Korner section of the library where students can ask questions, give suggestions, or offer general comments to their peer authors.

Grades 6 through 8, Character Development

Activity 3: Character Charades: *Guess Who?*

Select a story or play that you've recently read in class. Using 3×5 note cards, describe the characters' appearance, mannerisms, and any other distinguishing features they may have. Now it's time to play the game. Ask for student volunteers to pick a card, any card, and let your students guess which character is being described by the student's pantomime of that character. For an added attraction, you may want to divide your class into two teams. Keep track of the points that each team gets. Perhaps a small prize would be in order for the winning team—maybe a no-homework pass.

Grades 6 through 8, Character Development

Activity 4: Voice Charades: *Whose Voice Is It Anyway?*

Think of a number of different popular actors and one-line sayings that they're famous for. Write them down on 3 × 5 cards and ask for student volunteers to read the lines with the correct accent and voice intonation. Have the class guess who the famous character actually is. Relate this activity to voice in writing. Ask your students if they can hear a character's accent or voice intonations as they read their narratives. What type of vocabulary needs to be used to describe this type of voice?

Grades 6 through 8, Character Development

Activity 5: Dress-up Charades: *Guess Who's Coming to Class?*

Many times, teachers will dress up in costumes from the time period of a character they are teaching. Students really enjoy this! Why not have a student dress up in the costume that a character from their class story would wear? Can the class guess which character the student has chosen? *Variation:* Another way to do this is to allow students to draw a picture of different characters from their literature book. Remind them to put in the details, then have them describe their drawing in words. This highlights the importance of describing a character with rich detail.

Grades 6 through 8, Character Dialogue

Activity 6: Written Language: *Comic Strip Dialogue*

Yes, that's right. You can teach character dialogue by having your students bring comic strips to class. Comic strips use easy-to-follow character dialogue in their character call-out boxes. Talk about dialogue while reading the call-out bubbles of the comic strips as you show them to the class. Then have your students create their own comic strips! They'll love this activity and learn about character dialogue at the same time.

Resources

The website Newspaper in Education, Middle School Writing gives plans on how to develop character dialogue using comic strips and editorials and editorial cartoons for middle school writing: http://litsite.alaska.edu/workbooks/midnewswrite.html.

Genre Format and Voice for Personal Narrative:
Format: A Story with a Beginning, Middle, and End

Grades 6 through 8, Format: A Story with a Beginning, Middle, and End

Activity 1: Oral Language Activity: *Backpack Story*

Ask students to reach into their backpacks and take out one interesting item. Then ask for student volunteers to tell a story about the item that they pulled out of their backpack. Remind them to tell interesting facts, and to have a beginning, middle, and end. If the student volunteer gets stuck, another student can take over to keep the story going, but has to follow the leader and add more to the middle or add the ending.

Resources

The following website is good for middle school students learning to write a story with a beginning, middle, and end. The website is called *abcteach* and is located at www.abcteach.com. You can also find a great lesson on this site at www.abcteach.com/directory/basics/writing.

Grades 6 through 8, Format: A Story with a Beginning, Middle, and End

Activity 2: Oral Language Activity: *Stories in the Round*

Have students sit in a circle in class. Give them a sentence or two of a narrative story prompt. Let each student add a section to the story; however, by the time the story reaches the last student it must have included all the parts of the story. As the students are telling you their class-composed story, record the events on a class Blueprint on the board. This will allow your students to visualize the details they have so far and what components need to be added to complete the story. Ask for a student volunteer to record this class story in written format. Maybe a no-homework pass would be a good reward for completing this task. Give all your students a copy of this story after it is recorded as an example to follow when they are writing their own personal stories.

Grades 6 through 8, Format: A Story with a Beginning, Middle, and End

Activity 3: Oral Language Activity: *Dubbing a Movie*

Have your students divide up into groups of four or five. Ask each group to pick a favorite movie that most students know. Have them retell the story of the movie by recording notes on a poster-size Blueprint that shows the beginning, middle, and end of the story. Have one member of each group dub the movie by telling about it from the Blueprint. Don't let them name the movie, because their classmates have to guess the title from the story line. This is good practice for writing notes about the beginning, middle, and end of a story.

Grades 6 through 8, Voice

Activity 4: Writing Activity: *Poster Portrait—Who Am I?*

Give each student a poster board or large piece of paper. Ask your students to write a story that describes themselves in an interesting way. They cannot say who they are, but use a rich description. Then hang all the stories on a wall and ask your class to identify the author of each piece of writing. This makes a good ice-breaking activity. It also helps students *hear* the voice of each of their classmates.

Grades 6 through 8, Voice

Activity 5: Oral Language Activity: *Speaking in Voices*

Middle school students will love this activity, but it will take some preparation on your part, and access to good computer equipment that has a microphone built in. Perhaps your computer lab will allow you some time and space to do this. Download Voice Changer software to an MP3 player or the computer. The website is located at www.audio4fun.com/voice-changer.htm. Parts of this website are free. Have each student prepare a current narrative writing selection that has plenty of voice in it. One by one, allow them to go to the computer lab and read their selection onto a CD using the Voice Changer software. Each student will have their own track, so keep a log of which student is reading for each track. Also, set a timer for how many minutes they have to record (this activity can be so motivating, they may not come back!). When all students have recorded their stories in another voice, burn the CD and have it handy in your classroom to use day by day after that. This can be the warmup activity for the following week as they try to guess whose voice they are hearing on the CD.

Skill-Building Activities for Learning Persuasive Writing Building Blocks

Genre Writing Technique for Persuasive Writing: Point of View: What's My Point of View?

Grades 6 through 8, Point of View

Activity 1: Oral Language Activity: *Walking in Their Shoes*

Select a short story or a historical speech. Have a student volunteer read this selection or speech to your class. Tell them their job is to assume the role of the person who actually wrote the selection. They are to read and act just as the true author would in this presentation. Ask the readers how they felt about this presentation. Were the words they used different from words they would have chosen themselves? What words or phrases had an impact on them? This activity will communicate point of view in writing. If you need copies of historical speeches to use, you can make copies from the following website: http://en.wikipedia.org/wiki/ list_of_speeches.

Grades 6 through 8, Point of View

Activity 2: Oral Language Activity: *Whose Problem Is It?*

Ask your students to share a story about a time when they got into trouble. Have them tell the story from their point of view. Then have them retell the same story from their parents' point of view. Is the story different? Are the words used to tell the story different? This activity will teach students that different people have different points of view for a shared experience.

Grades 6 through 8, Point of View

Activity 3: Oral Language Activity: *Optimist or Pessimist?*

Have you heard the expression, "It's all in how you look at it"? Help your students practice looking at a situation in two different ways—from the perspective of an optimist and a pessimist. The topic might be: *School starts at 8:30* A.M. First, have your students take the optimistic point of view and tell why this is a good thing. Then, have them take the pessimistic point of view and describe why this is a bad thing. Remind students that when writing a persuasive paper, they need to decide on their point of view and stay with that perspective throughout their paper.

Genre Format and Voice for Persuasive Writing: Taking a Stand and Three Good Arguments

Grades 6 through 8, Taking a Stand

Activity 1: Class Activity: *Survey Surprises!*

Students love school surveys. Use this to your advantage when teaching persuasive arguments. Pick a hot issue in your school, maybe one to do with cell phone use or the value of being allowed to use a calculator in math class. Together with your class, develop a persuasive question that can be used as a survey question. For example, "Should we be able to use our cell phones during lunch in the cafeteria?" or "Should students have to calculate every problem in math by hand or, after showing that they know how to do it, could they use a calculator?" Create a student worksheet and tell students they have two days to survey twenty-five students in their school regarding this question. When the students bring in their results, have them tally the number of students who were for or against the proposed question. Have students present their results to the class and give brief reasons for supporting each side of the question. This activity helps assist students in understanding how to take a stand and how to recognize the opposing side of an argument.

Grades 6 through 8, Taking a Stand

Activity 2: Oral Language Activity: *Court Case*

Create a mock courtroom in your class. Appoint a judge, jury, and audience. Select a topic of interest to your student that has a good argument on both sides. For example, "Should we have a dress code? If so, should it include body jewelry and tattoos?" Appoint two attorneys: one to argue the case for the topic and the other to argue the case against the topic. Let the jury and the audience vote on which attorney presented the better argument.

Grades 6 through 8, Taking a Stand

Activity 3: Oral and Written Language Activity: *Debate Team*

If you are a middle school teacher, there's one thing that you know for sure and that is that your students are great at arguing. For this reason, consider creating a school debate team. Students who participate on debate teams will learn the building blocks of a persuasive argument quickly and have a great time doing it. If you're unsure of where to begin with this task, look at the following website. It will give you all the information you need to organize and begin your school debate team: www.middleschooldebate.com/topics/topicwriting.htm.

Grades 6 through 8, Three Good Arguments

Activity 4: Oral Language Activity: *Three Reasons Why*

Give your students a debatable hot topic, such as "Should we be allowed to bring our iPods to school?" Tell students to take a stand, "Yes, I agree" or "No, I don't agree." Give them five minutes to think of three good reasons for their stand. Walk around the room and call on volunteers to share their reasons. Say to these students, "What do you think and why?" and hold up three fingers. The students should hold up one finger for each of their three reasons to match your three-finger prompt. Continue around the room.

Variation: Give each student a persuasive Blueprint and have them number the squares 1, 2, and 3. Ask them to take notes about their three good reasons in the squares.

Grades 6 through 8, Three Good Arguments

Activity 5: Written Language Activity: *Convince the Boss*

Select a hot issue in your school. It should be one that directly affects them, such as whether students should be given a three-day suspension for excessive tardiness. Tell them to compose a letter to the school principal to persuade the principal to accept their side of the issue. Explain that they must include three strong arguments to build their case. After the class has completed this assignment, invite the principal to class. Ask for student volunteers to read these letters directly to the principal. See if your students, through their letters, can persuade the principal to accept their side of the argument.

Skill-Building Activities for Learning Research Building Blocks

Genre Writing Techniques for Research Papers: Writing the Research Question and Finding the Information

Grades 6 through 8, Writing the Research Question

Activity 1: Oral Language Activity: *What Dontcha Know?*

Research papers should relate to a cross-curricular topic. What are your students learning in their science or social studies class? Talk with those teachers and plan to teach your unit on research writing to connect to their topic in one of those courses. Start with a cross-curricular experience focused on your topic. Write "What I would like to know more about" in the center of the Wheel of Thought. As students tell you areas they would like to learn more about, write those topics in a question format on the Wheel of Thought. The rays of the Wheel of Thought become possible research questions.

Grades 6 through 8, Writing the Research Question

Activity 2: Writing in Pairs: *How Do You Do That?*

Middle school students often explore new sports, games, and hobbies. Have students work in pairs. Have each student write a list of at least two or three sports, games, or hobbies that interest him or her. Then have the students trade papers with their partners. Each student should write a question asking how that specific activity is done. Return the papers to the original authors and have them circle the question that interests them the most. These are now potential research questions.

Resources

There is a website called *Essential Questions* where students can see samples of research questions written on various topics. This would be a good tool to use to stimulate students who are struggling to understand what a research question looks like. The website is located at www.bcps.org/offices/lis/models/middle.html.

Grades 6 through 8, Finding the Information

Activity 3: Field Trips: *Special-Interest Field Trips*

Many times middle school curricular requirements include a science or history research project. Take the time to visit local science and history museums that have displays that support your students' special topic research projects. A visit to a museum with a special exhibit is worth a month of research! Your students will take notes, ask questions, and be actively involved with seeking out information for their project.

Grades 6 through 8, Finding the Information

Activity 4: Virtual Search: *Finding Your Facts*

You shouldn't be surprised when we say that middle school students spend a lot of time at the computer. They are actually more prone to conduct a virtual search for information rather than visit a *real* media center. Knowing this, why not capitalize on your students' interests and skills? Today there are many websites that list excellent reference materials online. The following website provides students with language and grammar help, a link to find special quotes, information about specific popular authors, a link for research report writing, as well as an Ask the Expert link. It was designed specifically for middle school students: www.sldirectory.com/studf/language.html.

Resources

Here is a website that provides resources for literature, science, and social studies ideas. There is an electronic zoo, a firehouse museum, a Grand Canyon trip, and a dinosaur exhibit. There are many cool ideas for virtual trips. It is called Projects, Fun Sites, and Field Trips for Middle School: http://mathforum.org/sum95/math.forum/middle.projects.desc.html.

Grades 6 through 8, Finding the Information

Activity 5: Personal Interviews: *Have You Met This Person?*

Another great source of information for research projects is personal interviews. For example, if one of your students was interested in conducting a research project on World War II for his history class, why not hook him up with a World War II veteran who would be willing to answer his questions? Recording firsthand experiences in a narrative format provides an interesting and personal touch to a research project. A good way to start is to help your students develop a questionnaire that will answer their proposed research question. Assist them in finding people to interview who would be knowledgeable and willing to answer their questions. They will remember these interviews long after the assignment. As one student stated, "I visited the *USS Pennsylvania* through his eyes. He even showed me pictures that he had kept that were very old. I revisited history!"

Grades 6 through 8, Finding the Information

Activity 6: Cyber Trip: *Let's Search with Dewey!*

If some of your students who are at risk or academically challenged are not familiar with media center resources, lead them through this interactive cyber media search. This activity will familiarize them with the Internet as a source for finding valuable information. The following website will teach the Dewey decimal system used in media centers for source classification in an interactive way: http://thrall.org/dewey. For this activity you will need an Internet hookup in your media center with individual student computers or a digital media presentation method for class viewing. This website has three links: a check link, to test your knowledge regarding the Dewey classification system; a meet Dewey link, where information about the man that invented this system is shared; and a Dewey decimal system link, where you learn how to use this system interactively. After each cyber lesson, let your students see if they can "Do the Dewey" themselves in the school media center.

Genre Format and Voice for Research Papers: Developing Three Good Supporting Research Points

Grades 6 through 8, Three Good Supporting Research Points

Activity 1: Writing Activity: *Science Fairs*

When students present their science fair projects they are expected to include information on three parts of their researched exhibit. This creates a perfect connection to writing a research paper that coincides with a science fair project. Students who are participating in the science fair are encouraged to present their three documented points using graphs, tables, or charts. Again, this can relate to a written research project. By encouraging all students to work on a science fair project (even if they are not interested in entering the competition), they can also work on a research paper.

Resources

Need ideas for developing student science fair projects? Check out these two websites: www.isd77.k12.mn.us/resources/cf/ideas.html and www.homeworkspot.com/sciencefair

Grades 6 through 8, Three Good Supporting Research Points

Activity 2: Writing Activity: *Schoolwide Science Mini Conference*

This idea will unite your middle school grade levels through a science conference that can be conducted annually. Each student or group of students will be asked to choose a topic related to their favorite science class units. Working together between science and English classes, students will submit a research proposal that they want to investigate. The teachers will send a letter back to the students saying whether their proposal has been accepted. Those students whose proposal has been accepted will conduct a research investigation and prepare a final report that resembles a journal article that will be published schoolwide. Instruction in this format will be provided either during a class unit on journal writing or as after-school support.

Grades 6 through 8, Three Good Supporting Research Points

Activity 3: Computer Activity: *Kidspiration*

When your students are beginning to think about their research question and finding three good supporting points, a visual representation can often help them picture the steps they are taking. When they are in the computer lab, have them log on to Kidspiration software. Kidspiration is an interactive graphic organizer that helps structure a research project. They can use this Web activity to relate their research question graphically with their three support points. As they find information about these points they can add additional branches for supporting detail. Graphic organizers like this can help students understand a process visually that they don't comprehend through hearing.

Resources

Another resource is available for walking your students through the steps for writing a good research paper. It can serve to reinforce each step that needs to be done. This website is called Middle School Cross-Curricular Paid Site Research Projects: CompassLearning and it is located at www.compasslearning.com/solutions/middleschool/crosscurricular/index.aspx.

Skill-Building Activities for Learning Poetry Building Blocks

Genre Writing Techniques for Poetry: Using Rhyme and Rhythm

Grades 6 through 8, Rhyme and Rhythm

Activity 1: Limerick Contest: *There Once Was a Student from Kent*

To teach rhyme and rhythm, have students compose a limerick and conduct a contest. The winners can read their poems over the schoolwide PA system. You can have a prize for the funniest limerick, the most interesting word choice, and even the most interesting topic.

Resources

A wonderful list of humorous poetry is available online at www.carylibrary.org/children/pdfs/humormiddle.pdf.

Grades 6 through 8, Rhyme and Rhythm

Activity 2: Silly Poems: *Let's Have a Giggle*

Middle school students love a good joke. They enjoy being silly at times, so let's incorporate that into a poetry lesson. Select a song that everyone knows such as "Jingle Bells" or "Happy Birthday." Write the song on an overhead transparency or on the board, leaving off the last word of each line. Students then fill in the open-ended lines with their own words to create a silly poem. If you need help or examples of this activity, go to www.gigglepoetry.com.

Variation: Let students make up a whole song with new words, such as one used years ago to the tune of "Battle Hymn of the Republic": "Mine eyes have seen the glory of the burning of the school. We have tortured every teacher and have broken every rule." Students will have great fun with this and learn rhyme and rhythm. Just be careful to set the rules first or it can go downhill quickly!

Variation: Another variation is to allow students to devise a poem to the beat of a hip-hop rhythm. Students can find words, even silly ones, that tell their thoughts in that sing-song manner.

Grades 6 through 8, Rhyme and Rhythm

Activity 3: Listening Activity: *Can You Hear It Now?*

Just as with any other genre, your students will learn to write poetry if you create a poetry-rich classroom environment. Read a wide variety of poems to your students where rhyme and rhythm are present. Read poems to your students daily and ask them to listen for the rhyming words and poetry meter.

Resources

Are you unsure of where to find poetry that your students will enjoy? Look at one of our favorite poetry anthologies: Moger, S. 2006. *A Poem for Every Day!* New York: Scholastic. Are you interested in playing some children's poetry for your students to listen to in class? Try this website: http://poetryvlog.com.

Genre Format and Voice for Poetry: Unique Poetry Styles

Grades 6 through 8, Unique Poetry Styles

Activity 1: Acrostic Poems: *Fun with Names*

Students enjoy writing acrostic poems, in which the letters of a person's name or a key word begin each line of the poem. Each line of the poem must also be about the person or must relate to the key word. An online interactive tool that can help your students is located at http://www.readwritethink.org/_mat/.asp. This website will help your students brainstorm, write, and revise their poems as well as print their finished work.

Grades 6 through 8, Unique Poetry Styles

Activity 2: Diamante Poems: *They Are a Gem*

This type of poetry is fun because the seven lines in the poem form a diamond shape when complete. It is a good poem for practicing parts of speech, because it uses nouns in the first and seventh lines, adjectives in the second and fourth lines, and gerunds (active verbs ending in *-ing*) in the third and fifth lines to describe a central topic or two opposing topics (such as night and day, or wet and dry). There is a precise format for students to follow. A good online tool to help your students learn about and write these poems is available at www.readwritethink.org/student_mat/student_material.asp?id=53.

Grades 6 through 8, Voice in Poetry

Activity 3: Poetry Performances: *Catch the Refrain*

There are many interesting poems that have a strong mood about them, such as Edgar Allen Poe's "Annabel Lee." Have a group of students select a poem from a set of them you have collected for this activity. Have the students perform the poem as a choral reading in front of the class, after they have rehearsed it. Encourage your students to determine whether there is a refrain, where one or more voices chime in together, or whether there are parts that just the girls say or just the boys. Perform these poems for other classes as well. Do you want to try a different poet? Try Banjo Patterson's "A Man from Snowy River" (from Australia). Check out your literature books for a good selection as well.

Grades 6 through 8, Unique Poetry Styles

Activity 4: Poem Maker: *Try It, You'll Like It*

Would you like your students to work on a website that helps them write their own poems? Go to www.mape.org.uk/activities/index.htm.

Remedies for Common Grammar Errors

Grades 6 through 8, Common Student Writing Errors

Common Error 1: Writing Only Short, Simple Sentences

Students at this age level aren't very confident in their writing skills. Consequently, they often write short, choppy sentences. Does this type of student writing sound familiar to you?

Remedy 1: Visual Imagery: *Snap It!*

Stand in front of the class with a rubber band in your hands. Tell your students that the rubber band that you're holding represents the length of their sentences. Ask your students to read a few of their sentences out loud. If the sentence is short, just hold the rubber band in place. Ask another student to expand on the sentence that was just read. If the sentence is longer, stretch out your rubber band a little longer. Tell your students you want their sentence length to stretch or even break your rubber band. As their sentences grow, stretch the rubber band longer and longer.

Remedy 2: Sentence Combining Exercise: *Sentence Growing*

Create your own game! Write a number of simple sentences on 5 × 7 cards. Then write a number of conjunctions on 3 × 5 cards. Divide your class into groups of three students and call them *teams*. Set a timer for three minutes. Tell students to combine as many sentences as they can until the timer rings. When the timer goes off, say, "Stop!" The team with the largest number of correctly combined sentences wins a no-homework pass.

Remedy 3: A Board Game: *Scrabble Sentence Cube Game* (S & R Games)

Students will enjoy this board game and will learn to build complex sentences at the same time.

Common Error 2: Spelling Mistakes

Do your students misspell words frequently? Do they lose context meaning in their writing because of terrible misspellings? You're not alone. Students at this grade level may still be using inventive spelling when writing.

Section III

Remedy 1: Create Topical Dictionaries: *Spelling Help!*

Students just don't like looking up words in dictionaries. They *will* enjoy making their own topical dictionaries, however, and will use them! Before your class begins a topic, select a number of new vocabulary words that they may have difficulty spelling. Put these words in alphabetical order and write the definitions with your class. Put them in a folder with the name of the topic on the front. Let students keep these student-created dictionaries in their Rough Draft Writing Folders.

Remedy 2: Electronic Franklin Spelling Dictionaries: *Spelling Support*

For your students with special needs, allow them to use an electronic spelling device such as one of the Franklin spelling products. This will allow them to get the correct spellings of those difficult words.

Remedy 3: Class Scrabble Contest: *Academic Game Day*

You'll need multiple Scrabble games and a class willing to work in cooperative groups. Set a timer and have the groups play the game during this time. After a set time, have a final round and provide a prize for the winning person in each group. A variation for your at-risk learners is to allow them to have a small dictionary at their side to look up any word they need to spell correctly. This allows for supported practice for them rather than just losing the game to those who spell better.

Planning for the Future

Maintaining the Momentum

We commend you for seeking materials to improve your writing instruction. We believe the strategies in BEW are just what you are looking for because they are research based and because they produce results for general education students as well as students who are ELLs, at risk, or students with special needs. However, no program works in a vacuum. For a writing program really to succeed, the program must expand beyond your individual classroom and follow your students as they move from grade to grade and school to school. This requires a program that functions at all three levels: classroom, school building, and district.

At the Classroom Level

Up to now we have focused on how to plan and teach a single writing unit based on a genre unit. By following the steps in each of the five phases in BEW we have taken you from defining basic vocabulary to a published student document within a two- to three-week teaching cycle. We have stressed the importance of *consistency* in your teaching methods. Our emphasis is on *front-end loading*—spending time on the vocabulary and prewriting. We believe in direct instruction as we show students how to take notes on their Blueprints, use the notes on their Blueprints to deliver talking paragraphs, and then use those Blueprint notes again to write the complete sentences and paragraphs that become their rough drafts. This leads to the editing step, the most important step of all, where true learning begins. Finally, celebrate the publishing of student writing, for this is what it is all about. Sharing your thoughts with others makes the labor worthwhile.

Follow this process for each and every genre unit you teach in writing. Your students will get to know the jingles and hand jives for your writing vocabulary words. They'll learn the process and move more comfortably between each step and phase. Even your authors who have struggled before will begin to understand the expectations. That's the beauty of using the same system, the same vocabulary, the same jingles and hand jives, and the same graphic organizers. Even struggling learners catch on to the concept. Always model each step personally for each genre you teach!

Completing a writing cycle in a consistent manner for a single assignment leads to the next issue: How often should this cycle be repeated throughout an instructional year to maintain the momentum?

How many writing selections should your students do each year? This is a topic we need to address because it will make a big difference in the success your students have with the writing process. Should you do one per week or one for each required genre at your grade level? The answer is neither.

If you try to do one writing piece per week, students won't have the time to develop something to say, nor will they have the time to plan, write, or learn editing skills. Instead of publishing polished writing pieces, they will turn in poorly written essays by rote.

If you answered, "One writing selection per genre," then your students will only be writing one piece every month or two, depending on how many genres you are asked to teach at your grade level. They won't get the repetition they need and will have forgotten much of the writing process if there are big breaks between selections. They will miss the practice that teaching multiple cycles of each genre allows so that they can retain the specific elements of the genres.

We recommend that you plan your school year to include a writing selection every two to three weeks. Take a minute to go back and look at the two-week charts we included in this book. We show how you can arrange to teach the five phases over that period of time. You may need three weeks for your first writing assignment, but after students become acclimated, the two-week cycle should be adequate. Look at your literacy series and match writing units to the literature your students will be reading. Also, be sure to look at your science and social studies curricula, because you can connect informative or research writing, or even persuasive writing, to match those units. Cross-curricular writing is very helpful in assisting students to see that what they learn in one area has relevance and interconnections to other areas. They can read about a topic, do projects associated with it, and then write about it too. Then they can share their writing using one of our publishing suggestions.

So, how many writing selections should be taught each year based on our suggested writing cycle? If you have typical nine-week quarters, that's thirty-six weeks per school year. Doing writing units every two to three weeks means you should be teaching from twelve to eighteen essays per year with your students. If you shoot for fifteen, students will have enough time to move comfortably through the steps of each phase with your guidance. This will allow you to repeat many of the most important genres three or four times.

If you follow this plan (see our Blueprint lesson plan at the end of the chapter), you will have provided a consistent writing environment for your students for a year. What happens to that momentum if the process is not followed when your students have moved on to the next grade? You're right! It's back to square one. To be effective at teaching writing, it takes more than a classroom. It takes a building!

At the Building Level

Many schools across the nation are targeting expressive writing as an area that needs improvement. And this is for good reason. We know from the National Assessment of Educational Performance (NAEP) tests of 1998 and 2002 that writing scores across the nation are low. (The latest test was completed in March 2007 for grades 8 and 12 with results expected sometime after spring of 2008.) Although the results from 2002 showed an increase in proficient writing for grades 4, 8, and 12 since 1998, the overall percentage of students showing acceptable proficiency was only between 22 percent and 31 percent of the total student population. (Persky, Danne, and Ying Jin, 2003). When you look more closely at the NAEP results, you'll find that boys scored lower than girls, that African American and Hispanic students scored lower than Asian/Pacific Islander and white students, and that scores were lower for students who were ELLs, at risk, or had special needs. You aren't alone if your writing test results for your school and district are far below equivalent scores in reading, math, science, and social studies. (If you want to see more about the NAEP results, go to http://nces.ed.gov/nationsreportcard/writing.)

Because of this, we hope that many of you are involved with a school improvement program in your school and that your improvement program includes improving student achievement in the area of expressive writing. BEW strategies can be truly effective if they are used across the writing curriculum for your building. To begin, the members of the school improvement plan committee need to be made aware of the success of the BEW program used in classrooms in your school. How should you go about doing this?

First, join with other teachers in your school and begin talking up the success you are having with teaching writing using BEW strategies. Many of the publishing ideas we suggested will also help you build this awareness. Make it a point to show other teachers samples of your students' writing while having a cup of coffee in the teacher's lounge. Get some momentum started in your school by making a plan to work together in a focused way. We find teachers often start by sharing information with other teachers at the same grade level, but it is also critical that like-minded teachers at other grade levels become involved. Make it a point to invite your principal to a talking paragraph session. Invite the principal and parents when your students are reading their finished work. Share! Share! Share!

When you have stimulated sufficient interest, it's time to talk to the principal to help you set up training in your school. It's best if all the teachers in your school participate. It helps to have an incentive like a nice lunch. For those teachers who are skeptical, the success of your students in producing quality writing will begin to win them over, especially when they see the success of your students who are ELLs, at risk, or have special needs. Set a goal for your training. You are all busy teachers, and it takes time to learn and add new elements to your teaching.

Don't stop with the training. Set up peer support groups, where you meet at least once a month to share strategies that work the best. Bring ideas for what you have developed on your own to add to your teaching and what you can do together to keep the excitement of learning happening. Share literacy boxes, literacy bags, worksheets, and publishing ideas, especially those that involve participation of the whole school. Post writing-related banners and student work in the hallway. Communicate with parents. Celebrate your successes. Discuss the progress with your fellow faculty members at staff meetings, especially as you get test scores back. If you think students were progressing in your class when you started this idea, imagine what will happen when students start being taught with the same strategies in kindergarten that they will be using in first grade, second grade, and on up the educational ladder. There will be no stopping your students! Watch the momentum build.

At the District Level

Work with your curriculum director to bring more training to your district. Your school will be ready for the next level of training, but some schools will just be starting. That's a perfect setup. You can be the support system for the schools just starting their training. Invite teachers from other schools to come to your classrooms and watch how it looks in action. Model the strategies at your writing-focused grade-level meetings. Develop a districtwide activity that supports writing. You can turn around a district by building a program around research-validated programs plus strategies that support diverse learners. It all starts with one or two teachers finding a system that works and fostering it at the beginning in their classes. Go from there to other classrooms in your school, and then to other schools in your district.

Our Final Words

Some teachers now say . . .

"Teaching writing was easier this way."

"I had as much fun as my students did as we learned about our topics."

"Even my students who are at risk were able to write good essays."

"I finally get what makes a proficient writing sample!"

Some students now say . . .

"I like writing!"

"I love publishing our stories."

"Look! I can write stories with several paragraphs!"

"That Blueprint really helps me know where things go in my story."

Not the Closing . . . Just the Beginning

Some of you are reading this chapter and deciding how the BEW approach will work for you. Others of you may already be trying some of our strategies in your classrooms. We are positive that you will find success using our systematic approach to building proficient writers. How can we say this? Our strategies are based on research and they have worked for us for years. What is really fun for us is to watch our students get excited about writing. Not only will your students have fun with this, but you will too! Learning to use the tools that increase student writing ability is just the beginning. Where do we go from here?

In Your Classroom

The most important outcome of BEW is that students learn they love writing, and one of the biggest reasons why they love it is that they are successful doing it. Will you start by adding vocabulary training, jingles, and hand jives into your teaching? Will you spend time on all the prewriting steps? Did you get some ideas of how to structure a two-week writing unit with an authentic reason for writing and publishing? Are you modeling more for your students and leaving the graphic organizers up in your room to help your writers? Do you use a Blueprint? Wherever you start, the secret is to keep doing it. Be consistent. For each writing unit, use the same systematic process. Use the same vocabulary words and fun ways to remember the definitions. Use the same graphic organizer so students learn to organize their thoughts. Help students narrow their topics. Add new pieces when you are ready so that your lessons become more and more powerful. If you follow the pattern of having two- to three-week units, your students will have more than fifteen writing selections at the end of the school year. Their skills will improve more and more. Keep writing portfolios so that both you and your students can see the growth in their writing over time.

But don't stop there! When you find something that works for your students, you need to plant the seed for success so that it grows throughout your school and even your district! We have to work together to help students keep enthusiasm they've found in learning and being successful so they can continue to grow and learn.

At Your Grade Level

The wonderful thing about working in schools is that we talk to each other! We share the things that are going well and ask for ideas to help us when we are struggling. When the strategies in BEW have worked for you, pass the word along to your grade-level teachers. Become a support group for one another.

Plan your weekly BEW writing lessons with other teachers from your same grade level (use the BEW Lesson Planner, Figure 14.1, at the end of this chapter). Plan your two- to three-week units together and embed the BEW strategies. Publish in similar ways so that you can have grade-level readings of the selections your students have written and make DVDs of your students' performances.

Meet with your grade-level colleagues and talk about what a proficient writing sample looks like. Grade each other's student final copies so you can agree about the qualities that need to be present for a good paper. It is so important to reflect, refine, and retrain as we target an area in which we want to become better teachers. Do it for yourself, but reach out and gain the interest and support of your colleagues.

Writing Schoolwide

After your grade level is coordinating your writing program and teaching strategies in similar ways, share your success with teachers at other grade levels. Any program is stronger if students consistently hear the same concepts at each grade level so they can build their knowledge base and skills using the same vocabulary and teaching strategies. The graphic organizers in BEW, especially the Blueprint, can provide much-needed support for students who may be at risk for learning difficulties. We believe students need an opportunity to review vocabulary words related to writing every day. If teachers across grade levels use the same jingles, you will be amazed at the ease with which students pick up right where they left off the year before.

Include BEW strategies in your school improvement plan. The key to success is to teach in a consistent way and to spiral writing concepts from grade to grade. The reward will be students who enjoy writing.

Moving Forward toward Your Goal

We know that teaching is hard work. And we know that teaching writing effectively for our inclusive classrooms is difficult for many teachers. We have provided a systematic way to teach the writing process so that it supports all your students, including those most at risk for learning difficulties. The strategies in the BEW process can be added to any curriculum. You can combine them with concepts you have learned from other sources about teaching process writing. Most of all, we hope the ideas in this book will provide support for you as you teach this subject, so that both you and your students will find joy in writing. This is not the end. It is the beginning of a renewed passion for teaching writing. Enjoy!

Blueprint Lesson Plan

Instructor _____   Subject _____

Grade _____ Date _____   Genre _____

Phase I: Authentic Vocabulary	**A. Writing Vocabulary** **Words to teach and review** 1. 2. 3. 4. 5. 6. 7. 8. 9. 10.	**B. Grammar and Conventions** **Vocabulary Words to teach** **and review** 1. 2. 3. 4. 5. 6. 7. 8. 9. 10.	**C. Lesson Vocabulary Words** 1. 2. 3. 4. 5. 6. 7. 8. 9. 10.

Phase II:

Prewriting

1. Multisensory Activity

_____

_____

_____

_____

_____

2. Wheel of Thought

Theme/Central Idea _____

_____

Possible Student Topics _____

_____

_____

_____

_____

3. Genre Building Blocks (genre format and voice concepts):

◯ Introduction: _____

_____

☐ Details: _____

_____

☐ Details: _____

_____

☐ Details: _____

_____

☐ Summary/Conclusion: _____

_____

(See Genre Building Blocks on next page)

4. KEY: Students take notes on Blueprint and do Talking
Paragraphs

Personal Narrative	

Personal Narrative
Topic: narrow
Building Blocks:
a. Well-defined characters using dialogue
b. Vividly described setting
c. Story line with details
d. Plot
e. Story ending with a learned lesson
f. Voice usage

Persuasive Writing
Topic: area of strong feelings; take a stand
Building Blocks:
a. Three good reasons
b. Audience appeal
c. Expert opinion
d. Research support
e. End with position restated
f. Voice usage

Research Writing
Topic: find an area of interest, ask a question
Building Blocks:
a. Write research question
b. Gather information
c. Analyze information
d. Write supporting paragraphs
e. Write ending, restating question

Response to Reading
Topic: state an opinion
Building Blocks:
a. Use reading skills to comprehend the reading selections
b. Understand the question or writing prompt
c. Form an opinion on question or writing prompt
d. Support opinion with details from both selections

Phase III:

Writing

1. **Writing the Draft**
   Post all Web of Words   Provide supportive material
   _____
   _____

2. **Title Writing**
   Tell a fact   Ask a question   Same sounding words
   _____

3. **Topic Sentence Writing**
   Ask a question   Interesting fact   Riddle   Use imagery
   _____

Phase IV:

Editing

1. **Create editing rubric as a class activity** (student ideas)
   a. Genre format/voice (e.g., paragraphs, building blocks, and voice):_____
   b. Vocabulary and Usage (e.g., words, sentences): _____
   c. Grammar (e.g., grade level skills): _____

2. **Self-editing** _____   Use the   **3. Peer Editing** _____
   _____   Rubric!   _____

4. **Teacher Conference** (use editing rubric and personalize needs for students) _____
   _____

Phase V:

Publishing

Have an authentic purpose for the writing assignment; make it special!
   _____
   _____

Section III

Appendix A

BEW and Research-Validated Practices

NCLB and Teaching to Diverse Learners

The Federal mandate No Child Left Behind (NCLB) requires school districts to improve student achievement by implementing instructional strategies that are *research validated*. By incorporating research-validated practices in day-to-day instruction, educators will ensure higher achievement levels for *all* learners.

National Center to Improve the Tools of Educators (NCITE) analyzed the research and identified six principles for accommodating instruction for diverse learners that can level the playing field in classrooms across the nation (NCITE, 2001). Diverse learners are those students identified as at risk for learning, special needs students, or those ELL students who need academic support. These six accommodations are Big Ideas, Primed Background Knowledge, Conspicuous Strategies, Mediated Scaffolding, Judicious Review, and Strategies Integration. Many school districts in our country have found value in providing professional development focused on these accommodations to raise student achievement.

BEW is an excellent approach that provides strategies that align with this research in the area of expressive writing.

Principle 1: Big Ideas

Classroom instruction should be organized around *big ideas*. These ideas provide an overall umbrella for students to organize and understand information based on smaller related ideas. The big ideas in writing should include the following:

1. Writing is a process that, when followed, can produce a proficient finished product.

2. The genres in which students will write will have similarities and differences that can be applied to new learning experiences.

BEW Alignment: Students proceed through the five phases and multiple steps within each phase of the BEW Master Plan every two to three weeks as they receive instruction for grade-level curriculum genres. In addition, BEW's Blueprint graphic organizer helps students recognize that most genres have a format that includes an introductory paragraph, one or more detail paragraphs, and a summary paragraph.

Principle 2: Primed Background Knowledge

Diverse learners can have difficulty with a school curriculum because instruction doesn't connect to their background experiences. Teachers need to prime student learning with vocabulary and experiences related to the writing elements.

BEW Alignment: BEW strategies are used during the first two phases of the writing process to support diverse learners with language, vocabulary, and multisensory experiences that tie students' unique backgrounds to their self-selected writing topics. Vocabulary related to writing conventions and grammar is taught and reviewed daily.

Principle 3: Conspicuous Strategies

Using special techniques to trigger student memory helps diverse learners understand and recall key lessons and procedures connected to the big ideas of their lessons.

BEW Alignment: Consistent use of catchy jingles and hand motions for Big Ten vocabulary words helps diverse learners with abstract words in a concrete way. Three graphic organizers (the Web of Words, the Wheel of Thought, and the Blueprint) provide visual strategies to support vocabulary and promote understanding of different genre formats. The Blueprint uses shapes and colors to denote specific paragraph requirements.

Principle 4: Mediated Scaffolding

This strategy involves the teacher or a peer providing guidance, assistance, and support to diverse learners to help them gain a deeper understanding of a skill or concept. As students gain confidence, the assistance (or scaffolding) can be gradually withdrawn.

BEW Alignment: A feature called "Professor Write" helps teachers see how to use direct instruction and teacher modeling for each step in the BEW process. In addition, three different graphic organizers are used to plan and formulate writing selections for as long as they are useful to the writer.

Principle 5: Judicious Review

Research shows the value of teachers incorporating a way for students to review past learning systematically, so that skills are not lost and students can progress from that point. Judicious review must take on a variety of forms and must also relate back to the big idea.

BEW Alignment: Review occurs in multiple ways using the BEW strategies. The writing cycle of five phases is repeated every two to three weeks during a school year, providing practice in the writing process ten to fifteen times a year. Each writing period begins with a review of the Big Ten vocabulary words and genre-specific vocabulary. Student drafts are reviewed four times before final copies are written, through talking paragraphs, self-editing, peer editing, and teacher conferencing. Finally, editing requires students to construct a class rubric of learned skills for each writing unit during the year to demonstrate their cumulative growth in learning grammar and conventions.

Principle 6: Strategic Integration

To support students in progressing beyond the lessons themselves, it is important to provide opportunities for students to expand and experiment with new ways to use their skills. For this to occur, students need enough practice to be fluent with writing and opportunities to write for various reasons.

BEW Alignment: The BEW process is repeated more than ten times each school year, with students becoming more fluent over time. In addition, each unit introduces a series of more challenging assignments as the school term progresses, including teaching writing genres that cross into science and social studies units. This ensures that students will see a writing pattern develop and will understand the expectations of proficient writing in different genres as the term progresses.

Appendix B

Classroom Instruction

BEW is aligned with *research-validated* strategies for classroom instruction. The Association for Supervision and Curriculum Development (ASCD) is a good resource for research on *best practices* in education. Robert Marzano, a leading researcher, has conducted an in-depth analysis of more than 395 research studies that identify nine essential instructional strategies that promote student learning across all content areas and grade levels. These strategies involve meta-cognitive skills and active student engagement.

Meta-cognition skills are difficult to include in daily classroom instruction because they don't occur naturally. Teachers need to plan and call student attention to these skills. When they are taught to students through active student involvement, an ideal learning situation is created. Marzano defines his strategies as "those direct and indirect activities orchestrated by the teacher to expose students to new knowledge, to reinforce knowledge, or to apply knowledge" (Marzano, 1998, p. 62). These nine strategies are further explained in his book *Classroom Instruction that Works* (Marzano et al., 2004). When these nine essential strategies for instruction are lined up with BEW strategies, it's a perfect match. All nine strategies are used in BEW: Strategy 1: Identifying Similarities and Differences, Strategy 2: Summarizing and Note Taking, Strategy 3: Reinforcing Effort and Providing Recognition, Strategy 4: Homework and Practice, Strategy 5: Nonlinguistic Representations, Strategy 6: Cooperative Learning, Strategy 7: Setting Objectives and Providing Feedback, Strategy 8: Generating and Testing Hypotheses, Strategy 9: Cues, Questions, and Advance Organizers. BEW aligns with all nine strategies for effective instruction.

Strategy 1: Identifying Similarities and Differences

When students dissect a concept into similar and dissimilar attributes, it affords them the opportunity to learn more complex problem-solving skills.

BEW Alignment: The prewriting strategies in Phase II of BEW teach each writing genre by helping students compare and contrast the building blocks of a specific genre against other genres. In addition, Chapter 10 in this book provides specific teaching strategies for comparing or contrasting reading selections based on a theme.

Strategy 2: Summarizing and Note Taking

With this strategy, students are required to synthesize concepts and to sort out unimportant details from important ones. Research also suggests that conforming to a specific format for note taking is more effective for student mastery.

BEW Alignment: Phase II in the BEW process emphasizes this important skill. To compose a writing assignment in sequential order, students are asked to write their notes in the appropriate places on their Blueprint graphic organizer. As they write their notes, they sort out trivial concepts from important details. Different genres require students to summarize their selections using a standard format. The Blueprint graphic organizer provides a format that is common for all genres.

Strategy 3: Reinforcing Effort and Providing Recognition

Research has shown that students frequently don't recognize the importance of effort; therefore, classroom instruction should show the positive link between effort and concept mastery. Student effort should be rewarded and reinforcement should be personal and meaningful to the student.

BEW Alignment: All five phases of the BEW process recognize effort. Students are taught using a quick-paced explicit instruction format with teacher questions and rapid student response. Students are praised for sharing their responses. In talking paragraphs (Phase II), students are applauded as they speak their stories aloud from their notes. In Phase V, all finished student assignments are celebrated as students share the purpose of their writing with an audience, whether in writing or vocally. By keeping writing portfolios, keepsakes, and student-written books in the library, students feel recognized by the display of these symbols of their efforts.

Strategy 4: Homework and Practice

Research shows there is real value in providing opportunities for homework and practice. Homework should be grade-level appropriate. It must be completed independently, with minimal parental assistance. Feedback on homework is a must.

BEW Alignment: Homework in BEW is nontraditional, although thought provoking and practical. For instance, a homework assignment for young students or diverse learners might require students to bring in artifacts or pictures to support their story topics. Students might be asked to share the new vocabulary words they learned at the dinner table. Older students might be asked to research ideas at home or conduct Internet searches on a topic. More advanced writers could be required to write their final copy at home or to type it on a computer.

Strategy 5: Nonlinguistic Representations

We know from research that information is stored in memory two ways: linguistically and non-linguistically. Testing has shown that nonlinguistic instructional strategies stimulate the intellectual process for learning. Suggestions for classroom applications of this principle include using strategies that involve hands-on activities, using physical movement in learning, using models for examples, and using symbols to represent concepts.

BEW Alignment: In BEW, nonlinguistic representations are woven throughout all phases and steps. For example, during Phase I, our hand jives and jingles serve as memory triggers for important writing vocabulary concepts. During Phase II, we recommend stimulating student ideas and language by using literacy bags and boxes, cyber trips, and many other multisensory activities to set the stage for learning. In Section III of this book, you'll find quick references for a variety of hand motions, jingles, and other activities that can add to student learning.

Strategy 6: Cooperative Learning

Learning is enhanced by having students work in small heterogeneous groups for instruction. This technique promotes peer support and helps increase student motivation and positive social inter-actions. This strategy eliminates competition between students and encourages cooperation among group members.

BEW Alignment: During Phase IV, peer editing provides an opportunity for students to evaluate one another's work in a small-group setting. In addition, Section III of this book gives a multitude of small-group activities that promote the acquisition of writing skills.

Strategy 7: Setting Objectives and Providing Feedback

Teachers set their own goals and objectives for daily, weekly, monthly, and semester expectations. When students share the teacher's objectives, they know where they are going, and their progress can be reinforced by giving feedback. Feedback can be given in many ways, but it's important that it be delivered quickly so that students can take action and not fall behind in their instruction. In classroom applications, an excellent research-validated method for generating student feedback is achieved by using rubrics.

BEW Alignment: In BEW, a rubric is class generated for every writing assignment and it covers all old and new concepts. The rubric not only reflects the teacher's objectives, but in addition it provides feedback to the teacher regarding whether these objectives are being achieved. This is because the rubric is student generated and captures what the student has learned. This may be different from what the teacher believes has been taught. This rubric is then used during the assessment process. In this way, students provide self-editing feedback and then receive feedback from peers and the teacher. The teacher also receives feedback and consequently knows whether certain lessons need to be retaught.

Strategy 8: Generating and Testing Hypotheses

Research shows us that instruction is enhanced if students are encouraged to think by using higher level analysis, problem solving, decision making, experimental inquiry, and invention. Deductive reasoning is an excellent instructional tool to use when teaching about generating and testing hypotheses. For example, the teacher might ask students to predict an answer to a question such as, "What do you think would happen if. . . . " Teachers use open-ended questions when they ask students to think, and use their own experiences to formulate a hypothesis.

BEW Alignment: In the BEW process, a fictional character, Professor Write, is used to provide a model for asking open-ended questions that require hypothesis formation.

Strategy 9: Cues, Questions, and Advance Organizers

Teachers can increase student learning by using all these strategies to help trigger student memories and stimulate thinking.

BEW Alignment: Section III of this book provides many suggestions for the use of hand motions and jingles to trigger student memory for key vocabulary words and genre definitions. In addition, we suggest the use of a variety of student worksheets to stimulate writing ideas prior to initiating a writing selection.

Glossary

alliteration repeating of consonant sounds, usually in the beginning of a word

antonym words that have opposite meanings

assonance a poetic technique that occurs when the vowel sound in the middle of a word is repeated in the middle of a second word

authentic editing interactive process between teacher and students whereby the teacher solicits student input to create a scoring rubric for a specific writing selection

authentic vocabulary all vocabulary words that pertain to the writing process

BEW acronym for Blueprint for Exceptional Writing

blank verse lines of poetry that do not have rhyme or rhythm

Blueprint a graphic organizer used in prewriting across all genres

character development the author's way of making the characters come alive through their detailed description

character dialogue the words characters speak in a story

characters people portrayed in a story

cross-text writing writing selections that compare main ideas from two or more reading selections, finding a common theme

detailed paragraph(s) paragraph(s) that follow the introduction, providing the specific details or information that build the content of the story by explaining and providing support for the topic

diction in poetry, the author's choice of words, their arrangement, and their accuracy, power, and distinction to paint a picture

edit correcting errors and revising writing selections to produce a high-quality final product

ethos a persuasive argument that is based on a person's credibility

final copy a completed writing selection

genre the kind of writing; communicating a purpose to a specific audience

genre format organizational structure for a writing selection dictated by its specific genre

homonym two words that are pronounced the same (and can be spelled the same) but have different meanings

imagery language that is used to create a specific image

introduction paragraph the first paragraph that sets the tone and topic of the writing selection

irony a way to convey a meaning by saying one thing, but meaning the opposite

kairos argument a persuasive argument based on urgency

literacy bags and boxes teacher-created bags and boxes containing materials that help generate ideas, multisensory experiences, and language about a topic

logos argument a persuasive argument that uses data, relevant facts, or logic to support the author's claim

metaphor associating two different objects as being the same

meter measured pattern of accents contained within a poem

multisensory experiences activities related to a topic that appeal to the senses (hands-on activities, music or sounds, smells, tastes, or visuals)

onomatopoeia words that sound like the word's meaning

pathos argument a persuasive argument that uses emotion to appeal to the audience

peer edit evaluating a peer's writing selection for changes or corrections

personal narrative writing a story written about the author or author's experiences; "my story"

persuasive writing writing selection in which the author's intent is to change the mind of the audience

plot the rising and falling action contained within a story that leads to problem resolution or some new level of understanding

poetry rhythmic writing that expresses thoughts in a creative, imaginative, or symbolic way

publish sharing finished writing selections whether in writing or by reading them aloud

recursive process a writing cycle whereby changes are repeatedly made to improve the selection by editing and rewriting until a polished copy is completed

research writing finding the answer to a sought-after question based on existing information or a new discovery

rhyme matching final consonant or vowel sounds in two or more words

rhythm the repeated beat created by stressed or accented syllables in poetry

rough draft student learning copy in which corrections are repetitively made

rough draft writing folder a folder used to keep all writing information together for a particular writing assignment

self-edit evaluating one's own writing for changes or corrections

setting where the story takes place

simile comparing two unlike things using the words *like* or *as*

stanza a group of lines that creates a division in poetry

student portfolio a collection of student writing selections either in hard or electronic copy

summary paragraph an ending paragraph in a writing selection with a specific purpose based on the genre that restates key information or draws the story to a close

symbol an item in writing that stands for something beyond its own meaning

synonym words that have the same meaning

talking paragraph a process whereby students use their notes to speak their potential paragraphs aloud prior to writing them

teacher conference a meeting between teacher and student to evaluate a writing selection prior to assessment

theme the big idea or major concept for the writing selection

topic a specific or personal aspect of a theme that becomes the focus of a writing selection or paragraph

topic sentence a sentence that introduces the main idea of the paragraph and acts as a hook to draw the audience into the story

transition sentence a connecting sentence between paragraphs or topics to assist the reader in moving from one idea to the next

verse one line of poetry

voice student's (or character's) personality in written form; the amount of voice is based on the genre or style of writing

Web of Words a graphic organizer with a center square used for vocabulary development

Wheel of Thought a graphic organizer with a center circle used for generating student ideas on a topic or narrowing a topic in BEW prewriting

Bibliography

Andrade, H. G. 2003. *Rubrics and Self-Assessment Project*. Project Zero: Harvard University. Accessed March 2006. Online. www.pz.harvard.edu/Research/RubricSelf.htm.

Burke, M. D., S. L. Hagan, and B. Grossen. 1998. "What Curricular Designs and Strategies Accommodate Diverse Learners?" *Teaching Exceptional Children,* 31(1), 34–38.

Butler, D., and P. Winnie. 1995. "Feedback and Self-Regulated Learning: A Theoretical Synthesis." *Review of Educational Research,* 65(3), 200–281.

Calkins, L. M. 1994. *The Art of Teaching Writing*. Portsmouth, NH: Heinemann.

Clayton, H. 2003. *Great Genre Writing Lessons*. New York: Scholastic.

Clemmons, J., L. Lasse, D. Cooper, N. Areglado, and M. Dill. 1993. *Portfolios in the Classroom: A Teacher's Sourcebook*. New York: Scholastic.

Cohen, A. 1998. *Strategies in Learning and Using a Second Language*. London: Addison Wesley Longman.

Crawford, L. W. 1993. *Language and Literacy Learning in Multicultural Classrooms*. Boston: Allyn & Bacon.

Dean, N. 2000. *Voice Lessons: Classroom Activities to Teach Diction, Detail, Imagery, Syntax, and Tone*. Gainesville, FL: Maupin House.

Dornyei, A. 2001. *Motivational Strategies in the Language Classroom*. Cambridge, UK: Cambridge University Press.

Echevarria, J., M. E. Vogt, and D. Short. 2004. *Making Content Comprehensible for English Learners*. Boston: Pearson.

Evans, J., and J. E. Moore. 1985. *How to Make Books with Children*. Monterey, CA: Evan Moor.

Fletcher, R., and J. Portalupi. 2001. *Writing Workshop: The Essential Guide*. Portsmouth, NH: Heinemann.

Gardner, H. 1993. *Multiple Intelligences: The Theory in Practice*. New York: Basic Books.

Genesee, F. 1994. *Educating Second Language Children: The Whole Child, the Whole Curriculum, the Whole Community*. New York: Cambridge University Press.

Gibaldi, J. 2003. *MLA Handbook for Writers of Research Papers*. 6th ed. New York: Modern Language Association of America.

Gillet, J., and L. Beverly. 2001. *Directing the Writing Workshop: An Elementary Teacher's Handbook*. New York: The Guilford Press.

Harwayne, S. 2001. *Writing through Childhood: Rethinking Process and Product*. Portsmouth, NH: Heinemann.

International Reading Association. 2002. *What Is Evidence-Based Reading Instruction?* A position statement of the International Reading Association. Accessed May 2006. Online. www.reading.org/downloads/positions/ps1055_evidence_basedpdf.

Johnson, K. 2004. *Writing Like Writers: Guiding Elementary Children through a Writer's Workshop*. Austin, TX: Prufrock Press.

Kagan, S. 1994. *Cooperative Learning and Language Arts*. San Diego, CA: Moore Data Management Services.

Kame'enui, E. J., D. W. Carnine, R. C. Dixon, D. C. Simmons, and M. D. Coyne. 2002. *Effective Strategies for Teaching Students That Accommodate Diverse Learners*. Columbus, OH: Merrill.

Kooy, M., and J. Wells. 1996. *Reading Response Logs*. Portsmouth, NH: Heinemann.

Kovacs, D., and J. Preller. 1993. *Meet the Authors and Illustrators*. New York: Scholastic.

Lane, B. 1993. *After the End: Teaching and Learning Creative Revision*. Portsmouth, NH: Heinemann.

Marzano, R. J., D. J. Pickering, and J. E. Pollock. 2004. *Classroom Instruction That Works: Research-Based Strategies for Increasing Student Achievement*. Alexandria, VA: Association for Supervision and Curriculum Development.

Moger, S. 2006. *A Poem for Every Day!* New York: Scholastic.

National Center to Improve the Tools of Educators. 2001. Accessed April 2008. Online. idea.uoregon/edu/~ncite.

No Child Left Behind Act of 2001. 107th Congress of the United State of America. Accessed April 2006. Online. www.ed.gov/legislation/ESEA02/107-10.pdf.

Persky, H., M. Daane, and Ying Jin. 2003. *The Nation's Report Card: Writing 2002*. Accessed Feb. 2008. Online. http://nces.ed.gov/nationsreportcard/pubs/main2002/2003529.asp.

Petty, K., and J. Maizels. 2006. *Perfect Punctuation Pop-Up*. New York: Dutton Children's Book.

Robb, L. 1999. *Brighten up Boring Beginnings and Other Quick Writing Lessons*. New York: Scholastic.

Schrecengost, M. 2004. *Voice Wizardry*. Gainesville, FL: Maupin House.

Silverstein, S. 1964. *The Giving Tree*. New York: Harper Collins.

Spandel, V. 2008. *Creating Writers through 6-Trait Writing Assessment and Instruction*. (4th ed.) New York: Allyn and Bacon.

Sunflower, C. 1993. *75 Creative Ways to Publish Students' Writing*. New York: Scholastic.

Temple, C., and J. W. Gillett. 1996. *Language and Literacy*. New York: Harper Collins.

Terban, M. 1996. *Scholastic Book of Idioms*. New York: Scholastic Trade.

Tucker, S. 1995. *Painting the Sky*. Parsippany, NJ: Good Year Books.

Yagelski, R. P. 2000. *Literacy Matters: Writing and Reading the Social Self*. New York: Teachers College Press.

Young, S. 2006. *Scholastic Rhyming Dictionary*. New York: Scholastic.

Index

Page numbers followed by a *t* indicates a table.

A

alignment with curriculum
    BEW and 6 Traits, xxi, xxii*t*
    BEW and Writing Workshops, xxiii, xxiv*t*
authentic assessment rubrics, development
    general rubric development, 63
    personal narrative, 103
    persuasive writing, 134
    poetry, 198
    research paper, 175
    response to reading, 220
authentic assessment rubrics, samples
    personal narrative, fifth grade, 105
    personal narrative, middle school, 106
    personal narrative, second grade, 104
    persuasive, first grade, 135
    persuasive, middle school, 137
    persuasive, third grade, 136
    research paper, fifth grade, 177
    research paper, middle school, 178
    research paper, second grade, 176

B

Big Ten vocabulary words, 4
    Blueprint, 9
    central theme, 7
    editing, 11
    final copy, 12
    genre, 5
    illustration, 9
    publishing, 14
    rough draft, 10
    student portfolio, 15
    topic, 7
Blueprint graphic organizers
    colors and shapes, 44
    detail squares, 47

early elementary, 26
middle school, 31
personal narrative, 119
persuasive writing, 154
poetry, 210
Professor Write, 42
research paper, 186
response to reading, 226
upper elementary, 28
Building Blocks for genres
    personal narrative, 91*t*
    persuasive writing, 122*t*
    poetry, 189*t*
    research paper, 159*t*
    response to reading, 213*t*

C

central theme
    defined, 7
    Professor Write, 7
character sketch
    character sketch, 100*t*
    defined, 99
common writing mistakes
    personal narrative, 90
    persuasive writing, 124
    poetry, 188
    research paper, 159
    response to reading, 213
cyber trips
    defined, 36
    writing tips: multisensory experiences, 36

D

detail paragraphs
    defined, 42
    Professor Write, 42

draft writing
    defined, 54
    Professor Write, 54
    writing tips: draft writing, 58

E

editing
    peer editing, 68
    self-editing, 67
    teacher conference, 69

F

final copy
    defined, 70
    writing tips: teaching final copy writing, 71

G

genre
    defined, 5
    Professor Write, 6
    writing tips: genre, 6
genre format and voice
    defined, 40
    Professor Write, 41

I

interactive creative strategies for teaching writing
    elementary (K–2)
        genre elements, 231
        genre format, 229
        personal narrative, character development, 232
        personal narrative, point of view, 237
        personal narrative, story format, 234
        personal narrative, voice, 237
        persuasive writing, taking a stand, 238

persuasive writing, three arguments, 238
poetry, connecting with your senses, 245
poetry, rhyme and rhythm, 243
poetry, word choice, 244
remedies for grammar errors, 246
research papers, finding the information, 242
research papers, supporting points, 243
research papers, writing the research question, 240
grades 3–5
  genre elements, 250
  genre format, 249
  personal narrative, character development, 253
  personal narrative, story format, 254
  personal narrative, voice, 256
  persuasive writing, point of view, 256
  persuasive writing, taking a stand, 257
  persuasive writing, three arguments, 258
  poetry, connecting with your senses, 265
  poetry, rhyme and rhythm, 263
  poetry, word choice, 264
  remedies for grammar errors, 266
  research papers, finding the information, 261
  research papers, supporting points, 262
  research papers, writing the research question, 259
grades 6–8
  genre elements, 271
  genre format, 269
  personal narrative, character development, 273
  personal narrative, story format, 275
  personal narrative, voice, 273
  persuasive writing, point of view, 277
  persuasive writing, taking a stand, 278
  persuasive writing, three arguments, 279
  poetry, rhyme and rhythm, 283
  poetry, voice, 285
  poetry, word choice, 285

L

lesson plan, 295
lined paper
  middle school, 32
  upper elementary, 29
literacy bags/boxes
  defined, 37
  Professor Write, 37
  writing tips: multisensory experiences, 38

M

master plan (BEW Phases), xiii

N

note taking
  Professor Write, 45

P

paragraphs
  defined, 17
  paragraphs, word wrap, 18
  Professor Write, 17
peer editing
  defined, 68
  Professor Write, 69
personal narrative
  defined, 88
  personal narrative, genre building blocks, 91
  personal narrative, hand jive, 229
  Professor Write, 99
persuasive writing
  defined, 120
  persuasive writing, genre building blocks, 122
  persuasive writing, hand jive, 229
  Professor Write, 130
remedies for grammar errors, 286
research papers, finding the information, 280
research papers, supporting points, 282
research papers, writing the research question, 280

poetry
  defined, 187
  diction, 191
  elements of, 192
  hand-jive, 229
  Professor Write, 197
  types taught in grades K through 8, 195
  word choice and vocabulary builder, 193t
publishing
  defined, 73
  publishing, for the community, 82
  publishing, student portfolios and keepsakes, 84
  publishing, within the school, 74
  writing tips: class-made books, 85
  writing tips: media center sharing, 75
  writing tips: meeting with professional authors, 77
  writing tips: professional storytelling, 79
  writing tips: public readings, 76
  writing tips: school newspaper, 78
  writing tips: school plays, 80
  writing tips: school publishing website, 77
  writing tips: school write-a-thon, 81
  writing tips: school writing assemblies, 76
  writing tips: sharing across grade levels, 75
  writing tips: sharing with the class, 74

R

research-based BEW strategies
  BEW and NCLB, xvii, 297
  Nine Effective Instructional Strategies, xx, 300
  Six Accommodations for Diverse Learners, xix, 297
research paper
  bibliography guide, MLA, 161
  bibliography note-card guide, 169
  defined, 156
  Professor Write, 171
  research paper, genre building blocks, 159
  research paper, hand jive, 229

transition words, 164*t*

    writing tips: multisensory experiences, 165

rough draft writing folder

    defined, 3

    early elementary, sample, 25

    middle school, sample, 30

    upper elementary, sample, 27

rubrics (*see* authentic assessment rubrics)

S

self-editing

    defined, 67

    Professor Write, 67

sensory log, 205

sentences

    defined, 16

    Professor Write, 17

    writing tips: teaching sentence writing, 16

show don't tell, 101*t*

student worksheets

    2.1 wheel of thought, 50

    2.2 blueprint with just squares, 51

    6.1 writing sensory details, 117

    6.2 character details, 118

    6.3 blueprint for personal narrative, 119

    7.1 art of persuasion, 146

    7.2 who is my audience?, 147

    7.3 fact versus opinion chart, 148

    7.4 current event opinion inventory, 149

    7.5 personal planning sheet, 150

    7.6 topic sentence strategies, 151

    7.7 voice of authority, 152

    7.8 types of arguments, 153

    7.9 blueprint for persuasive writing, 154

    7.10 talking paragraphs, 155

    8.1 who is my audience?, 184

    8.2 ready, set, go!, 185

    8.3 blueprint for research paper, 186

    9.1 sensory log, 205

    9.2 rhyming worksheet, 206

    9.3 blueprint for cinquain, 207

    9.4 blueprint for haiku, 208

    9.5 blueprint for diamante, 209

    9.6 blueprint for poetry, 210

    10.1 blueprint for response to reading, 226

summary or ending paragraphs

    defined, 43

    Professor Write, 43

T

talking paragraphs

    defined, 47

    Professor Write, 48

    writing tips: talking paragraphs, 49

teaching schedule

    personal narrative, 113

    persuasive, 143

    poetry, 202

    research paper, 183

    response to reading, 223

    typical two week genre unit, xvii

title writing

    defined, 58

    strategies of, 58

topic

    defined, 7

Professor Write, 8

    writing tips: teaching topic, 8

topic sentence

    defined, 18

    Professor Write, 19

    teaching strategies, 19

    writing tips: teaching topic sentence writing, 20

transition sentences

    defined, 20

    Professor Write, 21

V

voice

    defined, 44

    writing tips: voice, 44

W

web of words

    defined, 24

    graphic organizer, 24

    Professor Write, 23

    writing tips: web of words, 22

wheel of thought

    defined, 38

    graphic organizer, 50

    Professor Write, 40

    writing tips: wheel of thought, 38

writing prompts

    personal narrative, 114

    persuasive, 144

    poetry, 203

    response to reading, 224